THE
COLLECTED WORKS
of
W. H. HUDSON

IN TWENTY-FOUR
VOLUMES

THE BOOK OF A NATURALIST

THE BOOK
OF
A NATURALIST

BY

W. H. HUDSON

AMS PRESS
NEW YORK

Reprinted with the permission of J. M. Dent and Sons, Ltd.
From the edition of 1923, London
First AMS EDITION published 1968
Manufactured in the United States of America

Library of Congress Catalogue Card Number: 68-58908

AMS PRESS, INC.
New York, N.Y. 10003

PREFACE

IT is necessary that a book should have a title, and important that this should be descriptive of the book: accordingly, I was pleased with my good fortune and myself when I hit upon one which was not merely descriptive but was attractive as well.

This was a long time ago when these studies, essays and sketches of animal life began to accumulate on my hands and I foresaw the book. Unhappily, long before my book was ready my nice title had occurred to someone else and was duly given by Sir E. Ray Lankester to his *Diversions of a Naturalist*—a collection of papers on a vast variety of subjects which had been appearing serially under another title. I was very much annoyed, not only because he is a big man and I am a little one and my need was therefore greater, but also because it appeared to me better suited to my book than to his. He deals with the deep problems of biology and is not exactly a naturalist in the old original sense of the word—one who is mainly concerned with the "life and conversation of animals," and whose work is consequently more like play than his can be, even when it is *Science from an Easy Chair*.

What then was I to do, seeing that all possible changes had been rung on such general titles as Journals, Letters, Notes, Gleanings, and what not, of a Naturalist? There was no second string to my bow since *Recreations* had already been used by my friend J. E. Harting for his book. In sheer desperation I took this title, which would fit any work on natural history ever published. Doubtless it would have

been an improvement if I could have put in the " Field "
before " Naturalist " to show that it was not a compilation,
but the title could not be made longer even by a word.

Some of the chapters in this volume now appear for the
first time; more of them, however, are taken from or based
on articles which have appeared in various periodicals: the
Fortnightly Review, *National Review*, *Country Life*, *Nation*,
the *New Statesman*, and others. I am obliged to the Editors
of the *Times* and *Chambers's Journal* for permission to use
two short copyright articles on the Rat and Squirrel which
appeared in those journals.

CONTENTS

ix

THE
BOOK OF A NATURALIST

CHAPTER I

LIFE IN A PINE WOOD

People, Birds, Ants

SOME years ago a clever gentleman, a land-owner no doubt with pine plantations on his property, made the interesting discovery that the ideal place to live in was a pine wood, owing to the antiseptic and medicinal qualities emanating from the trees. You could smell them and began to feel better the moment you entered the wood. Naturally there was a rush to the pines just as there had been a rush to the hill-tops in response to Tyndall's flag-waving and exultant shouts from Hindhead, and as there had been a rush over a century earlier to the seaside in obedience to Dr. Russell's clarion call. I have no desire myself to live among pines, simply because I cannot endure to be shut off from this green earth with sight of flocks and herds. Woods are sometimes good to live in: I have spent happy months in a woodman's cottage in a forest; but the trees were mostly oak and beech and there were wide green spaces and an abundant wild life. Pine

woods, especially plantations, are monotonous because the trees are nearly all pines and one tree is
like another, and their tall, bare trunks wall you in,
and their dark stiff foliage is like a roof above you.
I, too, like being in a pine wood, just as I like being
by the sea, for a few hours or a day, but for a place
to live in I should prefer a moor, a marsh, a sea-
salting, or any other empty, desolate place with a
wide prospect.

In spite of this feeling I actually did spend a
great part of last summer in such a place. It is an
extensive tract, which when the excitement and rush
for the medicinal pines began, was first seized upon
by builders as being near London and in a highly
aristocratic neighbourhood. Immediately, as by a
miracle, large ornate houses sprang up like painted
agarics in the autumn woods—houses suitable for
the occupation of important persons. The wood
itself was left untouched; the houses, standing a
quarter of a mile or more apart, with their gardens
and lawns, were like green, flowery oases scattered
about in its sombre wilderness. Gardens and lawns
are a great expense, the soil being a hungry sand,
and for all the manuring and watering the flowers
have a somewhat sad and sickly look, and the lawns
a poor thin turf, half grass and half moss.

As a naturalist I was curious to observe the effect
of life in a pine wood on the inhabitants. It struck
me that it does not improve their health, or make
them happy, and that they suffer most in summer,
especially on warm windless days. They do not walk

in their woods; they hasten to the gate which lets them out on the road and takes them to the village —or to some point from which they can get a sight of earth outside the pines. They are glad to escape from their surroundings, and are never so happy as when going away on a long visit to friends living no matter where, in the country or abroad, so long as it was not in a pine wood. I should imagine that Mariana herself, supposing that she had survived to the present day and had been persuaded to come down south to try the effect of living in a pine wood, would soon wish to go back to her moated grange on a Lincolnshire flat, for all its ancient dust and decay, with no sound to break the sultry noonday brooding silence save the singing of the blue fly i' the pane and the small shrill shriek of the mouse behind the rotting wainscot.

So much for the human dwellers among the "crepuscular pines." I am quoting an expression of the late lamented Henry James, which he used not of pine woods generally but of this very wood, well known to him too when he was a guest in the house. But he didn't love it or he would have been a more frequent visitor; as it was, he preferred to see his dear friends—all his friends were very dear to him —when they were away from the twilight shelter of their trees in ever bright and beautiful London.

I was perhaps more interested in the non-human inhabitants of the wood. The wood that was mine to walk in, the part which belonged to the house and which as a fact I alone used, covered an area of about sixty acres and was one with the entire wood, only divided from the rest by oak palings. When one turned from the lawns and gardens into the wood it was like passing from the open sunlit air to the twilight and still atmosphere of a cathedral interior. It was also a strangely silent place; if a thrush or chaffinch was heard to sing, the sound came from the garden I had quitted or from some other garden in the wood still farther away. The only small birds in these pines were those on a brief visit, and little parties of tits drifted through. Nevertheless, the wood—the part I was privileged to walk in—had its own appropriate fauna—squirrels, wood-pigeons, a family of jays, another of magpies, a pair of yaffles, and one of sparrow-hawks. Game is not preserved in these woods which are parcelled out to the different houses in lots of a dozen to fifty or more acres; consequently several species which are on the gamekeeper's black list are allowed to exist. Most of the birds I have named bred during the summer—the hawks and yaffles, a dozen or more pairs of wood-pigeons, and a pair each of magpies and jays. The other members of the family parties of the last two species had no doubt been induced by means of sharp beaky arguments to go and look for nesting-places elsewhere.

But not one small bird could I find nesting in the wood. This set me thinking on a question which has vexed my mind for years—How do small birds safeguard their tender helpless fledgelings from the ants? This wood swarmed with ants: their nests,

half hidden by the bracken, were everywhere, some
of the old mounds being of huge size, twelve to
fourteen feet in circumference, and some over four
feet high. As their eggs were not wanted the ants
were never disturbed, and the marvel was how they
could exist in such excessive numbers in a naked pine
wood, which of all woods is the poorest in insect life.

I have said to myself a hundred times that birds,
especially the small woodland species that nest on
or near the ground, such as the nightingale, robin,
wren, chiff-chaff, wood and willow wrens, and tits
that breed low down in old stumps, must occasionally
have their nestlings destroyed by ants; yet I have
never found a nest showing plainly that such an
accident had occurred, nor had I seen anything on
the subject in books about birds; and of such books
I had read hundreds.

The subject was in my mind when I received
evidence from an unexpected quarter that tender
fledgelings are sometimes destroyed by ants. This
was in an account of the wren by a little boy which
I came upon in a bundle of Bird and Tree Competition essays from the village schools in Lancashire,
sent on to me to read and judge from the Royal
Society for the Protection of Birds. The boy states
in his essay that having selected the wren as his
subject he watched the birds and looked for nests;
that among the nests he found one containing five
eggs, and that four young were hatched but were
destroyed the same day by ants. I wrote to the
master of the school, at Newburgh, near Wigan, and

to the boy, Harry Southworth, asking for full particulars. The master's reply gave a satisfactory account of Harry as a keen and careful observer, and Harry's answer was that the nest was built in a small hole in a bank beside a brook, that he had kept his eye on it during the time the bird was sitting on her five eggs, that on his last visit he found the parent bird in a terrified state outside the nest, and that on examination he found that four young birds had been hatched, and were all dead but still warm, and swarming with small reddish-brown ants which were feeding on them.

This goes to show that not only do ants sometimes attack the fledgelings in the nest, but also that the parent birds in such cases are powerless to save their young from destruction. My conclusion was that small ground-nesting birds have an instinctive fear of ants and avoid building at places infested by them.

But how does it happen, I now asked, that the larger birds that nest high up in the pines escape the danger? The ants go up the tallest and smoothest trunks with the ease and at the same rate of speed as when moving on the surface. They are seen ascending and descending all day long in countless numbers, so that the entire tree-top must be swarming with them, searching every twig and every needle; and being ants and ready to fasten their jaws on any provender, dead or alive, without regard to the size of the object, the newly-hatched young wood-pigeons or magpies can be no safer in their lofty cradles than the robin or willow-wren fledgelings in their nest on the ground. Unfortunately, when I got to this point it was too late in the season to follow the matter much further, since most of the birds had finished breeding. Whether all or most of them had been successful or not I was not able to discover; however, the young were not yet out of the one nest which interested me the most. This was the sparrow-hawks', and was in the lowest branches of a tall, slim pine about forty-five feet from the ground. It was an exceptionally big nest. The birds, I knew, had brought off their young successfully in this same wood in the three previous years, and I came to the conclusion that the same nest had been used every time and had grown to its present size by the addition of fresh materials each season. By standing on a high mound situated at a distance of fifty yards from the tree I could, with my binocular, get a perfect sight of the four young hawks on their platform, looking like owls with their big round heads and their fluffy white down.

As their feathers grew they became more active; they were less and less inclined to sit in a close bunch; they would draw as far apart as they were able and sit on the extreme edge of the nest, and from that high perch they would stare curiously down at me when I looked up at them. The habits of the parent birds were unlike those of sparrow-hawks breeding in woods and wild places where people are rarely seen. Instead of displaying intense anxiety and screaming at the sight of a human form, causing the young birds to squat low down in the nest, they would slink off in silence and vanish from the scene. This extreme secretiveness was, in the circumstances, their safest policy, to express it in that way, but, of course, it had one drawback—it left the young uninstructed as to the dangerous character of man. That lesson would have to come later, when they were off the nest.

As the hawks grew, the supply of food increased, and the birds supplied were so carefully plucked, not a feather being left, also the head removed, that in some instances it was actually difficult to identify the species; but I think that most of the birds brought to the nest were starlings. The young hawks had now to feed themselves on what was on the table, and when one felt peckish he would take up a bird and carry it to the edge of the big nest so as to be out of the way of the others, and setting a foot on it, go to work to tear it to pieces. But he sometimes mismanaged the business, and when transferring the bird from his beak to his claws he would drop it over the edge and lose it. The dropped bird would be quickly found and attacked by the ants, and before many hours it would be a well-cleaned skeleton.

But the ants never ascended this tree. It then occurred to me that ants are always seen swarming up certain trees—always the same trees; and that a vast majority of the trees were never invaded by them at all. I now began going round and visiting all the trees where I distinctly remembered having seen ants ascending, and on all those trees I found them still swarming up in immense numbers as if to some place containing an inexhaustible supply of food. It was now, however, too late in the season to make sure that they do not from time to time invade fresh trees. That they should go on from day to day for weeks, and perhaps for the whole season, ascending the same trees strikes one as very strange; yet such a fact would accord with what we know of these puzzling insects—their almost incredible wisdom in their complex actions and system of life, coupled with an almost incredible stupidity. Or do the ants know just why they go up this particular tree and not any of the surrounding trees? Can it be that on this particular tree they have their carefully tended flocks and herds to supply them with honey-dew—their milk, butter and cheese? Such flocks and herds they do keep and tend on oak trees, as I discovered in Harewood Forest; and I wish that readers of this chapter who live in or near a pine wood and are the happy possessors of ladders forty or fifty feet long will make some further investigation into the matter.

My conclusion for the present is that wood-pigeons and other birds that breed in the pines do not build their nests in trees used by the ants.

Let us now follow the fortunes of the young sparrow-hawks, bred in a wood where people inhabit.

I watched them day by day, and, gradually, as their fluffy coat was replaced by feathers, and their lumpish appearance changed to the sharp-cut hawk figure, they grew more adventurous and would mount upon a branch accessible from the nest, the maturest bird taking the lead, the others, one by one, slowly and cautiously following. Finally, all four would be on the branch at a distance of six to ten inches apart, the one nearest the nest being always the least hawk-like in appearance—more lumpish and with more down on it than the others.

One morning in September I found the nest empty; the young had been persuaded to leave for good early that morning. Just how they had been persuaded —feelingly, perhaps with sudden smart blows—it would have been a great thing to witness, but I had never looked for it on account of the vigilance and extraordinary secretiveness of the parent birds. Never once had they uttered a sound or allowed themselves to be seen. Now that their young were out and able to fly, they no longer found it necessary to make themselves invisible on the appearance of the human form in the wood. At all events, after keeping the young concealed for the space of three or four days, they began to show themselves openly, pursued by the young, wailing and screaming to be fed. All day long these whining cries were heard, and it was plain that a new system had been adopted by the parent birds at this stage, which was to keep their young on short commons, instead of supplying them with more food than they could consume. The result was that the young, instead of sitting idly waiting for small birds, properly plucked, to be brought and dropped at their feet, were driven by hunger to fly after the parent birds, who led them an endless chase in and out and above the trees. It all looked like a great waste of energy, but it had an important use in teaching the young to fly and to develop the wing muscles by incessant exercise. These exercises continued for five or six days in the wood, then followed a fresh move; every morning early the wood was quitted by the whole family, the young, no doubt, being conducted to a clump on one of the extensive tracts of heath in the neighbourhood. There they would have other and more important lessons to learn. The young hawk would have to pluck the feathers out himself or else swallow them along with the flesh; the next stage would be that the bird would be delivered alive, but partially disabled, and he would have to kill it himself; finally, he would have to capture his own prey—the last and most difficult lesson of all.

That they were still kept on short commons was evident from the perpetual hunger-cries of the young when they returned each evening to their roosting-place in the wood. From the moment of their arrival an hour before sunset, until it was almost dark, the clamour went on, the young birds following their parents the whole time. This continued for a fortnight, and during the last few evenings the parent birds introduced yet another new subject or feature into their educational system. They would rise over the trees, both male and female, but keeping wide apart, followed by the clamouring young; and floating and circling up with easy harrier-like movement, they would mount to a height of two or three hundred yards above the tree-tops, then suddenly hurl themselves down like stones and vanish among the trees, still followed at a long distance by the young. Once down beneath the tree-tops it was marvellous to see them, dashing at their topmost sparrow-hawk speed hither and thither among the tall, naked boles, with many sudden sharp twistings which apparently just enabled them to escape being dashed to death against a trunk or branch. Every time I witnessed this seemingly mad violent action, yet accomplished with such ease, such certainty, such grace, I was astonished afresh.

This would be the last act in the day's business, for immediately afterwards they would fly to the roosting-place and the hungry young would hush their cries.

Then at the end of the third week in September the whole family disappeared. The young had now to learn that they could not always stay in the one place which they knew, soon to be followed with the last and hardest of all their lessons, that they must make their own living or else starve.

Note.—Since this paper appeared in the *National Review*, my idea concerning the destructiveness of ants to young birds has received further confirmation from two widely separated quarters. One, oddly enough, is contained in another country schoolboy essay, for a Bird and Tree Day Competition, in this case from a village in Hampshire. The skylark was the bird observed, and on one of the visits the little observer paid to the nest, when the nestlings were a few days old, he found them outside of the nest covered with small red ants and in a dying condition.

The second case is contained in a letter from one of my correspondents in Australia, Mr. Charles Barrett, well known in the Colony and in this country as a student of the native avifauna. He had in reading seen an extract from my paper on "Life in a Pine Wood," and wrote: "I believe that in Australia, where ants of many species swarm in the dry regions, large numbers of nestlings fall victims to these insects. Of course it is the birds that nest on the ground that suffer the most, but some of the ants ascend trees and attack the fledgelings in nests in the highest branches. . . . In November I noticed a stream of large reddish ants streaming up a gum sapling, and found it was pouring into a nest of wood swallows, *Artamus sarolida*, which contained three chicks about a week old. They were being devoured alive by ants. . . . I put the nestlings out of their misery, but felt miserable myself for the remainder of that golden afternoon, thinking that many similar tragedies to that were being enacted in the Bush. The odour and fragrance of the wattle-bloom along the creek and the blithe songs of birds failed to cheer for the time."

He also described finding the nest of a song-thrush (our English bird) with nestlings in a similar state.

CHAPTER II

IT has occurred to me that a few hints or wrinkles on the subject of adder-seeking might prove serviceable to some readers of this work, seeing that there are very many persons desirous of making the acquaintance of this rare and elusive reptile. They wish to know it—at a safe distance—in a state of Nature, in its own home, and have sought and have not found it. Quite frequently—about once or twice each week in summer—I am asked by someone for instructions in the matter.

One of my sweetest-tempered and most benevolent friends, who loves, he imagines, all things both great and small, pays the children of his village sixpence for every dead adder or grass-snake they bring him. He does not distinguish between the two ophidians. It is to be hoped that no such lover of God's creatures, including His "wild wormes in woods," will take advantage of these hints. Let him that finds an adder treat it properly, not without reverence, and his finding it will be to his gain in knowledge of that rare and personal kind which cannot be written or imparted in any way. That which we seek is not the viper, the subject of Fontana's monumental work, the little rope of clay or dead flesh in the British Museum, coiled in its bottle of spirits, and labelled "*Vipera berus*, Linn."

We seek the adder or nadder, that being venerated of old and generator of the sacred adder-stone of the Druids, and he dwells not in a jar of alcohol in the still shade and equable temperature of a museum. He is a lover of the sun, and must be sought for after his winter sleep in dry incult places, especially in open forest-lands, stony hill-sides, and furze-grown heaths and commons. After a little training the adder-seeker gets to know a viperish locality by its appearance. It is, however, not necessary to go out at random in search of a suitable hunting-ground, seeing that all places haunted by adders are well known to the people in the neighbourhood, who are only too ready to give the information required. There are no preservers of adders in the land, and so far as I know there has been but one person in England to preserve that beautiful and innocuous creature, the ringed-snake. Can anyone understand such a hobby or taste? Certainly not that friend of animals who pays sixpence for a dead snake. He, the snake-saviour, our unknown little Melampus, paid his village boys sixpence for every one they brought to him alive and uninjured, and to inspire confidence in them he would go with half a dozen large snakes in his coat pockets into the village school, and pulling his pets out, would play with and make the children handle them and take note of their beautiful form and motions.

This snake-lover possessed at Aldermaston one of

the largest parks in southern England, abounding in oak trees so ancient and of so noble a growth that they are a wonder to all who see them. This vast park was his snake-preserve, and in moist green places, by running waters, he planted thickets for their shelter. But when his time came and he died, the son who succeeded him thought he would get more glory and sport by preserving pheasants, and accordingly engaged a little army of men and boys to extirpate the reptiles. There is nothing now to recall the dead man's "fantastic hobby" but a stained-glass window—I wish it had been done by a better artist—placed by his pious widow in the beautiful parish church, where you can see him among angelic figures surrounded by a company of birds and beasts and reptiles of many shapes and colours, and at the margins the familiar words, *He prayeth best who loveth best*, etc.

Let us return to our quest. The trouble is when you have arrived at the adder-haunt to find the adder. A man may spend years, even a lifetime, without seeing one. Some time ago I talked to an aged shepherd whose flock fed in a wide furze-grown hollow in the South Downs where adders were not uncommon. He told me he had been shepherding forty years in that place, and during the entire period had found three adders! If he had said three hundred I should not have been surprised. The man on the soil does not often see an adder, because for one thing he does not look for it, and still more because of the heavy boots he wears, with which he pounds the earth like a dray-horse with its ponderous iron-shod hoofs. Even men who walk lightly and wear light foot-gear make, as a rule, an amazing noise in walking over dry heathy places with brittle sticks and dry vegetable matter covering the ground. I have had persons thrust their company on me when going for a stroll on ground abounding in adders, and have known at once from their way of walking in an unaccustomed place that the quest would prove an idle one. Their lightest, most cautious tread would alarm and send into hiding every adder a dozen or twenty yards in advance of us.

In spring the adders are most alert and shyest. Later in the season some adders, as a rule the females, become sluggish and do not slip quickly away when approached; but in summer the herbage is apt to hide them, and they lie more in the shade than in March, April, and the early part of May. In spring you must go alone and softly, but you need not fear to whistle and sing, or even to shout, for the adder is deaf and cannot hear you; on the other hand, his body is sensitive in an extraordinary degree to earth vibrations, and the ordinary tread of even a very light man will disturb him at a distance of fifteen or twenty yards. That sense of the adder, which has no special organ yet may serve better than vision, hearing, smell, and touch together, is of the greatest importance to it, since to a creature that lies and progresses prone on the ground and has a long brittle backbone, the heavy mammalian foot is one of the greatest dangers to its life.

Not only must the seeker go softly, but he must have a quick-seeing, ever-searching eye, and behind the eye a mind intent on the object. The sharpest sight is useless if he falls to thinking of something else, since it is not possible for him to be in two places at once. To empty the mind as in crystal-gazing is a good plan, but if it cannot be emptied, if thought will not rest still, it must be occupied with adders and nothing else. The exercise and discipline is interesting even if we find no adders; it reveals in swift flickering glimpses a vanished experience or state of the primitive mind—the mind which, like that of the inferior animals, is a polished mirror, undimmed by speculation, in which the extraneous world is vividly reflected. If the adder quest goes on for days, it is still best to preserve the mood, to think of adders all day, and when asleep to dream of them. The dreams, I have found, are of two sorts—pleasant and unpleasant. In the former we are the happy first finders of the loveliest and most singular serpents ever looked upon; in the second we unwittingly go up barefooted into a place from which we cannot escape, a vast flat region extending to the horizon, littered with adders. We have lifted a foot and don't know where to set it, for there is not one square foot of ground which is not already occupied by an adder coiled in readiness to strike.

In adder-seeking, the main thing is to find your adder without disturbing it, so as to be able to stand near and watch it lying quiescent in the sun. The

best plan is to come almost to a stop as soon as the
creature has been caught sight of, then to advance
so slowly and stealthily as to appear stationary, for
the adder although unalarmed is, I believe, always
conscious of your presence. In this way you may
approach to within two or three yards, or nearer,
and remain a long time regarding it.

But what is the seeker to do if, after long searching, he discovers his adder already in retreat, and
knows that in two or three seconds it will vanish
from his sight? As a. rule, the person who sees an
adder gliding from him aims a blow at it with his
stick *so as not to lose it.* Now to kill your adder *is*
to lose it. It is true you will have something to show
for it, or something of it which is left in your hands,
and which, if you feel disposed, you may put in a
glass jar and label "*Vipera berus.*" But this would
not be an adder. Must we then never kill an adder?
That is a question I do not undertake to answer,
but I can say that if we are seeking after knowledge,
or something we call knowledge because it is a convenient word and can be made to cover many things
it would be difficult to name, then to kill is no profit,
but, on the contrary, a distinct loss. Fontana dis-
sected forty thousand adders in his long and busy
day, but if there is anything we want to know about
the adder beyond the number of scales on the integu-
ment, and the number, shape, and size of the bones
in the dead coil, he and the innumerable ophiologists
and herpetologists who came after him are unable to
tell us. We can read about the scales and bones in

a thousand books. We want to know more about the living thing, even about its common life habits. It has not yet been settled whether or not the female adder swallows its young, not, like the fer-de-lance, to digest them in her stomach, but to save their threatened lives. It is true that many persons have, during the last half-century, witnessed the thing and have described what they saw in *The Zoologist, Land and Water, Field* and other journals; nevertheless the compilers of our natural histories regard the case as not yet proved beyond a doubt.

Here, then, we have one of several questions which can only be answered by field-naturalists who abstain from killing. But a better reason for not killing may be given than this desire to discover a new fact— the mere satisfying of a mental curiosity. I know good naturalists who have come to hate the very sight of a gun, simply because that useful instrument has become associated in their case with the thought and the memory of the degrading or disturbing effect on the mind of killing the creatures we love, whose secrets we wish to find out.

Alas! it took me a long time to discover the advantages of not killing. The following account of killing an adder—the last time I did such a thing —may serve to throw a little light on the question. Adders were common at a place where I was staying at a farm in the New Forest, but I had never seen one near the house until one sultry afternoon in July, when coming into a path which led from the farm-yard into and through a hazel copse, I came

upon one lying in the middle of the path. It was
a large adder, so sluggish that it made no attempt
to escape, but turned and struck at me when I
approached it. I thought of the little children, for
this was the very spot where they came to play and
hunt for fowls' eggs every afternoon; the adder, if
left there, might be a danger to them; it was necessary either to kill or remove it. Then it occurred to
me that to remove it would be useless, since if the
creature's place was there, it would infallibly return
to it from any distance. The homing instinct is
strong in the adder and in most serpents. And so
to end the matter I killed and buried it, and went
on my way. My way was through the copse and
over a fence and ditch on the other side, and I was
no sooner over the ditch than I beheld a second
adder, bigger than the last and just as sluggish. It
was, however, not strange, as in July the female
adder is often like that, especially in sultry thunderous
weather. I teased it to make it move away, then
picked it up to examine it, after which I released
it and watched it gliding slowly away into the shadow
of the bushes. And, watching it, I became conscious
of a change in my mental attitude towards the living
things that were so much to me, my chief happiness
having always been in observing their ways. The
curiosity was not diminished, but the feeling that
had gone with it for a very long time past was
changed to what it had been when I was sportsman
and collector, always killing things. The serpent
gliding away before me was nothing but a worm

with poison fangs in its head and a dangerous habit
of striking at unwary legs—a creature to be crushed
with the heel and no more thought about. I had
lost something precious, not, I should say, in any
ethical sense, seeing that we are in a world where
we must kill to live, but valuable in my special case,
to me as a field-naturalist. Abstention from killing
had made me a better observer and a happier being,
on account of the new or different feeling towards
animal life which it had engendered. And what was
this new feeling—wherein did it differ from the old
of my shooting and collecting days, seeing that since
childhood I had always had the same intense interest
in all wild life? The power, beauty, and grace of the
wild creature, its perfect harmony in nature, the
exquisite correspondence between organism, form and
faculties, and the environment, with the plasticity
and intelligence for the readjustment of the vital
machinery, daily, hourly, momentarily, to meet all
changes in the conditions, all contingencies; and
thus, amidst perpetual mutations and conflict with
hostile and destructive forces, to perpetuate a form,
a type, a species for thousands and millions of years!
—all this was always present to my mind; yet even
so it was but a lesser element in the complete feeling.
The main thing was the wonderfulness and eternal
mystery of life itself; this formative, informing
energy—this flame that burns in and shines through
the case, the habit, which in lighting another dies,
and albeit dying yet endures for ever; and the
sense, too, that this flame of life was one, and of my

kinship with it in all its appearances, in all organic shapes, however different from the human. Nay, the very fact that the forms were unhuman but served to heighten the interest;—the roe-deer, the leopard and wild horse, the swallow cleaving the air, the butterfly toying with a flower, and the dragon-fly dreaming on the river; the monster whale, the silver flying-fish, and the nautilus with rose- and purple-tinted sails spread to the wind.

Happily for me the loss of this sense and feeling was but a temporary one, and was recovered in the course of the next two days, which I spent in the woods and on the adjacent boggy heath, finding many adders and snakes, also young birds and various other creatures which I handled and played with, and I could afford once more to laugh at those who laughed at or were annoyed with me on account of my fantastic notions about animals. My next great adventure with an adder, which came a year later, gave me so good a laugh that I am tempted to go further with this digression to give an account of it.

The adventure was the finding of my biggest adder. It was in a tract of ground overgrown with furze and thorn, at a spot not far from the turnpike road that runs from Salisbury to Blandford. Having dis-covered that this spot, with an area of several hundred acres, teemed with interesting wild life, I made it a haunt for several weeks. I soon found out that it was a valuable game preserve and that the keeper had strict orders from the shooting tenant not to allow any person on the land. However, I approached him in the proper way, and he left me to enjoy myself in my own fashion.

Never had I seen adders so abundant as at this spot, yet the keeper assured me that he had been trying for years to extirpate them, and often killed as many as half a dozen in a day.

One morning, near the end of June, I found my big adder, and picking it up, held it suspended by the tip of its tail for nearly half an hour, until, exhausted with its vain wriggling, it allowed itself to hang limp and straight. Then I got out my tape-measure and set about the difficult task of getting the exact length; but the adder would not have it, for invariably when the tape was dropped at its side it drew itself up into a series of curves and defeated me. Tired of the long business, I set it down at length and stunned it with a rap on its head with my stick, then setting the tape on its flat head and pressing it with my thumb, I pulled the body straight and succeeded in getting the exact length. It was twenty-eight inches. The biggest adder I had hitherto found was twenty-five and a half; this was in the New Forest, in the wildest part, where it is most thinly inhabited and adders are most abundant. None of the other biggest adders I had measured before and since exceeded twenty-four inches.

We see that the adder, when we come to measure it, is not a big snake; it looks bigger than it is, partly on account of its strange conspicuous colouring, with the zigzag shape of the band, and its reputation as a dangerous serpent; this makes an adder two feet long look actually bigger than the grass-snake of three feet—the size to which this snake usually grows.

In a minute or two my adder recovered from the effects of the tap on his head and was permitted to glide away into the furze bushes. And leaving the spot I went on, but had not gone forty yards before catching sight of another adder lying coiled up. I stopped to look at it, then slowly advanced to within about five feet of it, and there remained standing still, just to see whether or not my presence so close to it would affect it in any way. Presently, hearing a shout, I looked up and saw two horsemen coming up over the down in front of me. They pulled up and sat staring down at me—a big man on a big horse, and a rather small man on a small horse. The big man was the shooting tenant, and the shout was evidently meant for me, but I took no notice. I kept my eyes on my adder, and soon the two horsemen came down at a gallop to me, and of course, before they were fifty yards from me, the thunder of the hoofs had sent the creature into hiding. Sitting on their horses they stared in angry silence at me, and finding I had to speak first, I apologised for being in the preserve, and said the keeper, knowing me to be a harmless naturalist, had given me permission to come there to find a flower I was interested in—also an adder. What, he demanded, did I want with adders? Just to see them, I said; I had found one and was watching it when his approach had driven it away. I then added that adders were exceedingly abundant on this land of his, that I had just found and measured one which was twenty-eight inches long—the biggest adder I had ever found.

"Where is it!—let's see it!" shouted both men, and I had to tell them that I had released it, and it had gone into a bush about forty yards from where we stood.

They stared at me, then exchanged glances, then the big man asked me if I meant what I had said —if I had actually caught a big adder only to release it unharmed?

That, I said, was what I had done.

"Then you did wrong," almost yelled the second man. "To catch and release an adder that might bite and kill someone any day — I consider it a crime."

I laughed and said I didn't mind being a criminal in that way, and I also thought people greatly exaggerated the danger of adder bites.

"You are wrong again!" he yelled, quite in a temper now. "As a naturalist, you ought to know better. Let me tell you that last summer I nearly lost my little son through an adder bite. He was in the Isle of Wight with his nurse, and trod on the thing and was bitten on the leg. For a whole day his life was trembling in the balance, and you dare to tell me that adders are not a danger!"

I apologised for having made light of the subject. He was right and I was wrong. But I couldn't explain to him why I could not kill adders — or anything else.

Let us now return to the adder-seeker who has unwittingly disturbed the adder he has found, and who sees it about to vanish into the brake. He has been waiting all this time to know what to do in such a case. He must let it vanish, and comfort himself with the thought that he has discovered its haunt and may re-find it another day, especially if he is so fortunate as to scare it from its favourite bed on which it is accustomed to lie sunning itself at certain hours each day until the progress of the season will make it too warm or otherwise unsuitable, when the old basking-place will be changed for a new one. But should he not be satisfied to lose sight of the adder immediately after discovering it, he must be provided with some simple contrivance for its capture.

My plan, which cannot be recommended to timid persons liable in moments of excitement to get flustered and awkward, is to catch the retreating adder quickly by the tail, which is a perfectly safe proceeding if there is no blundering, since the creature when going from you is not in a position to strike.

I confess I am always a little reluctant to offer such an indignity to the adder as grasping and holding it up, enraged and impotent, by the tail, although such treatment may be to its advantage in the end. We have a naturalist in England who picks up every adder he finds and pinches its tail before releasing it, just to teach it caution. The poor creeping thing with a zigzag band on its back to advertise its dangerous character has of all creatures the fewest friends among men. My sole object in picking up an adder by the tail is to be able to look at its under-surface, which is often the most beautiful part. As a rule the colour is deep blue, but it varies; the darkest specimens being blue-black or even quite black, while the exceedingly rare light blue is too beautiful for words. Occasionally we find an adder with the belly-plates of the same ground colour, a dull or pale straw yellow, as the upper part of the body, with the dark blue colour in broken spots and dots and lines inscribed on it. These markings in some cases resemble written characters, and it was said of old that they formed the words:

> If I could hear as well as see,
> No man of life would master me.

Probably these letter-like markings on the creature's belly, like the minute black lines, resembling writing, on the pale bark of the holly tree, suggested some other more important meaning to the priests of an ancient cult, and gave the adder a peculiarly sacred character.

To conclude, let me relate here how I once had to congratulate myself on having hurriedly snatched at and captured an adder at the moment of seeing it, and of its attempted escape. I was cautiously strolling along, hoping to see some good thing, in a copse in private grounds in the New Forest, a place abounding in adders and other interesting creatures. Night-jars were common there, and by-and-by one rose almost at my feet over the roots

of an oak tree, and casting my eyes down at the
spot from which it had risen, I spied a large adder,
which, alarmed either at my step or the sudden
flight of the bird, was gliding quickly away over
the bed of old dry bleached leaves to its refuge at
the roots of the tree. Oddly enough, it was not the
first occasion on which I had come upon a night-jar
and adder dozing peacefully side by side. It was
a beautiful adder of a rich tawny yellow hue, with
an intensely black broad zigzag mark, and as there
was no time to lose, I dashed at and managed to
catch it; then holding it up by the tail, what was
my surprise and delight at finding its under-surface
of a colour or "shade" I had never previously seen
—the lovely blue I have mentioned. There was no
break in the colour; every belly-plate from the neck
to the tip of the tail was of a uniform exquisite
turquoise blue, or considering that turquoise blues
vary in depth and purity, it would be more exact
to describe the colour as most like that of the forget-
me-not, but being enamelled, it reminded me rather
of the most exquisite blue one has seen on some
priceless piece of old Chinese pottery. I think that
if some famous aged artist of the great period, a
worshipper of colour whose life had been spent in
the long endeavour to capture and make permanent
the most exquisite fleeting tints in Nature, had seen
the blue on that adder he would have been overcome at the same time with rapture and despair.
And I think, too, that if Mother Nature in turning
out this ophidian had muddled things, as she is apt

to do occasionally, and had reversed the position of the colours, putting the tawny yellow and black zig-zag band on the belly and the blue above, the sight of the creature would have given rise to a New Forest myth. It would have been spread abroad that an angelic being had appeared in those parts in the form of a serpent but in its natural celestial colour.

After keeping it a long time in my hand, I released it reluctantly, and saw it steal away into the cavity at the roots of the oak. Here was its home, and I fondly hoped to see it again many times. But it was not there when I called on many successive days—neither serpent nor night-jar; but though we three shall meet no more, I remember the finding of that adder as one of the loveliest experiences I have met with during all the years I have spent in conversing with wild animals.

CHAPTER III

BATS

THE bat was formerly looked upon as an uncanny sort of bird, and described as such in the old natural histories. Oh, those ever delightful old natural histories, and the vision of the wise old naturalist examining a recently-taken specimen through his horn-bound spectacles, and setting it gravely down in his books that it is the only known bird which was clothed in fur in place of feathers! Or, as Plinius puts it, the only bird which brings forth and suckles its young, just as we say that the Australian water-mole is the only mammal which lays eggs. The modern ornithologist will have nothing to do with the creature; but after his expulsion from the feathered nation it was his singular good fortune not to sink lower in the scale; he was, on the contrary, raised to the mammalians, or quadrupeds, as our fathers called them; then on the discovery being made that he was anatomically related to the lemurs, he was eventually allotted a place in our systems next after that ancient order of fox-faced monkeys. And thus it has come to pass that when someone writes a book on the mammals of this island, which has no monkeys or lemurs, and man cannot be included in such works on account of an old convention or prejudice, he is obliged to give the proud first place to this very poor relation.

It is his misfortune, since it would have been more agreeable to the general reader if he could have led off with some imposing beast—the extinct wolf or tusky wild boar, for example—or, better still, with the white cattle of Chillingham, or the roaring stag with his grand antlers. The last is an undoubted survival, one which, encountered in some incult place where it is absolutely free and wild, moves us to a strange joy—an inherited memory and a vision of a savage, prehistoric land of which we are truer natives than we can ever be of this smooth sophisticated England. The science of zoology could not have it so, since it does not and cannot take man and his mental attitude towards other forms of life into account—cannot consider the fact that he is himself an animal of prey, several feet high, with large eyes fitted to look at large objects, and that he measures and classifies all creatures by an instinctive rule and standard, mentally pitting his strength and ferocity against theirs. What a discrepancy, then, between things as seen by the natural man and as they appear in our scientific systems, which make the small negligible bat the leader of the procession of British beasts — even this repulsive little rearmouse, or flittermouse, that flits from his evil-smelling cranny, in appearance a misshapen insect of unusual size, to pursue his crooked, broken-boned, squeaky flight in the obscurity of evening.

Imagine the effect of this modern rearrangement of the mammals on the mammals if they knew! The white bull of Chillingham would shake his frowning front and the stag his branching antlers in scorn; the wolf, in spite of being extinct, would howl; the British seal bark; the wild cat snarl, and the badger make free use of his most underground expressions of rage at such an insult; rabbit and hare would exchange looks of astonishment and apprehension; the hedgehog would roll himself into a ball with disgust; the mole sink back into his run; the fox smile sardonically; and the whole concourse, turning their backs on the contemptible leader thrust on them, would march off in the opposite direction.

Now the imaginary case of these beasts offended in their dignity fairly represents that of humanity angry at the intolerable insult implied in the Darwinian notion. But we have now so far outgrown that feeling that it is no longer an offence for the zoologist to tell us not only that we are related to the lemur with its luminous opalescent or topaz eyes, that are like the eyes of angels and are instinct with a mysterious intelligence when they look at us with a strange friendliness in them as if they knew what we, after thousands of years of thinking, have only just found out—not only that this animal is our relation, but even such a creature as the bat!

Look on this picture, and on this! On the eyes, for instance, of these two beasts, and we see at once that the bat is an example of extreme degeneration; also that it is the most striking example in the animal world of a degenerate in which the downward process has at length been arrested, and instead of extinction a new, different, and probably infinitely longer life given to it.

We are reminded of the flea—the remote descendant, as we deem, of a gilded fly that was once free of the air and feasted at the same sunlit flowery table with bright-winged butterflies and noble wasps and bees.

There are those who have doubts about this genealogical tree of the bat, and would have it that he is an insectivore related to moles, shrews, and such-like low-down animals, but the main facts all point the other way. And we may assume that the bat—our familiar flittermouse, since we are not concerned with the somewhat different frugivorous bats of the tropics—is the remote descendant of a small degenerate lemur that inhabited the upper branches of high trees in the African forest; that he became exclusively insectivorous and developed an extreme activity in capturing his winged prey, and was in fact like the existing small lemur, the golago, which in pursuing insects "seems literally to fly through the air," as Sir H. Johnston has said. Finally, there was the further development, the Ovidian metamorphosis, when the loose expanding membrane of the hands and arms and sides grew to wings.

But albeit like a bird in its faculty of flight, the bat was a mammal still, and was rather like a badly constructed flying-machine, at best an improvement on the parachute. This then was a risky experiment on Nature's part, seeing that to launch a mammal on the air is to put it into competition with birds, and throw it in the way of its rapacious bird enemies, natives of that element and infinitely its superior in flying powers. But Nature, we see, takes risks of this kind with a very light heart; her busy brain teems with thousands, millions, of inventions, and if nine hundred and ninety-nine in a thousand go wrong, she simply scraps them and goes cheerfully on with her everlasting business. An amusing person! One can imagine some Principality or High Intelligence, a visitor from Aldebaran, let us say, looking on at these queer doings on her part and remarking: "My dear, what a silly fool you are to waste so much energy in trying to do an impossible thing."

And — nettled at his air of superiority — her sharp reply:

"Oh yes, now you say that, I'm reminded of a visitor I once had from—oh, I don't know exactly where—somewhere in the Milky Way—just when I was experimenting with my snake idea. To make a vertebrate without any organs of progression, yet capable of getting freely about—ha, ha, ha, how very funny! I'd like him to come back now to show him a tree-snake with a cylindrical body two yards long and no thicker than a man's middle finger, green as a green leaf and smooth as ivory, going as freely about in a tree as a cat or a monkey. Also my blue sea-snake, cleaving the water like a fish; also my ground-serpents of numberless types, moving swiftly over the earth with a grace surpassing that of creatures endowed with organs of progression."

But not a word did she say about the flying-fish, which was not a great success.

Then he: "Well, I should advise the person from the Milky Way to keep out of *your* way. No doubt you have done clever things, but the snake problem was not so very difficult after all. You thought of the rib and the scale, and the thing was done."

And she: "Yes, it was quite simple, and so when I wanted to make reptiles fly I thought of this and of that and of something else and the thing was done."

Then he: "Yes, yes, my dear lady—that was clever, too, no doubt; only your flying lizard wasn't wound up to go on for ever—not as a lizard at all events; and what I should like you to tell me is: When you have got your little beast in the air how are you going to get him to stay there?"

Her sharp reply was: "By thinking," for she was angry at his supercilious Aldebaran airs. And, put on her mettle, it was only by sheer hard thinking that she finally succeeded in accomplishing her object —this, too, as it were, by means of a subtle trick. For the bird problem had been a very different one; her experiments with flying lizards had suggested it, and she was able to create this new and finer being an inhabitant of the air by giving it ·its peculiar pointed wedge shape, its covering of feathers, with feathers for flight—hard as steel, light as gossamer, bloodless, nerveless. And correlated with shape and flight and life in the air, a development of power of vision which, compared with that of mammals and reptiles, is like a supernatural faculty.

Her subtle trick, in the case of the bat, was to reverse the process followed in building up the bird; to suspend her beast head down by the toes instead of making him perch with his head up to keep it cool; to neglect the vision altogether as of little or no account; and, on the other hand, instead of the light, hard, nerveless feather wings, to make the flying apparatus the most sensitive thing in nature, barring the antennæ of insects; a bed and field of nerves, so closely placed as to give the membrane the appearance of the finest, softest shot silk. The brains of the creature, as it were, are carried spread out on its wings, and so exquisitely delicate is the sensitiveness of these parts that in comparison our finger-tips are no more quick of feeling than the thick tough hide of some lumbering pachyderm.

I have handled scores of bats in my time, and have never had one in my hand without being struck by its shrinking, shivering motions, the tremors that passed over it like wave following wave, and it has seemed to me that the touch of a soft finger-tip on its wing was to the bat like a blow of a cheese- or bread-grater on his naked body to a man.

Now anyone, even the intelligent foreigner from Aldebaran, would have imagined that such a creature so constructed would not have maintained its exist-ence in this rough world: a sudden storm of rain or hail encountered in mid-air would have destroyed it, and in its pursuit of insects in leafy places it would have been exposed every minute to disabling accidents. But it did not happen so. That exquisite super-sensitiveness, that extra sense, or extra senses, since we do not know how many there are, not only kept it in the air, able to continue the struggle of life in the particular forest, the district, the region, the continent where it came into being, but sent it abroad, an invader and colonist, to other lands, other continents all over the globe, including those far-off isolated islands which had been cut off from all connection with the rest of the earth before mammalian life was evolved, and had no higher life than birds, until this small beast came flying over the illimitable ocean on his wings, to be followed a million years later by his noble relation in a canoe.

We see then that the bat is a very wonderful creature, one of Nature's triumphs and masterpieces, and on this account he has received a good share of attention from the zoologists. Nevertheless, after looking through a large amount of literature on the subject, the old idea persists that we know little about the bat—little, that is to say, compared with all there is to be known. How very little my own researches can add to its life history these meagre observations and comments will serve to show.

Walking by the Test, near Longparish, one evening, I noticed a number of noctules, our great bat, gathered at a spot where some high trees, elms and beeches, grew on the edge of a wet meadow. The bats were flying up and down in front of the trees, feasting on the moths and other insects that abounded there. I wondered how it came about that these big bats had this rich table all to themselves, seeing that the small common bat is by far the most numerous species in that locality. After I had stood there watching them for a few minutes a common bat appeared, and at once began flying to and fro among them; but very soon he was spotted and attacked by a big bat, and then began the maddest chase it was possible to see, the little one doubling wildly this way and that, now mounting high in the air, then plunging downward to the grass, anon losing himself in the trees, to reappear in a few moments with his vicious persecutor sticking so close that the two often seemed like one bat. Finally, they went away out of sight in the distance, and keeping my eyes in the direction they had gone, I saw the big one return alone in about seven or eight minutes and resume his flying up and down with the others. It struck me that if I could have followed or kept them in sight to the finish I should probably have witnessed a little tragedy: the terror of the one and the fury of the other suggested such an end. The keen teeth once fixed in his victim's neck, the noctule would wash his supper of moths and beetles down with a draught of warm blood, then drop the dead body to the earth before returning to his companions. This is conjecture; but we know that bats have carnivorous propensities, and that in some exotic kinds the big will kill the little, even their own young.

Probably they all have something of the vampire in them. The female bat is a most devoted parent, carrying her young about when flying, wrapping them round with her silken wings as with a shawl when in repose, suckling them at her breast even as the highest of the mammalians do. One would not be surprised to learn that the deadliest enemy of her little ones, the one she fears most, is her own consort.

Whether bats migrate or not has long been a moot question, and Millais, our latest authority, and certainly one of the best, has answered it in the affirmative. But the migration he describes is nothing but a change of locality—a retirement from their summer haunts to some spot suitable for hibernation, in some instances but a few miles distant. Other hibernating creatures—serpents, for example—have the same habit, and though compelled to travel on their bellies, they do nevertheless return year after year to the old laying-up places. The question of a seasonal movement in bats, similar to migration in birds, greatly exercised my young mind in former years in a country where bat had no business to be. This was the level, grassy, practically treeless immensity of the pampas, where there were no hollow trunks, nor caves and holes for bats to shelter in, nor ruins and buildings of brick and stone which would be a substitute for natural caverns. Human dwellings were mostly mud and straw hovels, and the only trees were those planted by man, and were not large and could not grow old. The violent winds swept this floor of the world, which was unsheltered like the sea. Yet punctually in spring the bats appeared along with the later bird migrants, and were common until April, when they vanished, and then for six months no bat would be seen in or out of doors. Clearly, then, they were strictly migratory, able like birds to travel hundreds of miles and to distribute themselves over a vast area. They were, in fact, both migrants and hibernators, since we cannot but suppose that they forsook the pampas only to find some distant place where they could pass their inactive period in safety.

At one point, about two hundred miles south of Buenos Ayres city, the level pampa is broken by a range of stony hills, or sierras, standing above the flat earth like precipitous cliffs that face the sea. On my first visit to that spot I travelled with a party of eight or nine gauchos, and evening coming on near our destination, we camped about a league from the foot of the hills and built a big fire. Just as we had got a good blaze a loud cry of "Murciélagos!" (bats) from one of the men made us look up, and there, overhead, appeared a multitude of bats, attracted by the glare, rushing about in the maddest manner, like a cloud of demented swifts. In a few moments they vanished, and we saw no more of them. Bats, I found, were extremely abundant among these hills, and here they were probably non-migratory.

But the main question about bats is always that of their sense-organs, in which they differ not only from all other mammalians but from all vertebrates, and if in this there is any resemblance or analogue to any other form of life it is to the insect. As to insect senses we are very much in the dark. The number of them may be seven or seventeen, since insects appear to be affected by vibrations which do not touch us. We exist, it has been said, in a bath of vibrations; so do all living things; but in our case the parts by which they enter are few; so too with all other vertebrates except the bat alone, and a puzzle and mystery he remains. What, for example, are the functions of the transverse bands on the wings formed of minute glands; the enormous expanse of ears in the long-eared bat; the earlet, a curious development of the tragus; and the singular leaf-like developments on the nose of the horseshoe bat? We suppose that they are sense-organs, but all we know, or half know, about the matter is ancient history; it dates back to the eighteenth century, when Spallanzani, finding that bats were independent of sight when blinded and set flying in winding tunnels and other confined places, conjectured that they were endowed with a sixth sense. Cuvier's explanation of these experiments was that the propinquity of solid bodies is perceived by the way in which the air, moved by the pulsations, reacts on the surface of the wings. Thus the sixth sense was a refinement, or extension, of the sense of touch—an excessive sensitiveness in the membrane. Blind men, we know, sometimes have a similar extreme sensibility of the skin of the face. I have known one who was accustomed to spend some hours walking every day in

Kensington Gardens, taking short cuts in any direction among the trees and never touching one, and no person seeing him moving so freely about would have imagined that he was totally blind.

My own experiments on bats in South America were inconclusive. I used to collect a dozen or twenty at a time, finding them sleeping by day on the trees in shady places, and after sealing up their eyes with adhesive gum, liberate them in a large room furnished with hanging ropes and objects of various sizes suspended from the rafters. The bats flew about without touching the walls, and deftly avoiding the numerous obstacles; but I soon discovered that they were able when flying to use the hooked claw on the wing to scratch the gum away and pull the eyelids open, and whenever one came to grief I found that its lids had not been opened.

One can see at once that an experiment of this kind is useless. The irritation of the gum and the efforts being made to remove it by the animal while flying cloud the extra sense or senses, and it loses its efficiency.

What the bat can do I discovered by chance one summer afternoon in an English lane. It was one of those deep Hampshire lanes one finds between Selborne and Prior's Dean, where I was walking just before sunset, when two common bats appeared flying up and down the lane in quest of flies, and always on coming to me they circled round and then made a vicious little stoop at my head as if threatening to strike. My brown and grey striped or mottled tweed

caps and hats have often got me into trouble with
birds, as I have told in a chapter in *Birds and Man*,
and it was probably the colour of my cap on this
occasion that excited the animosity of this pair of
bats. Again and again I waved my stick over my
head on seeing one approach, but it had not the
slightest effect—the bat would duck past it and pass
over my cap, just grazing it boldly as ever. Then
I thought of a way to frighten them. My cane was
a slim pliable one, which gave me no support, and
was used merely to have something in my hand—
a thin little cane such as soldiers carry in their hands
off duty. Holding it above my head, I caused it to
spin round so rapidly that it was no longer a cane
in appearance, but a funnel-shaped mist moving with
and above me as I walked. "Now, you little rascal,"
said I, chuckling to myself as the bat came; then
making the usual quick circle he dashed down through
the side of the misty obstruction, made his demon-
stration over my cap, and passed out on the other
side. I could hardly credit the evidence of my own
eyes, and thought he had escaped a blow by pure
luck, and that if he attempted it a second time
he would certainly be killed. I didn't want to kill
him, but the thing was really too remarkable to be
left in doubt, and so I resumed the whirling of the
stick over my head, and in another moment the
second bat came along, and, like the first, dashed
down at my cap, passing in and out of the vortex
with perfect ease and safety! Again and again they
doubled back and repeated the action without touch-

ing the stick, and after witnessing it a dozen or fifteen times I could still hardly believe that their escape from injury was anything but pure chance.

Here I recall the most wonderful flying feat I have witnessed in birds—a very common one. Frequently when standing still among the trees of a plantation or wood where humming-birds abounded, I have had one dart at me, invisible owing to the extreme swiftness of its flight, to become visible—to materialise, as it were—only when it suddenly arrested its flight within a few inches of my face, to remain there suspended motionless like a hover-fly on misty wings that produced a loud humming sound; and when thus suspended, it has turned its body to the right, then to the left, then completely round as if to exhibit its beauty—its brilliant scale-like feathers changing their colours in the sunlight as it turned. Then, in a few seconds, its curiosity gratified, it has darted away, barely visible as a faint dark line in the air, and vanished perhaps into the intricate branches of some tree, a black acacia perhaps, bristling with long needle-sharp thorns.

The humming-bird is able to perform this feat a hundred times every day with impunity by means of its brilliant vision and the exquisitely perfect judgment of the brilliant little brain behind the sight. But I take it that if the bird had attempted the feat of the bat it would have killed itself.

It is a rule in wild life that nothing is attempted which is not perfectly safe, though to us the action may appear dangerous in the extreme, or even

impossible.   At all events, I can say that these bats
in a Selborne lane taught me more than all the books
—they made me see and understand the perfection
of that extra sense.

But it is just that same sense which Spallanzani
and Cuvier wrote about, and we cannot but think
that the bat has something more than this.   That
peculiar disposition of glands and nerves on the
wings, the enormous size of the ear in the great-
eared bat, the ear-leaf, and leaf-nose, and the other
developments and excrescences on the face which
give to some species a more grotesque countenance
than was ever imagined by any mediæval artist in
stone—these are doubtless all sense-organs, and the
question is, are these all additions to the one sense
we know of—an extension and refinement of the
sense of touch?   I think they are more than that,
and there are a few facts that incline one to believe
that knowledge comes to the bat through more ports
than one—knowledge of things far as well as near.
One observation made by Millais points to this conclusion.   He noticed that a crowd of noctule bats
that sheltered in a hollow tree by day, on issuing
in the evening all took flight in the same direction,
and that the line of flight was not the same, but
varied from day to day; that on following them up
to the feeding area he discovered that insects were
always most abundant at that spot on that evening.
It came to this—that on issuing from the hollow
tree every bat in the crowd, issuing one or two at
a time and flying straight away, knew where to go,

south, east, west, or north, to some spot a mile or
two away. The bat too, then, like the far-seeing
vulture, is "sagacious of his quarry from afar," but
what Nature has given him in place of his dim,
degenerate eyes to make him sagacious in this way
remains to be found out.

CHAPTER IV

BEAUTY OF THE FOX

IT is only by a fortunate chance, a rare con-
junction of circumstances, that we are able to
see any wild animal at its best. And by animal
it must be explained is here meant a hair-clothed vertebrate that suckles its young and goes on four feet.

Chiefly on this account it would be hard in any
company of men well acquainted with our fauna
to find two persons to agree as to which is the
handsomest or prettiest of our indigenous mammals.

Undoubtedly the stag, one would exclaim: another would perhaps venture to name the field-mouse,
or the dormouse, or the water-vole, that quaint
miniature beaver in his sealskin-coloured coat, sitting erect on the streamlet's margin busily nibbling
at the pale end of a polished rush stalk which he has
cut off at the root and is now holding clasped to his
breast with his little hands. Anyone who had thus
seen him, the brown sunlit bank with its hanging
drapery of foliage and flowers for background, reflected in the clear water below, could well be
pardoned for praising his beauty and giving him
the palm. Another would champion the squirrel, that
pretty, passionate creature, most birdlike of mammals; and some white-haired veteran sportsman

would perhaps speak in glowing terms of the wild cat as seen in a tearing rage. A word, too, would be spoken for the otter, and the weasel, and the hare, and the harvest-mouse, and the white Chillingham bull, and the wild goat on the Welsh mountains. These two last, after some discussion, would doubtless be disqualified, and the roe and fallow deer entered instead; but no person would say a word about the wolf and wild boar, the last of these noble quadrupeds having been slain by some Royal hunter half a thousand or more years ago. And no one would mention the marten, or even know whether or not, like the wolf and boar, it had become "part and parcel of the dreadful past." Someone would, however, put in a plea for the hermit badger—one with sharper sight or more patient than the others, or perhaps more fortunate; and the company would be highly amused.

The rough, grizzled brock, our little British bear, would perhaps be better described as a fearsome or sublime than a beautiful beast. At all events, I lately had a singular instance of the terrifying effect of a badger related to me by a rural policeman in West Cornwall, a giant six feet six in height, a mighty wrestler, withal a sober, religious man, himself a terror to all evil-doers in the place. His beat extends on one side to the border of a wide, level moor, and one very dark night last winter he was at this desolate spot when he heard the distant sound of a horse cantering over the ground. The heavy rains had flooded the land, and he heard the splash of the hoofs as the horse came towards him. "Who could this be out on horseback at twelve o'clock on a dark winter night?" he asked himself; and listened and waited while the sound grew louder and louder and came nearer and nearer, and he strained his eyes to see the figure of a man on horseback emerging from the gloom, and could see nothing. Then it suddenly came into his mind that it was no material horseman, but a spirit accustomed to ride at that hour in that place, and his hair stood up on his head like the bristles on a pig's back. "It almost lifted my helmet off," he confessed, and he would have fled, but his trembling legs refused to move. Then, all at once, when he was about to drop fainting with extreme terror, the cause of the sound, appeared—an old dog badger trotting over the flooded moor, vigorously pounding the water with his feet, and making as much noise as a trotting horse with his hoofs. The badger was seven or eight yards away when he first caught sight of him, and the badger, too, then saw a sublime and terrifying creature standing motionless before him, and for a few moments they stared at one another; then the badger turned aside and vanished into the darkness.

To return. It was the sight of a fox that set me speculating on this subject. I have seen more foxes than I can remember, but never one that was the equal of this one; yet he was, I daresay, an ordinary specimen, with nothing to distinguish him from any other large dog fox in good condition with a fine coat of hair and a thick brush. It was in

Savernake Forest that, on emerging from a beech-wood, I noticed at a distance of seventy to eighty yards away on the wide green level open space before me a number of rabbits sitting up at the mouths of their burrows, all staring in wide-eyed alarm in one direction. Not at me, but towards a patch of dead rust-red bracken, some clumps of which were still standing, although the time was now the end of March. At intervals some of the rabbits would drop their fore-feet down and begin nibbling at the grass; then in a moment they would all start up and stare once more at the patch of bracken. I walked slowly to this red patch, and when I approached it a large fox got up and moved reluctantly away. The rough red fern on which he had been lying had made him invisible to me until he moved; but he had been plainly visible to the rabbits all the time. He trotted quietly away to a distance of about forty yards, then stopped, and half turning round, stood regarding me for some time. Standing on that carpet of vivid green spring grass, with the clear morning sunlight full on him, his red colour took an intensity and richness never previously seen. In form he appeared no less distinguished than in colour. His sharp, subtle face, large, leaf-shaped pointed ears, black without and white within, and graceful bushy tail, gave him the appearance of a dog idealised and made beautiful; and he was to the rough brown or red common dog what the finest human type— a model for a Phidias or a Praxiteles—is to a Connemara peasant or a Greenlander.

CHAPTER V

A SENTIMENTALIST ON FOXES

IT was inevitable in these tremendous times that among the many voices suggesting various drastic measures for our salvation, those of Mr. Brown and Mr. Smith, the poultry farmers, should be heard loud as any advocating the extirpation of foxes, a measure, they say, which would result in a considerable addition to the food supply of the country in the form of eggs and chickens. Even so do the fruit-growers remind us in each recurring spring that it would be an immense advantage to the country if the village children were given one or two holidays each week in March and April, and sent out to hunt and destroy queen wasps, every wasp brought in to be paid for by a bun at the public cost. That the wasp, an eater of ripe fruit, is also for six months every year a greedy devourer of caterpillars and flies injurious to plant life, is a fact the fruit-grower ignores. The fox, too, has his uses to the farmer, seeing that he subsists largely on rats, mice, and voles, but he has a greater and nobler use, as the one four-footed creature left to us in these islands to be hunted, seeing that without this glorious sport we should want horses for our cavalry, and men of the right kind on their backs, to face the Huns who would destroy us.

Apart from all these questions and considerations, which humanitarians would laugh at, the fox is a being one cannot help loving. For he is, like man's servant and friend the dog, highly intelligent, and is to the good honest dog like the picturesque and predatory gipsy to the respectable member of the community. He is a rascal, if you like, but a handsome red rascal, with a sharp, clever face and a bushy tail, and good to meet in any green place. This feeling of admiration and friendliness for the fox is occasionally the cause of a qualm of conscience in even the most hardened old hunter. "By gad, he deserved to escape!" is a not uncommon exclamation in the field, or, "I wish we had been able to spare him!" or even, "It was really hardly fair to kill him."

Here let me relate an old forgotten fox story—a hunting incident of about eighty years ago—and how it first came to be told. When J. Britton, a labourer's son in a small agricultural village in Wiltshire, and in later life the author of many big volumes on the "Beauties of England and Wales," came up to London to earn a precarious living as bottle-washer, newspaper office boy, and in various other ways, it was from the first his ambition to see himself in print, and eventually, because of his importunity, he was allowed by a kindly editor to write a paragraph relating some little incident of his early years. What he wrote was the fox story—a hunting incident in the village that had deeply impressed his boy mind. The fox, hard pressed, and running for dear life, came into the village and took refuge in a labourer's cottage, and entering by the kitchen door, passed into an inner room, and, jumping into a cradle where a baby was sleeping, concealed himself under the covering. The baby's mother had gone out a little way, but presently seeing the street in a commotion, full of dogs and mounted men, she flew back to her cottage and rushed to the cradle and plucking off the coverlet saw the fox snugly curled up by the side of her child, pretending to be, like the baby, fast asleep. She snatched the sleeping child up, then began screaming and beating the fox, until, leaping out of the cot, he fled from that inhospitable place, only to encounter the whole yelling pack at the threshold, where he was quickly worried to death.

The editor was so pleased with the anecdote that he not only printed it but encouraged the little rustic to write other things, and that is how his career as a writer began.

Now, albeit a sentimentalist, I would not say that the fox took refuge in a cradle with a sleeping baby and pretended to be asleep just to work on the kindly, maternal feelings of the cottage woman and so save his life, but I do say, and am pretty sure that not one of the Hunt and not a villager but felt that the killing of that particular fox was not quite the right thing to do, or not altogether fair.

This incident has served to remind me of another from South America, told to me by an Anglo-Argentine friend as we sat and talked one evening in Buenos Ayres, comparing notes about the ways of beasts and birds. The fox of that distant land is not red like his English cousin; his thick coat is composed of silver-white and jet-black hairs in about equal proportion, resulting in an iron-grey colour, with fulvous tints on the face, legs and under parts. If not as pretty as our red fox, he is a fine-looking animal, with as sharp a nose and as thick a brush, and, mentally, does not differ in the least from him. He is not preserved or hunted in that country, but being injurious to poultry, is much persecuted.

My friend had been sheep-farming on the western frontier, and one winter evening when he was alone in his ranch he was sitting by the fire whiling away the long hours before bed-time by playing on his flute. Two or three times he thought he heard a sound of a person pressing heavily against the door from the outside, but being very intent on his music, he took no notice. By-and-by there was a distinct creaking of the wood, and getting up and putting down his flute he took up the gun, and, stepping to the door, seized the handle and pulled it open very suddenly, when down at his feet on the floor of the room tumbled a big dog fox. He had been standing up on his hind legs, his fore-feet pressed against the door and his ear at the keyhole, listening to the dulcet sounds. The fox rolled on the floor, frightened and confused by the light; then, picking himself up, dashed out, but before going twenty yards he pulled up and looked back just when the gun was at my friend's shoulder. There had been no time for reflection, and in a moment Reynard, or Robert as we sometimes call him, was on the ground bleeding his life out.

I did not like the end of his story, and I fancied, too, from his look that he rather hated himself for having killed that particular fox, and regretted having told me about it.

In another instance which remains to be told, the fox, in England this time, who had got into trouble, and was in dire danger, was saved not once, but twice, just because there was time for reflection. It was told to me at Sidmouth by an old fisherman well known to the people in that town as "Uncle Sam," a rank sentimentalist, like myself, to whom birds and beasts were as much as human beings. It chanced that in 1887 he was occupied in collecting materials for a big bonfire on the summit of Barrow Hill, a high hill on the coast west of the town, in preparation for Queen Victoria's first Jubilee, when one day, on coming down from his work, he met a band of excited boys, all armed with long, stout sticks, which they had just cut in the adjacent wood.

Uncle Sam stopped them and told them he knew very well what they were after; they had got their sticks to beat the bushes for birds, and he was determined to prevent their doing such a thing. The boys all cried out, denying that they had any such intention, and told him they had found a fox caught in a steel trap with one of its fore-legs crushed, and as it would perhaps be a long time before the keeper would come round, they were going to kill the fox with their sticks to put it out of its misery. Uncle Sam said it would be better to save its life, and asked them to take him to the spot. This they did willingly, and there, sure enough, was a big fine fox held by one leg, crushed above the knee. He was in a savage temper, and with ears laid back and teeth bared he appeared ready to fight for his life against the crowd. Uncle Sam made them place themselves before the tortured beast, and tease him with their sticks, pretending to aim blows at his head. He in the meantime succeeded in setting the end of his stick on the shaft of the gin, and, pressing down, caused the teeth to relax their grip, and in a moment the fox was free, and, darting away, disappeared from their sight in the wood.

A year or so later, Uncle Sam heard of his rescued fox, a three-legged one, the crushed limb having fallen or been gnawed off. He had been seen near that spot where he had been caught. This was close to the highest part of the wall-like cliff, and he had a refuge somewhere among the rocks in the face of it some forty or more feet below the summit. Those, too, who walked on the sands beneath the cliff sometimes saw his tracks—the footprints of a three-legged fox. Doubtless he had modified his way of life, and subsisted partly on small crabs and anything eatable the sea cast up on the beach, and for the rest on voles and other small deer obtainable near the cliff. At all events he was never met with at any distance from the sea, and was in no danger from the Hunt, as he was always close to his fortress in the precipitous cliff.

One day a farmer, the tenant of the land at that spot, who was out with his gun and walking quickly on the narrow path in the larch wood close to the cliff, looking out for rabbits, came face to face with the three-legged fox. He stopped short, and so did the fox, and the gun was brought to the shoulder and the finger to the trigger, for it is a fact that foxes *are* shot in England by farmers when they are too numerous, and in any case here was a useless animal for hunting purposes, since he had but three legs. But before the finger touched the trigger, it came into the man's mind that this animal had done him no harm, and he said, "Why should I kill him? No, I'll let him keep his life," and so the fox escaped again.

More was heard from time to time about the three-legged fox, and that went on until quite recently—about four years ago, I was told. If we may suppose the fox to have been two or three years old when caught in a trap, and that he finished his life four or five years ago, he must have lived about twenty-six years. That would be a much longer period than the domestic dog has, and for all I know the fox may be living still, or, if dead, he may have ended his life accidentally.

CHAPTER VI

THE DISCONTENTED SQUIRREL

HURRYING along the street the other day, intent on business, I was brought to a sudden full stop by the sight of a heap of old books in tattered covers outside a second-hand furniture shop. I didn't want old books, and had no time to spare; the action was purely automatic, like that of the old horse ridden or driven by a traveller who often refreshes himself, in stopping short on coming to a public-house on the roadside. On the top of the heap was a small pamphlet or booklet in blue covers, entitled *The Discontented Squirrel*, and this attracted my attention. It seemed to touch a chord, but a chord of what I did not know. I picked it up, and, opening it, saw on the first page an ancient rude woodcut of a squirrel eating a nut.

The old picture looked familiar, but I was still at a loss until I read the first few lines of the letter-press, and then I immediately dropped the booklet and hastened on faster than ever, to make up for a wasted minute.

Why, of course, the Discontented Squirrel, that dear little ancient beastie! The whole of the child's tale came back with a rush to memory, for I had read and re-read it when my age was seven; though

I had never since met with it in the hundreds of boxes of old books turned over in my time, or in any collection of children's books of the early nineteenth century. I once made a small collection of such literature myself, and others have collected and still collect it in a large way. I sometimes wonder why some enterprising publisher doesn't start an Every Child's Library, and rescue many of the most charming of these small publications from total oblivion. Undoubtedly he would find the best period was from 1800 to about 1840.

Once upon a time—so ran the story as I remembered it, and retold it to myself while walking on —a squirrel lived in a wood, as plump and playful and happy a squirrel as one would wish to see. He had a favourite tree, an old giant oak, which was his home, and when summer was nearing its end he began to amuse himself by making a warm nest in a cavity down at the roots; also by hoarding a quantity of hazel-nuts, which were plentiful just then in the wood. This he did, not because he had any reason for doing it, or thought there was any use in it, but solely because it was an old time-honoured custom of the squirrel tribe to do these things.

While occupied in this way he all at once became aware of a new restlessness and excitement among the birds, and when he asked his feathered neighbours what it was all about, they were surprised at his innocence, and answered that it was about migration. And what was migration? A funny question to put to a bird! However, they condescended to inform their ignorant young friend that migration meant going away from the country in order to escape the winter. For now winter was coming, that sad season of leafless trees and of short, dark days; of wet and wind and bitter, bitter cold, when lakes and streams would be frozen over, and the earth buried in white, awful snow.

And where would they go to escape these awful changes?

They would go to a land where there was no winter; where the trees were green all the year round, with flowers always blooming, and fruit and nuts always ripening.

"Oh beautiful land! oh happy birds!" thought the squirrel. "But where is that desirable country?" he asked.

"Over that way," replied the birds, pointing to the south, just as if it were a place quite near. "It was," they added, "beyond the ridge of blue hills one could see on that side."

These tidings threw the squirrel into a great state of excitement, and he spent his whole time running after and questioning every bird he knew. "When," he asked, "would the migration begin?"

They laughed at the question, and said it had begun some time ago, and was going on at the present moment. The swift had long been gone; so had the night-jar; the cuckoo too; and others were beginning to follow.

The cuckoo—his own neighbour and familiar friend! Ah, that was why he hadn't seen him for some days past! And then began an unhappy time for the squirrel, and every day and every hour increased his discontent. The yellowing leaves, the chillier evenings, and long nights filled him with apprehension of the coming change, and at last he resolved that he would not endure it. For why should he stay in such a land when all his feathered neighbours and friends were now hurrying away to a better one?

Having made up his mind to migrate, he set out at dawn of day, and travelled many miles toward those blue hills in the south, which turned out to be much farther than he had thought. It was not until the late afternoon that he arrived at the foot of the ridge, feeling more tired and sore-footed than he had ever been in his life. Nevertheless he was determined not to give in, but to cross the hills before dark, and in crossing them perhaps view from the summit that beautiful land to which he was travelling. And so up and ever up he went, finding it more fatiguing every minute, until he began to despair of ever reaching the summit. And he never did; it was too high, and he was now spent with hunger and weakness after his long fatiguing day. Furthermore, the hillside grew more and more barren and desolate as he got higher, until he found himself in a place where it was all stony, without trees and bushes or even grass; and there was no food to be found, and no shelter from the cold, violent wind.

He could go no farther, and the summit was still far, far above him. Hunching himself up on the stony ground, with his nose down between his paws and his bushy tail spread along his back, he began to reflect on his condition.

Why had he not taken into account that he could not travel like a bird with wings to bear him through the air, and over hills and rivers and long stretches of rough country? And when he asked the birds how long it would take them to reach that happy land of everlasting sunshine beyond the blue ridge, had they not answered in a careless way, as if they thought little of it, "Oh, not long; two or three weeks, according to one's powers"? And it never occurred to him that a bird can fly farther in half an hour than a squirrel can travel in a whole day! Now, when it was too late, when he could not go forward, and his home was too far, far behind him, he remembered and considered these things. Oh poor squirrel! Oh miserable end of all your happy dreams!

And while he was sitting hunched up, shivering with cold and thinking these bitter, desponding thoughts, a passing kite spied him, and swooping down, snatched him up in his talons and carried him off. Little strength had he now to struggle, and at his least movement the sharp, crooked claws tightened their grasp; and even if he had been able to free himself, it would only have been to fall that vast distance through the void air and be crushed on the earth.

Then all at once the bird's flight grew swifter and rose higher, for now a second kite had appeared, and had given chase to the first to deprive him of his prey.

The first, burdened with the squirrel, could not escape from his persecutor, and they were soon at close quarters. The marauding bird now began making furious swoops at the other, aiming blows at his back with his claws, and every time he swooped down he uttered savage cries and mockings. "Aha!" he cried, "you can't save yourself with all your speed and all your doublings. Drop that squirrel if you don't want your back cut into strips. Do you remember, you red rascal, that you found me carrying home a duckling I had picked up at a farm, and made me drop it? Do you remember what you said on that occasion—that I was burdened while you were free, so that you had the advantage of me, and would claw my back to ribbons unless I dropped the duckling? Well, robber—pirate! who has the advantage now?"

It was awful, that battle in the sky; the blows, the shrieks, the dreadful imprecations they hurled at one another; but in the end the kite was obliged to drop the squirrel to defend himself with his claws, and the poor little beastie fell earthward like a stone, and would have been crushed if he had fallen upon the ground; but, luckily, he first struck a close mass of twigs and foliage on the top of a large tree. This broke the violence of the fall, and he came down gently to the branches beneath, when he managed to catch hold of a twig and come to a stop. He was bruised and bleeding, and half-dead with the shock;

but by-and-by he revived, and then what was his relief and joy to discover that he was at home—that he had fallen into his own favourite old oak-tree! On recovering a little strength he crept down the trunk, and after satisfying his hunger with two or three hazel-nuts from his store, he crawled into his unfinished nest, where he coiled himself up, and drawing the blankets over his ears, mused drowsily on his unspeakable folly in having forsaken so comfortable a home. And as to migration—well, "Never again!" he murmured as he dropped off to sleep.

The story greatly pleased me as I retold it to myself, after having forgotten it for so many long years, since I now perceived that it was a fable of the right sort; that, in fact, it was a true story —in other words, true to the creature's character. Stories about reasoning and talking animals do not always conform to this rule, which has made the terse fables of Æsop a joy for ever. Whether the author knew it or not, it is a fact that the squirrel is subject to fits of discontent with his surroundings, which send him rushing off in quest of some better place to live in; and at such times he will make his way, or try to, over wide stretches of barren, un-promising country. Thus, when trees are planted in a treeless district, by-and-by squirrels make their appearance, even when their nearest known haunts are many miles distant. Nor is this only an occa-sional outbreak of a gipsy roving disposition of the animal, since he too is subject to migratory impulses at the same time of year as the birds. In some countries large numbers of squirrels are affected simultaneously in this way, and have been observed migrating, many perishing when attempting to cross rivers too wide or swift for them.

I also liked the story because it recalled a squirrel's adventure told to me a short time before by an old fisherman at Wells-next-the-Sea, in Norfolk. Wells lies at the edge of a marsh a mile and a quarter back from the sea, and has a harbour, a river or estuary which at full tide is deep enough to enable small vessels to come up to the town. Near the river's mouth there is a row of tall guiding poles in the channel, and one afternoon my informant noticed a squirrel sitting hunched up on the summit of the outermost pole, about thirty feet above the water. Evidently he had come through the pine plantation on the sand-dunes on the Holkham or north side of the river; but, anxious to continue his travels south-ward along the shore and over the vast flat saltings towards Blakeney, he had cast himself into the river, at low tide, and finding the current too strong, had just saved himself from being carried out to sea by climbing up the last pole. Now the current was the other way, and the river full from bank to bank: the poor squirrel on his pole-top was in the middle of the swirling current, and dared not venture into the water again, either to go forward or back to the wood.

The fisherman went home to his tea; but, two hours later, just about sunset, he strolled back to the sea-front, and there still sat the squirrel hunched up on the top of his pole. Presently a fishing-boat came in from the sea, with only one person, a young man, in it. The old man hailed him, and called his attention to the squirrel on the pole. "All right; I see him!" shouted back the young fellow. "I'll try to get him off!"

Then, as the swirling current carried the boat up to within about three yards of the pole, he leant forward and thrust out an oar until the blade touched the pole; and no sooner had it touched than down like lightning came the squirrel from his perch, leaped upon the oar, and from the oar to the boat, then quickly bounded up the mast and perched himself on the top.

The squirrel had not understood the man's friendly intentions, and his lightning-quick action appeared not to have been prompted either by reason or instinct, but rather by that intuitive faculty one is half-inclined to believe in, which causes an animal suddenly threatened with destruction to take instantly the one line by which it may be saved.

The boat went swiftly on, driven by the rushing tide, until it reached the quay at Wells, and no sooner did the keel touch the stones at the landing-stage than down the squirrel flew from the mast-top, and rushing to the bow, took a flying leap to the land, then dashed off toward the town at top-most speed. A number of children playing on the quay saw him, and with a wild cry of " Squirrel! squirrel!" went after him. Luckily there was no dog about; and the squirrel being faster than the boys, kept well ahead, and, dodging this way and that among coal-trucks and wagons and horses, and men occupied in unloading, got through them all, then crossing the lower or coast road, dashed into one of the wynds or narrow streets which run up to the higher part of the town. There more yelling children joined the hunt, and the people of the wynd ran out of their houses to find out what all the uproar was about.

The wynd ends at the upper street, and facing it is a long brick wall ten feet high, and up this wall went the squirrel without a pause or slip, as swiftly as when going over the level earth, and disappeared over the top into the orchard on the other side. There the loud advancing wave of young barbarians was stayed by the wall, as by an ocean-facing cliff.

It had been a dashing performance, and the squirrel could now have settled safely down in that sheltered spot among its fruit and shade trees, since the tenant, who lived a hermit life in the house, was friendly to all wild creatures, and allowed neither dogs nor cats nor fiends in shape of boys with loud halloo and brutal noise to intrude into his sacred grounds.

But this would not have suited the squirrel; the town noises and lights, the shrill cries of children at play in the evening, and the drum and fife band of the Boy Scouts would have kept him in a constant state of apprehension. Squirrels are nervy creatures. No doubt when the town was asleep and silent that night he scaled the back-wall and crossed other orchards and gardens until he came out to the old unkept hedge on that side, and followed it all the way to Holkham Park, a vast green solitude with many ancient noble trees, in one of which he probably first saw the light.

And there, at home once more, he perhaps resolved, like the Discontented Squirrel of the fable, never again to attempt to better himself by migrating.

CHAPTER VII

MY NEIGHBOUR'S BIRD STORIES

WE sometimes make mistakes, and I certainly made one about my neighbour over the way, Mr. Redburn, when I formed the conclusion that I had no use for him. For I was just then birding in an east-coast village, and when engaged on that business I look for some interest in the subject which absorbs me, some bird-lore in those I meet and converse with. If they are entirely without it, they are negligible persons; and Mr. Redburn, a retired bank manager and a widower, living alone in a house opposite my lodgings, fell quite naturally into this category. A kindly man with friendly feelings towards a stranger, one it was pleasant to talk with, but unfortunately he knew nothing about birds.

One day we met a mile from the village, he out for a constitutional, and I returning from a prowl; and as he seemed inclined to have a talk, we sat down on a green bank at the roadside and got out our pipes.

"You are always after birds," he said, "and I know so little about them!" Then to prove how little he knew of their ways and wants, he related the history of a thrush he once kept in a cage hanging at the back of his house, where there was

a garden, and where he amused himself by culti-
vating flowers and vegetables. The bird had been
taken from the nest and reared by hand; consequently it had never learnt to sing a true thrush song,
but had invented a song of its own, composed of
imitations—cackling fowls, whistling boys, and various other village noises, including those from the
smithy. The village postman, who lived close by,
had a peculiar shrill double whistle which he always
emitted when nearing his house, to bring his wife
to the door. This sound, too, the thrush mimicked
so cleverly that poor Mrs. Postman was always
running to the door for nothing, and at length had
to beg her husband to invent some other sound to
announce his approach.

Seeing that the bird was always cheerful and noisy,
it was a puzzle to Mr. Redburn that it never looked
well. It was supplied with clean water and good
food—bread and milk and crushed rape-seed—every
day; but it never seemed to enjoy its food, and its
plumage had a dry, loose, disarranged appearance,
and was without a gloss. It was a perfect contrast in this respect to a wild thrush that used to
visit the garden.

One day, when the bird had been in his possession
for a little over a year, he happened to be sitting in
his garden smoking, when this wild thrush came on
the scene and began running about the lawn looking for something to eat. By chance he noticed that
his thrush in its cage was watching the wild bird
intently. Presently the bird on the lawn spied a

worm which had incautiously put its head out of its hole, and dashed at and seized it, then began tugging away until it pulled it out, after which it proceeded to kill and devour it with a good appetite. The caged bird had watched all this with increasing excitement, which culminated when the worm was killed and swallowed.

"Now I wonder if he wants a worm too?" said Mr. Redburn to himself, and getting up he took a spade and dug up two big worms, which he placed in the cage as an experiment; and no sooner did the thrush see than he flew at and killed and devoured them as if mad with hunger. Every day after that he dug up a few worms for his thrush, and the sight of him with a spade in his hand would always start the bird hopping wildly about his cage.

As a result of this addition to his diet the thrush in due time took on a brighter, glossier coat.

Mr. Redburn had congratulated himself on having made a happy discovery—happy for his thrush. It had taken him a year of twelve months, but he had never made the more important discovery, which it appeared to me he had come so near making, that the one and only way to give perfect happiness to your captive thrush is to open the cage and let him fly to find worms for himself, and to get a mate, and with her assistance build a deep nest in a holly bush, and be the parent of five beautiful gem-like blue eggs spotted with black.

The only other bird he had ever possessed was a jackdaw, a charming fellow, full of fun, with uncut wings, so that he was free to go and come at will; but he was a home-loving bird, very affectionate, though loving mischief too, and never happier than when his indulgent master allowed him to use his head as a perch.

One day, when Mr. Redburn was busy in his study, his little daughter, aged seven, came crying to him to complain that Jack was plaguing her so! He wanted to pull the buttons off her shoes, and because she wouldn't let him he pecked her ankles, and it hurt her so, and made her cry. He gave her his stick, and told her, with a laugh, to give Jack a good smart rap on the head with it, and that would make him behave himself. He never for a moment imagined that such a clever, quick bird as Jack would allow himself to be struck by a little girl with a long walking-stick; nevertheless this incredible thing happened, and the stick actually came down on Jack's head, and the child screamed, and, running to her, he found her crying, and Jack lying to all appearance dead on the floor! They took him up tenderly and examined him, and said he was really and truly dead, and then tenderly, sorrowfully, put him down again. All at once, to their astonishment and delight, he opened his mischievous little grey eyes and looked at his friends standing over him. Then he got up on his legs and began rocking his head from side to side, after which he shook his feathers two or three times; then tried to scratch his poll with his claw, but didn't succeed. He was in a queer state, and didn't know what had happened to him; but he soon recovered, and was just as fond of his little playmate as ever, although he never again attempted to pull her buttons off or peck her ankles.

Some time after this Jack disappeared for a day or two, and was brought back by a boy of the village, who was warmly thanked and rewarded with a few pence. From that day every little boy who was so lucky as to find Jack out of bounds, and could catch him, expected a gratuity on taking him to the house; and as the little boys were all very poor and hungry for sweets, they were perpetually on the look-out for Jack, and went about with something in their ragged little pockets to entice him into their cottages. Every day Jack was lost and found again, until the good man, who was not rich, concluded that he could not afford to keep so expensive a pet; and so Jack was given to a gentleman who had a pet daw of his own and wanted another. In his new home he had nice large grounds with big trees, and Jack with a chum of his own tribe was very happy until his end, which came very suddenly. The two birds roosted side by side together on a tall tree near the house, and one summer night this tree was struck by lightning; next morning the two birds were found lying dead at the roots.

My neighbour had one more bird story, the best of all to tell, and this about rooks, the only wild birds he had ever observed with the object of finding out something about their habits. There was a small rookery in some elm trees growing at the bottom of the garden of the house he then lived in, and the way the birds went on during nest-building time moved his curiosity to such a degree that one Sunday morning he resolved to give the whole day to a careful inquiry into the domestic affairs of these black neighbours. No doubt, he thought, they were subject to a law or custom which enabled them to exist in a community, living and rearing their young in nests placed close together. Nevertheless it was evident that it was not an ideal society, and that the noise was not due merely to animal spirits, as in the case of a lot of boys out of school; there was a great deal of scolding and quarrelling, and from time to time a mighty hubbub, as if the entire colony had suddenly been seized with an angry excitement. What occasioned these outbursts? It was just to try to find this out that he planted himself in a chair near the trees on that Sunday morning. The nearest tree contained one nest only, a new one not yet finished, and eventually he thought it best to concentrate his attention on this point, and watch the movements of the one pair of birds. He had quickly found that it only worried and confused him to keep a watch on the movements and actions of several birds and their nests. The two birds he attended to went and came, sometimes together, then first one, and then the other, and sometimes one would remain at the nest during the absence of its mate. This went on for about three hours, and nothing unusual happened at the nest; at other points of the rookery there were little storms of noise and some shindies, but he was determined not to let his attention wander from his two birds. At length he was rewarded by seeing one of the pair fly to an unguarded nest about thirty yards away, on a neighbouring tree, and deliberately pull out a stick, which it brought back and carefully adjusted in its own nest. By-and-by the two birds who had been robbed returned together and immediately appeared to be aware that something was wrong with their home. Standing on the nest, they put their heads together, fluttering their wings and cawing excitedly, and presently they were joined by others, and others still, until almost the entire colony was congregated on the tree, all making a great noise. After two or three minutes they began to quarrel among themselves, and there were angry blows with beaks and wings, after which the tumult subsided, and the company broke up, every pair going back to its own nest. After that comparative peace and quiet continued for some time, but Mr. Redburn now noticed that one bird always remained on guard on the nest where the stick had been stolen. His two birds quietly continued to work and go and come, and by-and-by, about two hours after the commotion, they both flew away to the fields together, and no sooner were they gone than the bird they had robbed, keeping guard on his tree, flew straight to the nest they had left, and after what appeared like a careful examination took hold of a stick and tugged vigorously until he succeeded in pulling it out. With the stick in his beak he flew back to his nest and proceeded to adjust it in the fabric.

What would happen now, Mr. Redburn asked, when the dishonest couple came back and discovered that they had been deprived of their loot? He watched for their return with keen interest, and by-and-by they came, and, to his astonishment, nothing happened. They settled on their nest, looked it over in the usual way to see that it was as they had left it, and although they no doubt saw that it was not so they made no fuss.

The most remarkable thing in all this affair was, to Mr. Redburn's mind, that the robbed birds appeared to know so well who the thief was and where the stick could be looked for.

To me it was remarkable that my neighbour, who "knew nothing about birds," had yet, in one day's watching, succeeded in seeing something which throws a stronger light on the law of the rookery than any single observation contained in the ornithological books.

In this case, as he relates it, the robbed birds appeared to know very well who the culprit were among their neighbours. Why, then, were the robbers not attacked, and seeing that they waited their time and went quietly and recovered their own, why all that preliminary fuss? It sometimes happens, we know, that the entire rookery becomes infuriated against a particular pair; that in such cases they fall upon and demolish the nest, and in extreme cases expel the offenders from the rookery. I take it that such attacks are made only on the incorrigible ones, those that obtain all their materials by thieving, and so make themselves a nuisance to the community. It seems probable that in this instance the colony, although excited at the news of the robbery and the outcry made by the victimised pair, declined to take too serious a view of the matter, and after some discussion and quarrelling left the angry couple to manage their own affairs. We may think, too, that in a majority of cases an occasional offence is condoned among birds that have a social law but do not observe it very strictly. Thus, at home, the rook is a stealer of sticks when the occasion offers, and a wooer of his neighbour's wife when his neighbour is out of the way. Too severe a code would not do; it would, in fact, upset the whole community, and rooks would have to go and live like carrion crows, each pair by itself. At all events, in this instance we see that only after the angry outcry made by the victims had failed to bring about an attack they quietly waited their opportunity to recover their property. Then the meek way in which the robbers took it appears to show that they too understood the whole business very well indeed. They were in a dangerous position, and were quite ready to lose what they had taken and say no more about it.

CHAPTER VIII

THE TOAD AS TRAVELLER

ONE summer day I sat myself down on the rail of a small wooden foot-bridge—a very old bridge it looked, bleached to a pale grey colour with grey, green, and yellow lichen growing on it, and very creaky with age, but the rail was still strong enough to support my weight. The bridge was at the hedge side, and the stream under it flowed out of a thick wood over the road and into a marshy meadow on the other side, overgrown with coarse tussocky grass. It was a relief to be in that open sunny spot, with the sight of water and green grass and blue sky before me, after prowling for hours in the wood—a remnant of the old Silchester forest —worried by wood-flies in the dense undergrowth. These same wood-flies and some screaming jays were all the wild creatures I had seen, and I would now perhaps see something better at that spot.

It was very still, and for some time I saw nothing, until my wandering vision lighted on a toad travelling towards the water. He was right out in the middle of the road, a most dangerous place for him, and also difficult to travel in, seeing that it had a rough surface full of loosened stones, and was very dusty. His progress was very slow; he did not hop, but crawled laboriously for about five inches, then sat up and rested four or five minutes, then crawled and rested again. When I first caught sight of him he was about forty yards from the water, and looking at him through my binocular when he sat up and rested I could see the pulsing movements of his throat as though he panted with fatigue, and the yellow eyes on the summit of his head gazing at that delicious coolness where he wished to be. If toads can see things forty yards away the stream was visible to him, as he was on that part of the road which sloped down to the stream.

Lucky for you, old toad, thought I, that it is not market day at Basingstoke or somewhere with farmers and small general dealers flying about the country in their traps, or you would be flattened by a hoof or a wheel long before the end of your pilgrimage.

By-and-by another creature appeared and caused me to forget the toad. A young water-vole came up stream, swimming briskly from the swampy meadow on the other side of the road. As he approached I tapped the wood with my stick to make him turn back, but this only made him swim faster towards me, and determined to have my own way I jumped down and tried to stop him, but he dived past the stick and got away where he wanted to be in the wood, and I resumed my seat.

There was the toad, when I looked his way, just about where I had last seen him, within perhaps a few inches. Then a turtle-dove flew down, alighting

within a yard of the water, and after eyeing me
suspiciously for a few moments advanced and took
one long drink and flew away. A few minutes later
I heard a faint complaining and whining sound in
or close to the hedge on my left hand, and turning
my eyes in that direction caught sight of a stoat,
his head and neck visible, peeping at me out of the
wood; he was intending to cross the road, and seeing
me sitting there hesitated to do so. Still having
come that far he would not turn back, and by-and-
by he drew himself snake-like out of the concealing
herbage, and was just about to make a dash across
the road when I tapped sharply on the wood with
my stick and he fled back into cover. In a few seconds
he appeared again, and I played the same trick on
him with the same result; this was repeated about
four times, after which he plucked up courage enough
to make his dash and was quickly lost in the coarse
grass by the stream on the other side.

Then a curious thing happened: flop, flop, flop,
went vole following vole, escaping madly from their
hiding-places along the bank into the water, all swimming for dear life to the other side of the stream.
Their deadly enemy did not swim after them, and
in a few seconds all was peace and quiet again.

And when I looked at the road once more, the
toad was still there, still travelling, painfully crawling a few inches, then sitting up and gazing with
his yellow eyes over the forty yards of that weary
via dolorosa which still had to be got over before he
could bathe and make himself young for ever in

that river of life. Then all at once the feared and
terrific thing came upon him: a farmer's trap, drawn
by a fast trotting horse, suddenly appeared at the
bend of the road and came flying down the slope.
That's the end of you, old toad, said I, as the horse
and trap came over him; but when I had seen them
cross the ford and vanish from sight at the next
bend, my eyes went back, and to my amazement
there sat my toad, his throat still pulsing, his promi-
nent eyes still gazing forward. The four dread hoofs
and two shining wheels had all missed him; then at
long last I took pity on him, although vexed at
having to play providence to a toad, and getting off
the rail I went and picked him up, which made him
very angry. But when I put him in the water he
expanded and floated for a few moments with legs
spread out, then slowly sank his body and remained
with just the top of his head and the open eyes
above the surface for a little while, and finally
settled down into the cooler depths below.

It is strange to think that when water would
appear to be so much to these water-born and
amphibious creatures they yet seek it for so short
a period in each year, and for the rest of the time
are practically without it! The toad comes to it
in the love season, and at that time one is often
astonished at the number of toads seen gathered in
some solitary pool, where perhaps not a toad has
been seen for months past, and with no other water
for miles around. The fact is, the solitary pool has
drawn to itself the entire toad population of the

surrounding country, which may comprise an area of several square miles. Each toad has his own home or hermitage somewhere in that area, where he spends the greater portion of the summer season practically without water excepting in wet weather, hiding by day in moist and shady places, and issuing forth in the evening. And there too he hibernates in winter. When spring returns he sets out on his annual pilgrimage of a mile or two, or even a greater distance, travelling in the slow, deliberate manner of the one described, crawling and resting until he arrives at the sacred pool—his Tipperary. They arrive singly and are in hundreds, a gathering of hermits from the desert places, drunk with excitement, and filling the place with noise and commotion. A strange sound, when at intervals the leader or precentor or bandmaster for the moment blows himself out into a wind instrument—a fairy bassoon, let us say, with a tremble to it—and no sooner does he begin than a hundred more join in; and the sound, which the scientific books describe as "croaking," floats far and wide, and produces a beautiful, mysterious effect on a still evening when the last heavy-footed labourer has trudged home to his tea, leaving the world to darkness and to me.

In England we are almost as rich in toads as in serpents, since there are two species, the common toad, universally distributed, and the rarer natterjack abundant only in the south of Surrey. The breeding habits are the same in both species, the concert-singing included, but there is a difference in the *timbre* of their voices, the sound produced by the natterjack being more resonant and musical to most ears than that of the common toad.

The music and revels over, the toads vanish, each one taking his own road, long and hard to travel, to his own solitary home. Their homing instinct, like that of many fishes and of certain serpents that hibernate in numbers together, and of migrating birds, is practically infallible. They will not go astray, and the hungriest raptorial beasts, foxes, stoats, and cats, for example, decline to poison themselves by killing and devouring them.

In the late spring or early summer one occasionally encounters a traveller on his way back to his hermitage. I met one a mile or so from the valley of the Wylie, half-way up a high down, with his face to the summit of Salisbury Plain. He was on the bank at the side of a deep narrow path, and was resting on the velvety green turf, gay with little flowers of the chalk-hills — eye-bright, squinancy-wort, daisies, and milkwort, both white and blue.

The toad, as a rule, strikes one as rather an ugly creature, but this one sitting on the green turf, with those variously coloured fairy flowers all about him, looked almost beautiful. He was very dark, almost black, and with his shining topaz eyes had something of the appearance of a yellow-eyed black cat. I sat down by his side and picked him up, which action he appeared to regard as an unwarrantable liberty on my part; but when I placed him on my knee and began stroking his blackish corrugated back with my finger-tips his anger vanished, and one could almost imagine his golden eyes and wide lipless mouth smiling with satisfaction.

A good many flies were moving about at that spot—a pretty fly whose name I do not know, a little bigger than a house-fly, all a shining blue, with head and large eyes a bright red. These flies kept lighting on my hand, and by-and-by I cautiously moved a hand until a fly on it was within tongue-distance of the toad, whereupon the red tongue flicked out like lightning and the fly vanished. Again the process was repeated, and altogether I put over half a dozen flies in his way, and they all vanished in the same manner, so quickly that the action eluded my sight. One moment and a blue and red-headed fly was on my hand sucking the moisture from the skin, and then, lo! he was gone, while the toad still sat there motionless on my knee like a toad carved out of a piece of black stone with two yellow gems for eyes.

After helping him to a dinner, I took him off my knee with a little trouble, as he squatted close down, desiring to stay where he was, and putting him back among the small flowers to get more flies for himself if he could, I went on my way.

It is easy to establish friendly relations with these lowly creatures, amphibian and reptiles, by a few gentle strokes with the finger-tips on the back. Shortly after my adventure with this toad I was visiting a naturalist friend, who told me of an adventure he had had with a snake. He was out walking with his wife near his home among the Mendips when they spied the snake bathing in the sun on the turf, and at the same moment the snake saw them and began quietly gliding away. But they succeeded in overtaking and capturing it, and, although it was a large snake and struggled violently to escape, they soon quieted it down by stroking its back with their fingers. They kept and played with it for half an hour, then put it down, whereupon it went away, but quite slowly, almost as if reluctant to leave them.

So far this was a common experience; I have tamed many grass-snakes in the same way, and the only smooth snake I have ever captured in England was made tame in about ten minutes by holding it on my knee and stroking it. In the instance related by my friend, it would appear that the tameness does not always vanish as soon as the creature finds itself free again. About three days after the incident I have related he was again walking with his wife, and they again found the snake at the same spot, whereupon he, anxious to capture it again, made a dash at it, but the snake on this occasion made no attempt to escape, and when picked up did not struggle. They again kept it some time, caressing it with their fingers, then releasing it as before; later they saw their snake on several occasions, when it acted in the same way, allowing itself to be taken up and kept as long as it was wanted, and then, when released, going very slowly away.

That one first delightful experience of having its back stroked with finger-tips had made a tame snake of it.

CHAPTER IX

THE HERON: A FEATHERED NOTABLE

THE bird-watcher's life is an endless succession of surprises. Almost every day he appears fated to witness some habit, some action, which he had never seen or heard of before, and will perhaps never see again. Who but Waterton ever beheld herons hovering like gulls over the water, attracted by the fish swimming near the surface? And who, I wonder, except myself ever saw herons bathing and wallowing after the manner of beasts, not birds? At all events I do not remember any notice of such a habit in any account of the heron I have read; and I have read many. At noon, one hot summer day, I visited Sowley Pond, which has a heronry near it on the Hampshire coast; and peeping through the trees on the bank I spied five herons about twenty yards from the margin bathing in a curious way among the floating poa grass, where the water was about two feet deep or more. All were quietly resting in different positions in the water—one was sitting on his knees with head and neck and shoulders out of it, another was lying on one side with one half-open wing above the surface, a third had only head and neck out, the whole body being submerged; and it puzzled me to think how he could keep himself down unless it was by grasping the roots of the grass with his claws. Occasionally one of the bathers would shift his position, coming partly up or going lower down, or turning over on the other side; but there was no flutter or bird-like excitement. They rested long in one position, and moved in a leisurely, deliberate manner, lying and luxuriating in the tepid water like pigs, buffaloes, hippopotamuses, and other water-loving mammalians. I watched them for an hour or so, and when I left, two were still lying down in the water. The other three had finished their bath, and were standing drying their plumage in the hot sun.

This was not the first surprise the heron had given me, but the first was received far from this land in my early shooting and collecting days, and the species was not our well-known historical bird, the *Ardea cinerea* of Britain and Europe generally, and Asia and Africa, but the larger *Ardea cocoi* of South America, a bird with a bigger wing-spread, but so like it in colour and action that any person from England on first seeing it would take it for a very large specimen of his familiar home bird.

It happened that I was making a collection of the birds of my part of the country and was in want of a specimen of our common heron. A few of these birds haunted the river near my home, and one day when out with the gun I caught sight of one fishing in the river. It was deep there, and the bird was standing under and close to the bank, where the water came up to his feathered thighs.

Moving back from the bank I got within shooting
distance and then had a look at him and saw that
he was very intently watching the water, with head
drawn back and apparently about to strike. And
just as I pulled the trigger he struck, and stricken
himself at the same moment he threw himself up
into the air and rose to a height of about thirty feet,
then fell back to earth close to the margin and began
beating with his wings. When I came up he was at
his last gasp, and what was my astonishment to find
a big fish impaled by his beak. It was an uneatable
fish, of a peculiar South American family, its upper
part cased in bony plates; an ugly and curious-
looking creature called *Vieja* ("old woman") by the
natives. It was a common fish in our stream and a
nuisance when caught, as it invariably sucked the
hook into its belly. Now I had often found dead
"old women" lying on or near the bank with a hole
in their bony back and wondered at it. I had concluded that some of the native boys in our neighbourhood had taken to spearing the fish, and naturally
these useless ones they killed were thrown away.
Now I knew that they were killed by the heron with
a blow of his powerful beak; a serious mistake on
the bird's part, but an inevitable one in the circumstances, since even the shining, piercing eyes of
a heron would only be able to *surmise* the presence
of a fish a few inches below the surface in the muddy
streams of the pampas. To distinguish the species
would never be possible.

In this case the iron-hard dagger-like beak had

been driven right through the fish from the bone-plated back to the belly, from which it projected about an inch and a half. With such power had the blow been delivered that it was only by exerting a good deal of force that I was able to wrench the beak out. My conclusion was that the bird would never have been able to free himself, and that by shooting him I had only saved him from the torture of a lingering death from starvation. The strange thing was that bird and fish had met their end simultaneously in that way: I doubted that such a thing had ever happened before or would ever happen again. From that time I began to pay a good deal of attention to the dead "old women" I found along the river-bank with a hole in their back, and could never find one in which the beak had been driven right through the body. In every case the beak had gone in about half-way through—just far enough to enable the bird to fly to the shore with its inconvenient captive and there get rid of it.

Death by accident is common enough in wild life, and a good proportion of such deaths are due to an error of judgment, often so slight as not to seem an error at all. For example, a hawking swallow may capture and try to bolt a wasp or other dangerous insect without first killing or crushing it, and in doing so receive a fatal sting in the throat. The flight of hawking swallows and swifts is so rapid that it hardly gives them time to judge of the precise nature of the insect appearing before them which a second's delay would lose. This is seen in swallows and swifts so frequently getting hooked by dry-fly anglers. Birds of prey, too, occasionally meet their death in a similar way, as when a kite or falcon or buzzard or eagle lifts a stoat or weasel, and the lithe little creature succeeds in wriggling up and fixing its teeth in the bird's flesh. If they fall from a considerable height both are killed. Again, birds sometimes get killed by attempting to swallow too big a morsel, and I think this is oftenest the case with birds that have rather weak beaks and have developed a rapacious habit. I remember once seeing a Guira cuckoo with head hanging and wings drooping, struggling in vain to swallow a mouse stuck fast in its gullet, the tail still hanging from its beak. Undoubtedly the bird perished, as I failed in my attempts to capture it and save its life by pulling the mouse out. A common tyrant-bird of South America, *Pitangus*, preys on mice, small snakes, lizards and frogs, as well as on large insects, but invariably hammers its prey on a branch until it is bruised to a pulp and broken up. It will work at a mouse in this way until the skin is so bruised that it can be torn open with its long, weak bill, but it never attempts to bolt it whole as the cuckoo does.

One day when sitting on the bank of Beaulieu River in Hampshire I saw a cormorant come up with a good-sized eel it had captured and was holding by the neck close to the head, but the long body of the eel had wound itself serpent-wise about the bird's long neck, and the cormorant was struggling furiously to free itself. Unable to do so it dived, thinking perhaps to succeed better under water, but when it reappeared on the surface the folds of the eel appeared to have tightened and the bird's struggles were weaker. Again it dived, and then again three or four times, still keeping its hold on the eel, but struggling more feebly each time. Finally it came up without the eel and so saved itself, since if it had kept its hold a little longer it would have been drowned.

In my *Land's End* book I have given an account of a duel between a seal and a huge conger-eel it had captured by the middle of the body, the conger-eel having fastened its teeth in the seal's head.

An odd way in which birds occasionally kill themselves is by getting a foot caught in long horse-hair or thread used in building. I have seen sparrows and house-martins dead, suspended from the nest by a hair or thread under the nest in this way.

When I killed my heron, and by doing so probably saved it from a lingering death by starvation, it struck me as an odd coincidence that it was within a stone's throw of the spot where a few weeks before I had saved another bird from a like fate—not in this instance by shooting it. The bird was the painted snipe, *Rhynchæa semicollaris*, a prettily coloured and mottled species with a green curved beak, and I found it on the low grassy margin of the stream with the point of its middle toe caught in one of Nature's traps for the unwary—the closed shell of a large fresh-water clam. The stream at this spot was almost entirely overgrown with dense beds of bulrushes, and the clams were here so abundant that the bottom of the stream was covered with them. The snipe wading into the water a foot or so from the margin had set its middle toe inside a partially open shell, which had instantly closed and caught it. Only by severing the point off could the bird have delivered itself, but its soft beak was useless for such a purpose. It had succeeded in dragging the clam out, and on my approach it first tried to hide itself by crouching in the grass, and then struggled to drag itself away. It was, when I picked it up, a mere bundle of feathers and had probably been lying thus captive for three or four days in constant danger of being spied by a passing carrion-hawk and killed and eaten. But when I released the toe it managed to flutter up and go away to a distance of thirty or forty yards before it dropped down among the aquatic grasses and sedges on a marshy islet in the stream.

A large heronry is to the naturalist one of the most fascinating spectacles in the wild bird life of this country. Heaven be thanked that all our land-owners are not like those of South Devon, who are anxious to extirpate the heron in that district in the interest of the angler. On account of their action one is inclined to look on the whole fraternity of dry-fly fishers as a detestable lot of Philistines. Some years ago they raised a howl about the swallows—their worst enemies, that devoured all the mayflies, so that the trout were starved! Well, they can re-joice now to know that swallow and martin return to England in ever decreasing numbers each summer, and they must be grateful to our neighbours across the Channel who are exterminating these noxious birds on migration.

I have known and know many heronries all over England, and I think the one I liked to visit best of all was in a small wood in a flat green country in the Norfolk Broads district. It was large, containing about seventy inhabited nests—huge nests, many of them, and near together, so that it looked like a rookery made by giant rooks. And it has had a troubled history, like that of an old Norfolk town in the far past when Saxons and Danes were at variance. For this heronry had been established alongside of an old populous rookery, and the rooks hated the herons and mobbed them and demolished their nests, and persecuted them in every rookish way; but they refused to quit, and at length the rooks, unable to tolerate them, shifted their rookery a little farther away, and there was an uncomfortable sort of truce between the big black hostile birds and their grey ghostly neighbours with very long, sharp, and very unghostly beaks.

On the occasion of my last visit this heronry was in the most interesting stage, when the young birds were fully grown and were to be seen standing up on their big nests or on the topmost branches of the trees waiting to be fed. At some spots in the wood where the trees stand well apart I could count as

many as forty to fifty young birds standing in this
way, in families of two, three, and four. It was a
fine sight, and the noise they made at intervals was
a fine thing to hear. The heron is a bird with a big
voice. When nest-building is going on, and in fact
until most of the eggs are laid, herons are noisy birds,
and the sounds they emit are most curious — the
loud familiar squalk or "frank," which resembles the
hard, powerful alarm-note of the peacock, but is
more harsh, while other grinding metallic cries remind
one of the carrion-crow. Other of their loud sounds are
distinctly mammalian in character; there is a dog-
like sound, partly bark and partly yelp, swine-like
grunting, and other sounds which recall the peculiar,
unhappy, desolate cries of the large felines, especially
of the puma. One need not take it for granted that
these strange vocal noises are nothing but love calls.
They may be in part expressions of anger, since it
is hardly to be believed that the members of these
rude communities invariably respect one another's
rights. We see how it is with the rook, which has
a more developed social instinct than the lonely
savage heron.

During incubation quiet reigns in the heronry;
when the young are out, especially when they are
well grown and ravenously hungry all day long, the
wood is again filled with the uproar; and a noisier
heronry than the one I am describing could not have
been found. For one thing, it was situated on the
very edge of the wood, overlooking the green flat
expanse towards Breydon Water, where the parent

birds did most of their fishing, so that the returning
birds were visible from the tree-tops at a great
distance, travelling slowly with eel- and frog- and
fish-laden gullets on their wide-spread blue wings—
dark blue against the high shining blue of the sky.
All the young birds, stretched up to their full height,
would watch its approach, and each and every one
of them would regard the returning bird as its own
too-long absent parent with food to appease its own
furious hunger; and as it came sweeping over the
colony there would be a tremendous storm of wild
expectant cries—strange cat- and dog-like growling,
barking, yelping, whining, screaming; and this would
last until the newcomer would drop upon its own
tree and nest and feed its own young, whereupon
the tempest would slowly subside, only to be renewed
on the appearance of the next great blue bird coming
down over the wood.

One of the most delightful, the most exhilarating
spectacles of wild bird life is that of the soaring
heron. The great blue bird, with great round wings
so measured in their beats, yet so buoyant in the
vast void air! It is indeed a sight which moves all
men to admiration in all countries which the great bird
inhabits; and I remember one of the finest passages
in old Spanish poetry describes the heron rejoicing
in its placid flight. "Have you seen it, beautiful in
the heavens!" the poet exclaims in untranslatable
lines, in which the harmonious words, *delicado y
sonoroso*, and the peculiar rhythm are made to mimic

the slow pulsation of the large wings. Who has not seen it and experienced something of the feeling which stirred the old writer centuries ago:

Has visto hermosa en el cielo
La garza sonreirse con plácido vuelo?
Has visto, torciendo de la mano,
Sacra que la deribe por el suelo?

The most perfect example I know of in literature in which the sound is an echo to the sense. How artificial and paltry that ornament often seems to us in our poets, even in much-admired passages, such as Goldsmith's white-washed walls and nicely-sanded floor, and the varnished clock that clicked behind the door. The beauty of the passage quoted —the heavenward sublime flight of the heron and the furious zigzag pursuit of the falcon, who will presently overtake and hurl it back to earth—is in its perfect naturalness, its spontaneity, as if someone in delight at the spectacle had exclaimed the words.

This is one of the sights in bird life which makes me envy the sportsmen of the old time when falconry was followed and the peregrine was flown, not at skulking magpies, as the way is with our Hawking Club, but at noble heron. They saw the great bird at its best, when it mounts with powerful wing-beats almost vertically to a vast height in the sky. The heron, in these days, when all the hawks have been extirpated by our Philistine pheasant-breeders who own the country, has no need to exercise that instinct and faculty.

The question has sometimes come into my mind,

Why does the heron at all times, when, seen on the wing, it strikes us as beautiful, and when only strange or quaint-looking, or actually ugly, produce in some of us a feeling akin to melancholy? We speak of it as a grey, a ghost-like bird; and grey it certainly is, a haunter of lonely waters at the dim twilight hour; mysterious in its comings and goings. Ghostly, too, it is in another sense, and here we may see that the feeling, the sense of melancholy, is due to association, to the fact that the heron is a historical bird, part of the country's past, when it was more to the country gentleman than the semi-domestic pheasant and the partridge on the arable land and the blackcock and red grouse on the moors all together to the man of to-day. The memory of that vanished time, the thought that the ruder life of the past, when men lived nearer to Nature, had a keener flavour, is accompanied with a haunting regret. It is true that the regret is for something we have not known, that we have only heard or read of it, but it has become mixed in our mind with our very own experienced past—our glad beautiful "days that are no more." And when we remember that in those distant days the heron was a table-bird, we may well believe that men were healthier and had better appetites than now—that they were all and always young.

CHAPTER X

THE HERON AS A TABLE-BIRD

IN reading the Hampshire children's Bird and
Tree Essays for 1916 I came upon one by a little
boy which ends as follows: "One of our school-
boys had a heron given him, so his mother cooked
it and when it was done it was tough and had a
NASTY TASTE."

Mine are the capitals, but the concluding words
seemed crying for them; they also served to remind
me of a story about eating heron told me by the
only person I had ever met who had some first-hand
knowledge about the heron as a table-bird. It is a
rather long story; perhaps a painful one to persons
of a squeamish stomach, but as it is pure natural
history I must be allowed to tell it.

I was staying at Bath, and wishing to get some
work copied I set out with the name and address
of a lady typist, furnished by a bookseller of the
town, to look for her in the Camden Road. A long
road it proved. Like Pope's wounded serpent it
dragged its slow length along to the distant horizon
and beyond it. It also reminded me of Upper Wig-
more Street, as it seemed to poor dying Sydney
Smith, except that Camden Road was about a
thousand times longer. At length, a mile or so

99

short of the far end, I came to the number I was
looking for on the door of a small, pretty, old-
looking vine-clad cottage set well back from the road
with trees and flowers about it, and there I found
my typist and her sister—two little unmarried ladies,
no longer young, who in their gentle subdued manner,
low soft speech, and quiet movements appeared to
harmonise very well with the old-world little house
they lived in. They were, I fancy, somewhat startled
at the apparition of so big a man in their small
interior—one whose head came within an inch or
two of the low ceiling: they seemed timid and
troubled and anxious in their minds when I gave
them my scrawl to decipher and copy.

One day, wanting a good long walk, I paid them
a second visit, to find them less shy and reticent
than at first; and afterwards I went again on several
occasions, until we became quite friendly, and they
gratified my De Quincey-like craving to know everything about the life of every person I meet from its
birth onwards, by telling me all about themselves.

They had been left with very little to live on, and
one was an invalid; yet they had to do something,
and typewriting at home was the only thing, as
this enabled them to keep together, so that the
invalid would always have her sister with her.
The work they had done hitherto, they said, was
copying tradesmen's circulars, also some copying for
two of the local clergy and for an attorney of the
town. My work had come as a relief to them. The
very first thing I had given them was a paper about

the sheldrake. What a strange subject—they could hardly believe their eyes when they saw it. The sheldrake!—that bird about which they had so many memories, pleasant, and some not quite pleasant. It was all very wonderful. Before they came to Bath they lived with a bachelor brother who had come into a small farm, left him by a distant relation, on the Welsh coast. As he had nothing else in the world he went to live on it and work it himself, and kindly took them to keep house and do the indoor work. The farm was on a very wild, lonely spot, close to the sea, and abounded in birds of many kinds—sea and shore and land—they had never seen before. And though it was a rough place they loved it because of the sea and woods and hills and the birds, and they wished they had never had anything to do with the birds except just to see and admire them. But there was their brother, who was a great sportsman and who had some very strange ideas. One was that most birds were good to eat, and he was always shooting some queer-looking bird and bringing it in to them to dress and cook it for dinner. And the sheldrake was one he often shot. He said it was a sort of duck, and therefore just as good to eat as a mallard, or widgeon, or teal, and that it was nothing but a silly prejudice which prevented people from eating them. And though they never had one on the table that wasn't tough and dry and fishy-tasted he would still bring them in and argue that they were very good. "We loved," they said, "to see the sheldrakes flying about on

the coast, but how we hated to see them brought
in to be cooked for dinner! But he was always
very masterful with us and we never dared to go
against his wishes."

One day he brought in a heron, and they were
quite startled at the sight of such a huge, lank, grey,
loose-feathered creature with such immense legs and
such a dreadful beak. But when he said it would
be a grand experience for them to eat heron they
thought he must be joking, although it was not
a common thing for him to say anything in fun.
He was a very serious sort of man. Finally they
ventured to ask him if he really meant that this up-
setting bird was to be eaten? He was quite indignant:
of course it was to be eaten, he said; did they
imagine that he killed birds just for the pleasure of
killing them! He said it would be a grand day for
them when they sat down to a heron on the table.
Didn't they know that it was one of the most famous
birds of the old time—that the heron was regarded
as a noble, a royal bird, that it was a great dish at
the feast in baronial halls; and that's how he went
on until they were quite ashamed of their ignorance
of the old days and humbly promised to cook the
bird. Very well, he said, he was going to hang it in
the big empty room next the dairy and let it remain
until fit to cook. The longer it hung the more
tender it would be.

There was an iron hook in the central beam of
the big vacant room he had spoken of, and on this
hook he suspended the heron by its legs, its long

pointed beak nearly touching the tiled floor, and hanging there with nothing else in the room it looked bigger than ever. It troubled them greatly to have to go through this room many times a day, but it was far worse at night. They were accustomed, especially on moonlight nights, to go that way to the dairy without a candle; and they sometimes forgot about the bird, and then the sight of it in its pale grey plumage would startle them as if they had seen a ghost. How awful it looked, with its wings like great arms half-open as if to scare them!

Days and weeks went by, and still the heron was suspended in the big vacant room to make their life on the farm a burden to them, then one morning after finishing his breakfast their brother said that he had been looking at the heron and found it was just about in perfect condition to be cooked, and that they would have it for dinner that day. Then he added: "I don't mean at our twelve o'clock dinner. There would be no time to prepare it and it would not be proper to eat it at such an hour. To-day we must have a real eight o'clock dinner so as to do honour to the heron."

Then he went out and left them staring into each other's pale face. However, the painful task had to be performed, and they loyally went to work and plucked it, but in cleaning it received a shock at finding a trout about a foot in length in a semi-decomposed condition in its gullet. After refreshing themselves with sal-volatile and half an hour in the garden, they finished the hateful business by singeing it and pumping many gallons of water over its carcase, and then towards evening put it in the oven to roast or bake. The smell of it was very trying and not only made the kitchen atmosphere almost not to be borne but pervaded the whole house, causing them to look forward more and more apprehensively to the evening dinner. Still, they were determined to do everything to please their brother, and got out their best table-cloth and silver, flowers for decoration, and wine and coloured glasses; and the brother when he sat down smiled on them approvingly. Then the heron on a big dish was brought in, and the brother rose to carve it, and heaped their plates with generous slices of the lean black flesh, and helped himself even more generously. They having been helped first had to begin, but to put even the smallest morsel into their mouths was more than they could do. They pretended to cut and eat it while confining themselves to the vegetables on their plates. Their brother was not affected with such squeamishness and straightway started operations, and did honour to the heron by taking a tremendous mouthful. The sisters exchanged frightened glances and watched him furtively, wondering at his courage —wondering, too, if he would be able to keep it up and consume the whole monstrous plateful. Then something happened: a change came over his face, he turned pale, and stopped chewing; then, with mouth still full, he suddenly rose and fled from the room.

That was the end of their gorgeous dinner! Feeling pretty sure that he would not call for the cold remains of the bird next morning for breakfast they took it out and buried it in the garden, then threw all the doors and windows in the house open to get rid of the savour.   It was late that evening when they next saw their brother; he was looking pale as if but lately recovering from a serious illness; but he sauntered in with an air of not knowing anything about it, and remarked casually that he had been for a stroll and didn't know it was so late.   But never a word about the heron he had dined on, nor did he ever after allude to the subject.

CHAPTER XI

THE MOLE QUESTION

AS to whether the mole is injurious or not, the farmer appears not yet to have made up his mind. Mole clubs flourish throughout the country, which fact may be taken by some as proof that the creature is regarded as an enemy. Is it so? There are many farmers who subscribe to the local mole club, and occasionally have their grounds cleared, yet they say that they do not know that they are doing themselves any good, some are even inclined to think that it would perhaps be better to leave the moles alone. They go on subscribing to clubs in the same way that so many of us give our crowns or half-guineas year by year for objects we care nothing about, and do not know whether they are good or bad. All the other farmers in the place have paid their subscriptions, and Jones gives his so as not to be set down as a mean or singular person, and because it would be a bother to have any controversy over the subject. The others have probably subscribed for the same poor reason.

Occasionally we meet a farmer who is quite positive on one side or the other; he knows all about it, and is angry with his neighbours either because they do or do not kill their moles. There are always a few extremists. Every one has heard of Mr. Joseph Nunn, who maintains that the sparrow is the farmer's best feathered friend, and is carried by his zeal to the length of declaring that all those who shoot the sparrow ought themselves to be shot. I hear of another farmer who buys moles from mole-catchers to put on his land; he is convinced that their presence is wholly beneficial, that when those inhabiting the lands adjoining his farm have been killed off, his own moles flow out into these depleted grounds to enjoy the greater abundance of food they find there; and it is to make good this loss inflicted on him by the ignorance and stupidity of his neighbours that he is obliged to act as he does.

Recently I was with a man who takes the opposite view; one who revolves schemes and projects for the suppression of the mole. This enemy of the mole is in possession of three or four water - meadows, infested by these animals to an extraordinary degree. As he is partly dependent for a livelihood on a few milch-cows he keeps, the condition of this meadow land is a matter of importance to him; and he has come to the conclusion that he loses a large portion (a fourth, he imagines) of his grass crop on account of the uneven condition of the surface caused by the moles. It is true that he could roll the ground, and it would then probably be in a sufficiently level state at the next grass-cutting for the scythe, but by the following season it would again be in a hummocky condition, and repeated rollings would be a serious item in his expenses. He considers that if the damage thus inflicted on him in these small meadows where the scythe is used is sufficient to be seriously felt, the loss must indeed be great on large farms where the machine is used for mowing, and the ground must be kept in a smooth condition at considerable expense.

Pondering over these things, and fighting the moles, which, not content with making a sort of physical-geography raised map of his little grass meadows, nightly invade his garden to spoil his work there, he has come to look upon it as a tremendously important question. It is his conviction that he who invents a means of suppressing the mole will be a great benefactor to the country, and he has set himself to find out the means, and he has even strong hopes of success. So long (he argues) as we continued to fight the moles with the traps now in use, made to take one mole at a time, the very utmost we can do is to keep their numbers down with a great deal of trouble and at a considerable expense. They increase rapidly, and no sooner are our efforts relaxed than they again become abundant. We want a trap that will not take a single mole but as many moles as are accustomed to use the run in which it is placed. That a large number do constantly use the same main road by which they migrate from one hunting-ground to the other is to him a settled fact. One of his neighbours took thirty-two moles, one by one, in the course of a few days in a single trap placed at the same place in a run—a proof that all the moles in the place that range any day over an area of many acres have roads that are free to the colony. All we have got to do, then, is to find one of these principal roads, usually at the side of a hedge, and to place a trap capable of holding as many moles as may come into it, and the thing is done.

To inform my rural friend that he was not the first person to have great dreams anent the mole question I related to him the history of the famous Henri le Court, described by Bell in his *British Quadrupeds* as "a person, who having held a lucrative situation about the Court at the epoch of the French Revolution, retired from the horrors of that fearful period into the country, and there devoted the remainder of his life to a study of the habits of the mole, and of the most efficient means for its extirpation."

It surprised him to hear that men of brains had begun to occupy themselves with this question as long ago as the eighteenth century; but the thought that nothing important had resulted from their efforts in so long a time did not discourage him: it was simply the case that, brains or no brains, he had been so lucky as to hit upon the one efficacious means for the extirpation of the mole, which all before him had missed—to wit, *his* trap.

This frightful engine of destruction is not yet perfected, and perhaps the moles need not be in a hurry to say their prayers. In the meantime, while the farmers are waiting to be delivered from their subterranean enemy, I cannot help thinking that it is not much to the credit of the science of agriculture, and the Royal Agricultural Society, that some practical steps have not been taken before now to ascertain whether or not the mole is an injurious beast; or, to put it differently, whether the direct loss he causes by throwing up hills in meadows and grasslands exceeds any benefit that may result from his presence in draining and ventilating the soil and in clearing it of grubs.

With gardens and lawns we are not concerned; moles are a nuisance when they come too near, and if someone could devise a means to inflict sudden death on every underground intruder into such places it would be a great advantage. Experiments in a small way could be made at a very slight cost. For instance, take a meadow, like one of those belonging to my friend, very much infested with moles; divide it in two equal portions, one half to be open to moles, the other half to be strictly protected from them by means of a fence of fine wire-netting sunk to a proper depth in the soil. Then let the grass crops of the two portions be compared as to weight and quality for a period of four or five years. Such an experiment carried out by a number of farmers at the same time in different parts of the country would probably result in the settlement of this old vexed question.

CHAPTER XII

CRISTIANO: A HORSE

A GAUCHO of my acquaintance, when I lived on the pampas and was a very young man, owned a favourite riding-horse which he had named Cristiano. To the gaucho "Christian" is simply another word for white man: he gave it that name because one of its eyes was a pale blue-grey, almost white—a colour sometimes seen in the eyes of a white man, but never in an Indian. The other eye was normal, though of a much lighter brown than usual. Cristiano, however, could see equally well out of both eyes, nor was the blue eye on one side correlated with deafness, as in a white cat. His sense of hearing was quite remarkable. His colour was a fine deep fawn, with black mane and tail, and altogether he was a handsome and a good, strong, sound animal; his owner was so much attached to him that he would seldom ride any other horse, and as a rule he had him saddled every day.

Now if it had only been the blue eye I should probably have forgotten Cristiano, as I made no notes about him, but I remember him vividly to this day on account of something arresting in his psychology: he was an example of the powerful effect of the conditions he had been reared in and of the persistence of habits acquired at an early period after they have ceased to be of any significance in the creature's life. Every time I was in my gaucho friend's company, when his favourite Cristiano, along with other saddle horses, was standing at the *palenque*, or row of posts set up before the door of a native rancho for visitors to fasten their horses to, my attention would be attracted to his singular behaviour. His master always tied him to the *palenque* with a long *cabresto*, or lariat, to give him plenty of space to move his head and whole body about quite freely. And that was just what he was always doing. A more restless horse I had never seen. His head was always raised as high as he could raise it—like an ostrich, the gauchos would say—his gaze fixed excitedly on some far object; then presently he would wheel round and stare in another direction, pointing his ears forward to listen intently to some faint far sound, which had touched his sense. The sounds that excited him most were as a rule the alarm cries of lapwings, and the objects he gazed fixedly at with a great show of apprehension would usually turn out to be a horseman on the horizon; but the sounds and sights would for some time be inaudible and invisible to us on account of their distance. Occasionally, when the bird's alarm cries grew loud and the distant rider was found to be approaching, his excitement would increase until it would discharge itself in a resounding snort—the warning or alarm note of the wild horse.

One day I remarked to my gaucho friend that his

blue-eyed Cristiano amused me more than any other
horse I knew. He was just like a child, and when
tired of the monotony of standing tethered to the
palenque he would start playing sentinel. He would
imagine it was war-time or that an invasion of
Indians was expected, and every cry of a lapwing
or other alarm-giving bird, or the sight of a horseman in the distance would cause him to give a
warning. But the other horses would not join in
the game; they let him keep watch and wheel about
this way and that, spying or pretending to spy something, and blowing his loud trumpet, without taking
any notice. They simply dozed with heads down,
occasionally switching off the flies with their tails or
stamping a hoof to get them off their legs, or rubbing their tongues over the bits to make a rattling
sound with the little iron rollers on the bridle-bar.

He laughed and said I was mistaken, that Cristiano was not amusing himself with a game he had
invented. He was born wild and belonged to a
district not many leagues away but where there was
an extensive marshy area impracticable for hunting
on horseback. Here a band of wild horses, a small
remnant of an immense troop that had formerly
existed in that part, had been able to keep their
freedom down to recent years. As they were frequently hunted in dry seasons when the ground was
not so bad, they had become exceedingly alert and
cunning, and the sight of men on horseback would
send them flying to the most inaccessible places in
the marshes, where it was impossible to follow them.

Eventually plans were laid and the troop driven from their stronghold out into the open country, where the ground was firm, and most of them were captured. Cristiano was one of them, a colt about four or five months old, and my friend took possession of him, attracted by his blue eye and fine fawn colour. In quite a short time the colt became perfectly tame, and when broken turned out an exceptionally good riding-horse. But though so young when captured the wild alert habit was never dropped. He could never be still: when out grazing with the other horses or when standing tied to the *palenque* he was perpetually on the watch, and the cry of a plover, the sound of galloping hoofs, the sight of a horseman, would startle him and cause him to trumpet his alarm.

It strikes me as rather curious that in spite of Cristiano's evident agitation at certain sounds and sights, it never went to the length of a panic; he never attempted to break loose and run away. He behaved just as if the plover's cry or the sound of hoofs or the sight of mounted men had produced an illusion—that he was once more a wild hunted horse—yet he never acted as though it was an illusion. It was apparently nothing more than a memory and a habit.

CHAPTER XIII

MARY'S LITTLE LAMB

THIS is the history of a pet lamb that differed mentally from other lambs I have known. One does not look for anything approaching to marked individuality in that animal, yet sheep do show it on occasions though not in the same degree as cats and dogs. Goats exhibit more character than sheep, probably because we do not compel them to live in a crowd. Indeed, when we consider how our poor domesticated sheep is kept we can see that they have little chance of developing individuality of mind. A sheep cannot "follow his own genius," so to speak, without infringing the laws we have made for his kind. His condition in this respect is similar to that of human beings under a purely socialistic form of government: for example, like that of the ancient civilised Peruvians. In that state every man did as he was told: worked and rested, got up and sat down, ate, drank, and slept, married, grew old and died in the precise way prescribed. And I daresay if he tried to be original or to do something out of the common he was knocked on the head. So with our sheep. The shepherd, assisted by his dog, maps out his whole life for him, from birth to death, and he is not permitted to stray from the path in which he is made to walk. But if a lamb be taken from the flock and reared at a farm and given the same liberty that cats and dogs and even many goats enjoy, he will in almost every case develop a character of his own.

I remember a tame sheep we once had at my home on the pampas who in thieving could give points to many thievish dogs, not excepting the pointer himself, the most accomplished thief in the entire canine gang. Tobacco and books were the objects this mischievous beast was perpetually foraging for when she could get into the house. Tobacco was hard to come at even when she had a good long time to look for it before someone came on the scene to send her about her business with a good whack or a kick. But books were often left lying about on tables and chairs and were easily got at. She knew very well that it was wrong and that if detected she would have to suffer, but she was exceedingly cunning, and from a good distance would keep an eye on the house, and when she saw or cunningly guessed that no person was in the sitting- or dining-room or any other room with the door standing open, she would steal quietly in and finding a book would catch it hastily up and make off with it. Carrying it off to the plantation she would set it down, put her hoof on it, and start tearing out the leaves and devouring them as expeditiously as possible. Once she had got hold of a book she would not give it up—not all the shouting and chasing after her would make her drop it. Away she would rush until fifty yards or more ahead of her hunters; then she would stop, set it down and begin hurriedly tearing out the leaves; then when the hunt drew near with loud halloo she would snatch it up and rush on with it flapping about her face, and leave us all far behind. Eventually, when her depredations could no longer be tolerated, she was sent away to the flock.

An English settler in Patagonia I used to stay with when visiting that part kept a tame guanaco at his estancia, which had a habit resembling that of our book-stealing sheep. This animal had been captured when small by some guanaco-hunters, and my friend reared and made a pet of it. When grown up it associated with the sheep and other domestic animals and was friendly with the dogs, but spent much of its time roaming by itself over the plains. He had the run of the house as well, but at length had to be excluded on account of his passion for devouring any white linen or cotton which he could get hold of. But the guanaco, like our sheep, was cunning and would approach the house from the back and make his way into a bedroom to snatch up and make off with a towel, night-shirt, handkerchief, or anything he could find of linen or cotton, so long as it was white. One day my host came in to get himself ready to attend a meeting and dinner at a neighbouring estancia, and after putting out his linen on his bed he went into an adjoining room for a hot bath. Coming back to his bedroom he was just in time to see his pet guanaco pick up his beautifully-

got-up snow-white shirt from the bed and make a
dash for the open door.   He uttered a wild yell,
which had no effect, but he was determined not to
lose his shirt, for at that moment he remembered
that it was the only clean one he possessed;   he
rushed out just as he was with nothing but a towel
round him, and jumping on to his horse, which stood
saddled at the gate, started in pursuit.   Away he
went, shouting to the dogs to come and help him
recover his shirt.   His yell and shouts brought all
the men about the place on the scene, and running
out they too mounted their horses in hot haste and
started after him.   And away far ahead of them
went the guanaco at a pace no horse could equal,
the shirt held firmly in his teeth waving and flapping like a white banner in the wind.   But from time
to time he made a stop, and bringing the shirt down
to the ground would hurriedly tear a piece out of
it, then picking it up would rush on again.   The dogs
overtook him only to dance round him, barking joyfully to encourage him to run on and keep the fun
going.   He was their friend and playmate, and it
was to them nothing but a jolly sham hunt got up
by their sport-loving master for their amusement.
The chase led up the valley of the river, a great flat
plain, and continued for about four to five miles; by
that time the precious shirt had dwindled to something quite small—nothing in fact was left but the
hard starched front, which the guanaco found it
difficult to masticate and swallow.   Then at long last
the hunt was given up and my poor shirtless friend

in his towel rode mournfully home in the midst of laughing companions, attended, too, by a lot of dogs, lolling their tongues out and overflowingly happy at having had such an exciting run.

Let me now come to the subject I sat down to write about—namely, Mary's little lamb. It was little to begin with, when my youngest sister, who was not then very big herself, and was always befriending forlorn creatures, came in one day from the shepherd's ranch with a young lamb which had unhappily lost its mother. Oddly enough this little sister's name was Mary—one seldom hears it in these Doris-Doreen days, but in that distant Mary-Jane-Elizabeth period it was quite common. And the motherless lamb she had brought in grew to be her pet lamb, with fleece as white as snow; nor was the whiteness strange, seeing that it was washed every day with scented soap, its beauteous neck beribboned and often decorated with garlands of scarlet verbenas which looked exceedingly brilliant against the snowy fleece. A pretty, sweet-tempered and gentle creature it proved and never developed any naughty proclivities like the tobacco- and book-plundering sheep of an earlier date. They were very fond of each other, those two simple beings, and just as in the old familiar rhyme wherever Mary went her little lamb would go. But there was a little rift within the lute which by-and-by would widen till it made the music mute. The lamb was excessively playful and frisky, but its mistress had her little lessons and duties to attend to, and the lamb couldn't understand it, and often after frisking and jumping about to challenge the other to a fresh race in vain it would run away to get up a race or game of some sort with the youngest of the dogs. The dogs were responsive, so that they were quite happy together.

We kept eight dogs at that time; two were pointers, all the others just the common dog of the country, a smooth-haired animal about the size of a collie. Like all dogs allowed to exist in their own way, they formed a pack, the most powerful one being their leader and master. They spent most of their time lying stretched dog-fashion in the sun in some open place near the house, fast asleep. They had little to do except bark at strangers approaching the house and to hunt off the cattle that tried to force their way through the fences into the plantation. They would also go off on hunting expeditions of their own. Strange playmates and companions for Libby, as she was named, the pretty pet lamb with fleece as white as snow; yet so congenial did she find the dogs' society that by-and-by she passed her whole time with them, day and night. When they came to the door to bark and whine and wag their tails to call attention to their wants or to be noticed, the lamb would be with them but would not cross the threshold since the dogs were not permitted in the rooms. Nor would she come to her mistress when called, and having discovered that grass was her proper food she wanted nothing that human beings could give her. Not even a lump of sugar! She was no longer a pet lamb; she was one of the dogs. The dogs on their part, although much given to quarrels and fights among themselves, never growled or snapped at Libby; she never tried to snatch a bone from them, and she made them a comfortable pillow when they slept and slumbered for hours at a stretch. And Libby, just to be always with them and to do exactly as they did, would sleep too. Or rather she would lie stretched out on the ground pretending to sleep, always with the head of one of the dogs pillowed on her neck. Two or three or four of the other dogs who had failed to secure the pillow would lie round her with their heads pressed against her fleece. They would form a curiously amusing group. Then if a shrill whistle was emitted by someone, or the cry of "Up and at 'em," the lamb would spring like lightning to her feet, throwing the drowsy dog off, and away she would dash down the avenue to get outside the plantation and find out what the trouble was. Then the dogs, shaking off their sleep, would start off and perhaps overtake her a couple of hundred yards away.

Most amusing of all the lamb's acting was when the dogs had their periodical hunting fits, when they would vanish for half a day's vizcacha-hunting on the plain, just as fox-terriers and other dogs in which the hunting instinct still survives steal out of the village to chase or dig out rabbits on their own account.

The vizcacha is a big rodent and lives in communities, in warrens or villages composed of a group of huge burrows, and the native dogs are fond of assaulting these strongholds but seldom succeed in getting at their quarry. A dog no bigger than a fox-terrier can make his way in till he comes to grips with the vizcacha, usually with the result that he gets well punished for his audacity. Our dogs would simply labour to enlarge the burrows by scratching and biting away the earth and furiously barking at the animal inside who would emit curious noises and cries, which the dogs appeared to regard as insults and would only cause them to redouble their efforts.

On several occasions, when riding on the plain a mile or two from home, I would come on our dogs —the entire pack and the lamb with them, engaged in the siege and assault of a vizcacha village or earth. A funny sight! The dogs would jump up barking and wagging their tails as if to say, "Here we are, you see, just in the middle of our fight with no time to spare for friendly conversation." And back they would fly to their burrows. The lamb too would dance up to give me a welcome and then back to her duties. Her part was to go frisking about from burrow to burrow, now taking a flying leap over the pit-like mouth, then diving down to see how things were progressing inside, where the dog was tearing at the earth and trying to force himself in and keeping up a running dialogue of threats and insults with the beast inside.

But though Libby, in these her dog days, was a continual joy to us, we thought it best for her own

sake to put an end to them. For in spite of her
activities she was in very good condition, and any
poor gaucho who came upon her, hunting with our
dogs a few miles from home, would be justified in
saying: "Here is a good fat animal without an ear-
mark, consequently without an owner; and though
I find it in the company of Neighbour So-and-So's
dogs, it can't be his since he has put no mark on
it, and as I've found it I have a right to it, and I'm
quite sure from its appearance that its flesh when
roasted will prove tender and savoury."

Accordingly we took Libby away from her companions and put her with the flock, where in due
time she would learn that a sheep is a sheep and
not a dog.

There are, I imagine, few old sportsmen, field
naturalists, and observers of animal life generally
who have not met with similar instances of animals
of widely different natures, in some instances natural
enemies, living and even acting in harmony together.
We see it chiefly in the domesticated and in tamed
wild animals. When visiting a friend in Patagonia
I was greatly astonished one day, on going out with
a gun to shoot something, followed by the dogs, to
find a black cat in their company, and to see her
when I fired my first shot actually dashing off before
the dogs to retrieve the bird!

One of the amusing recollections of an old lady
friend of mine, a lover of animals, was of a pet cat
and rabbit which had been reared from babyhood

together and were always fed out of one saucer of milk, and, when they grew up, from one dish. It was common to see them exchange foods, and the cat would be seen laboriously gnawing at a cabbage stalk while the rabbit picked a bone.

My friend Mr. Tregarthen, author of *Wild Life at the Land's End*, has just kindly furnished me with two or three remarkable instances known to him of hunting and hunted animals living together in happy companionship. One is of a tame fox, taken when small and reared in the kennels with fox-hounds. When fully grown its great game when the dogs were taken out for exercise was to scamper off and give them a chase. Invariably when overtaken it would throw itself on its back and allow itself to be worried in fun. They never hurt it. Then there are two instances of otters reared from puppyhood with otter-hounds. In one case the otter would go otter-hunting with the hounds; in the second case the otter did not accompany the hounds, or was not allowed to go with them, but the hounds, although they hunted their quarry with all the zeal and fury natural to them, refused to bite or hurt it in any way when they got it. Their friendship with an otter had had a psychological effect on their otter-hound natures.

CHAPTER XIV

THE SERPENT'S TONGUE

"BUT now," says Ruskin, "here's the first thing, it seems to me, we've got to ask the scientific people—what use a serpent has for its tongue; since it neither works it to talk with, or taste with, or hiss with, nor, as far as I know, to lick with, and, least of all, to sting with—and yet, for people who do not know the creature, the little vibrating forked thread, flicked out of its mouth and back again, as quick as lightning, is the most striking part of the beast; but what is the use of it? Nearly every creature but a snake can do some sort of mischief with its tongue. A woman worries with it, a chameleon catches flies with it, a cat steals milk with it, a pholas digs holes in the rock with it, and a gnat digs holes in *us* with it; but the poor snake cannot do any manner of harm with it whatsoever; and what is *his* tongue forked for?"

The writer's manner in this paragraph, and the unexpectedness of the mocking question that leaps out at the end, suggest the idea that there are, in man, two sorts of forked tongues, and that one sort is not worked for mischief. Certainly few of these "vibrating forked threads" in literature have flickered more startlingly, like forked lightning, and to the purpose, than Ruskin's own. The passage is admirable, both in form and essence; it shines even in that brilliant lecture on *Living Waves* from which it is taken, and where there are very many fine things, along with others indifferent, and a few that are bad. But there is this fault to be found with it: after putting his question to the "scientific people," the questioner assumes that no answer is possible; that the stinging and hissing and licking theories having been discarded, the serpent's tongue can do no manner of mischief, and is quite useless. A most improbable conclusion, since the fact stares us in the face that the serpent does use its tongue; for instance, it exserts and makes it vibrate rapidly, but why it does so remains to be known. It is true that in the long life of a species an organ does sometimes lose its use without dwindling away, but persists as a mere idle appendage: it is, however, very unlikely that this has happened in the case of the serpent's tongue; the excitability and extreme activity at times of that organ rather incline one to the opinion that it has only changed its original use for a new one, as has happened in the case of some of the creatures mentioned in the passage quoted above.

"A chameleon," says Ruskin, "catches flies with its tongue," inferring that the snake has no such accomplishment. Yet the contrary has been often maintained. "The principal use of the tongue," says Lacépède in his *Natural History of Serpents*, "is to catch insects, which it catches by means of its double tongue." This notion about the use of the

double tongue is quite common among the older
ophiologists, and, along with it, the belief that snakes
prey chiefly on insects. And here I cannot resist
the temptation to quote a few more words touching
on this point from Lacépède—a very perfect example
of the teleological spirit in science which flourished a
century ago, and made things easy for the naturalist.
"We are not," he says, "to be amazed at the vast
number of serpents, both species and individuals,
which inhabit the intertropical countries. There
they find the degree of warmth which seems congenial to their natures, and the smaller species find
abundance of insects to serve them for food. In
those torrid regions, where Nature has produced an
infinite multitude of insects and worms, she has like-
wise produced the greatest number of serpents to
destroy the worms and insects; which otherwise
would multiply so exceedingly as to destroy all
vegetable productions, and to reduce the most fertile
regions of the earth into barren deserts, inaccessible
to man and animals; nay, even these noxious and
troublesome insects would be finally obliged to destroy
each other, and nothing would remain but their
mangled limbs."

Here the French naturalist pauses, aghast at
the frightful picture of desolation he has himself
conjured up.

When enumerating the uses to which a serpent
does *not* put its tongue, Ruskin might very well
have said that it is not used as a tactile organ. That
it is a tactile organ is a very modern supposition—

a small hypothesis about a small matter, but with a curious and rather amusing history. It was in the first place given out merely as a conjecture, but no sooner given than accepted as an irrefragable fact by some of the greatest authorities among us. Thus Dr. Günther, in his article on snakes in the *Encyclopædia Britannica*, ninth edition, says, "The tongue is exserted for the purpose of feeling some object, and sometimes under the influence of anger or fear."

Doubtless those who invented this use for the organ were misled by observing snakes in captivity, in the glass cases or cages in which it is usual to keep them; observing them in such conditions, it was easy to fall into the mistake, since the serpent, when moving, is frequently seen to thrust his tongue against the obstructing glass. It should be remembered that glass *is* glass, a substance that does not exist in nature; that a long and sometimes painful experience is necessary before even the most intelligent among the lower animals are brought to understand its character; and, finally, that the delicate, sensitive tongue comes against it for the same reason that the fly buzzes and the confined wild bird dashes itself against it in their efforts to escape. In a state of nature when the snake is approached, whether by its prey or by some large animal, the tongue is obtruded; again, when it is cautiously progressing through the herbage, even when unalarmed, the tongue is exserted at frequent intervals; but I can say, after a long experience of snakes, that the exserted organ never touches earth, or rock, or leaf, or anything whatsoever, consequently that it is not a tactile organ.

Another suggestion, less improbable on the face of it than the one just cited, is that the tongue, without touching anything, may, in some way not yet known to us, serve as an organ of intelligence. The serpent's senses are defective; now when, in the presence of a strange object or animal, the creature protrudes its long slender tongue—not to *feel* the object, as has been shown—does it not do so to *test* the air, to catch an emanation from the object which might in some unknown way convey to the brain its character, whether animate or inanimate, cold or warm blooded, bird, beast, or reptile, also its size, etc.? The structure of the organ itself does not give support to this supposition; it could not *taste* an emanation without some such organs as are found in the wonderfully formed antennæ of insects, and with these it is not provided.

Only by means of a sensitiveness to air waves and vibrations from other living bodies near it, in degree infinitely more delicate than that of the bat's wing—the so-called sixth sense of that animal—could the serpent's tongue serve as an organ of intelligence. Here, again, the structure of the tongue is against such an hypothesis; and if the structure were different it would only remain to be said that the instrument performs its work very badly.

Another explanation which has been put forward by two well-known writers on serpent life, Dr. Stradling and Miss Hopley, remains to be noticed. These observers came independently to the conclusion that the snake makes use of his tongue as a decoy to attract its prey.

In the case of one of these writers, the idea was suggested by an incident in our Zoological Gardens. A fowl was placed in a boa's cage to be eaten, and immediately began hunting about for food on the floor of the cage; the serpent—apparently seen merely as an inanimate object — protruded its tongue, whereupon the fowl rushed and pecked at it, mistaking it for a wriggling worm. Such a thing could not well happen in a state of nature. The tongue may resemble a wriggling worm, or, when vibrated very quickly, a fluttering moth; but we cannot assume that the serpent, however motionless it may lie, however in its colour and pattern it may assimilate to its surroundings, is not recognised as a separate and living thing by a bird or any other wild animal.

From the foregoing it will be seen that so far from being silent on this subject, as Ruskin imagined, the "scientific people" have found out or invented a variety of uses for the serpent's tongue. By turns it has been spoken of as an insect-catching organ, a decoy, a tactile organ, and, in some mysterious way, an organ of intelligence. And, after all, it is none of these things, and the way is still open for fresh speculation.

I have on numberless occasions observed the common pit-viper of southern South America, which is of a sluggish disposition, lying in the sun on a bed

of sand or dry grass, coiled or extended at full length.
Invariably, on approaching a snake of this kind, I
have seen the tongue exserted; that nimble, glistening organ was the first, and for some time the only,
sign of life or wakefulness in the motionless creature.
If I stood still at a distance of some yards to watch
it, the tongue would be exserted again at intervals;
if I moved nearer, or lifted my arms, or made any
movement, the intervals would be shorter and the
vibrations more rapid, and still the creature would
not move. Only when I drew very near would other
signs of excitement follow. At such times the tongue
has scarcely seemed to me the "mute forked flash"
that Ruskin calls it, but a tongue that said something, which, although not audible, was clearly understood and easy to translate into words. What it
said or appeared to say was: "I am not dead nor
sleeping, and I do not wish to be disturbed, much
less trodden upon; keep your distance, for your own
good as well as for mine." In other words, the tongue
was obtruded and vibrated with a *warning* purpose.

Doubtless every venomous serpent of sluggish
habits has more ways than one of making itself
conspicuous to and warning off any large heavy
animal that might injure by passing over and treading on it; and I think that in ophidians of this
temper the tongue has become, incidentally, a warning organ. Small as it is, its obtrusion is the first
of a series of warning motions, and may therefore
be considered advantageous to the animal; and, in
spite of its smallness, I believe that in very many

instances it accomplishes its purpose without the aid of those larger and violent movements and actions resorted to when the danger becomes pressing.

All large animals, including man, when walking on an open space, see the ground before them, with every object on it, even when the head is raised and when the animal's attention is principally directed to something in the distance. The motions of the legs, the exact measurement of every slight obstruction and object in the way—hillocks, depressions in the soil, stones, pebbles, sticks, etc.—are almost automatic; the puma may have nothing but his far-seen quarry in his mind, and the philosopher be thinking only of the stars, as they move, both quite unconscious of what their feet are doing; but the ground must be seen all the same, otherwise they could not go smoothly even over a comparatively smooth surface.

When the man or other animal progressing in this ordinary way comes to where a serpent, with a protective or assimilative colour and appearance, lies motionless in the path, he certainly sees it, but without distinguishing it as a serpent. The vari-coloured surface it rests on and with which it is in harmony is motionless, consequently without animal life and safe to tread on—a rough flooring composed of mould, pebbles and sand, dead and green herbage, withered leaves, twisted vines, and sticks warped by the sun, brown and grey and mottled. But if the smallest thing moves on that still surface, if a blade trembles, or a minute insect flutters or flies up, the

vision is instantly attracted to the spot and con-
centrated on a small area, and as by a flash every
object on it is clearly seen, and its character recognised. Those who have been accustomed to walk
much in dry, open places, in districts where snakes
are abundant, have often marvelled at the instan-
taneous manner in which something that had been
previously seen as a mere strip or patch of dull
colour on the mottled earth, as a part of its indeter-
minate pattern, has taken the serpent form. And
when once it has been recognised as a serpent it is
seen so vividly and in such sharp contrast to its
surroundings as to appear the most conspicuous and
unmistakable object in nature. Why, in such cases,
they ask in astonishment, did they not recognise its
character sooner? I believe that in such cases it is
the suddenly exserted, glistening, vibrating tongue
that first attracts the eye to the dangerous spot
and reveals the serpent to the mind.

This warning character is, I believe, as has already
been intimated, an incidental use of the tongue, probably confined, or at all events most advantageous, to
the vipers and to other venomous serpents of lethargic
habits. In the case of the extremely active, non-
venomous snake, that glides away into hiding on
the slightest alarm, the tongue would be of little use
or no value as a warning organ. Between a snake of
this kind and the slumberous pit-viper the difference
in habit is extreme. But at bottom, all ground snakes
are alike in disposition—all hate to be disturbed,
and move only when necessity drives; and we can

imagine that when the tremendous weapon of a lethal tooth had been acquired, when experience began to teach the larger mammalians to view the serpentine form with suspicion and to avoid it, the use of the tongue as a warning would react on the serpent, making it more and more lethargic in habit—as inactive, in fact, as every snake loves to be.

There is, I imagine, another and more important use of the tongue, older than its warning use, although this may date back in time to the Miocene period, when the viperine form existed—a use of the tongue common to all ophidians that possess the habit of exserting and vibrating that organ when excited. The subject is somewhat complicated, for we have not only to consider the tongue, but the whole creature of which the tongue is so small a part; its singularity and anomalous position in nature, and the many and diverse ways in which the animals it preys on are affected by its appearance. Furthermore, I have now in my mind two separate functions, the first of which occasionally, perhaps often, passes into and becomes one with the other.

When the common or ring snake pursues a frog, the chase would in most cases prove a very vain one but for that fatal weakness in the hunted animal, which quickly brings its superior activity to naught. The snake need not even be seen for the effect to be produced, as anyone can prove for himself by pushing his walking-stick, snake-wise, through the grass and causing it to follow up the frog's motions, whereupon, after some futile efforts to escape, the creature collapses, and stretching out its fore-feet like arms that implore mercy, emits a series of piteous, wailing screams. Thus, all that is necessary for this end to be reached is that the frog should be conscious of something, no matter what, pushing after it through the grass. There is here, apart from the question in animal psychology, a little mystery involved; for how comes it that in the course of the countless generations during which the snake has preyed on the frog, this peculiar weakness has not been eliminated by means of the continual destruction of the individuals most subject to it, and, on the other hand, the preservation of all those possessing it in a less degree, or not at all? It is hard for a good Darwinian to believe that the frog is excessively prolific for the snake's advantage rather than for its own. But this question need not detain us; there are vulnerable spots and weak joints in the defensive armour of all animals. What I wish to draw attention to is the fact that, speaking metaphorically, the serpent, of all creatures that kill their own meat, is the most *unsportsmanlike* in its methods, that it has found out and subtly taken advantage of the most secret and unsuspected weaknesses of the animals on which it preys.

We have seen how the common snake catches the frog; but frogs are found only in wet places, and snakes abound everywhere, and the sedentary snake of the dry uplands must feed on the nimble rodent, volatile bird, and elusive lizard. How does he manage to catch them? For considering how alert and quick-sighted these small hunted creatures are, it must, I think, be assumed that the snake cannot, except in rare instances, approach them unseen and take them unawares. I believe that in many cases the snake succeeds by approaching its intended victim while appearing to be stationary. This stratagem is not confined to the ophidians: in a somewhat different form it is found in a great variety of animals. Perhaps the most familiar example is afforded by the widely distributed hunting-spider. The plan followed by this spider, on a smooth surface where it cannot hide its form, is to advance boldly towards its prey, and when the fly, who has been suspiciously watching its approach, is about to dart away, to become motionless. This appears to excite the fly's curiosity, and he does not take flight; but very soon his restive spirit returns, he moves about this way and that, to see all round him, and each time he turns his bright eyes away the spider rapidly moves a little nearer; but when the fly looks again, appears motionless as before. In this way, little by little, the space is lessened, and yet the fly, still turning at intervals to regard the suspicious-looking object, does not make his escape, simply because he does not know that the space has been lessened. Seeing the spider always motionless the illusion is produced that it has not moved: the dividing distance has been accurately measured once for all, and no second act of judgment is required; the fly, knowing his own quickness and volatile powers, feels himself perfectly safe; and this goes on until by chance he detects the motion and instantly flies away, or else fails to detect it and is caught. Cats often succeed in capturing birds by a similar stratagem.

The snake, unlike the spider and cat, cannot make the final spring and rush, but must glide up to within striking distance: this he is able to do by means of the faculty he possesses of progressing so gradually and evenly as to appear almost motionless; the tongue which he exserts and rapidly vibrates at intervals when approaching his victim helps in producing the deception.

Long observation has convinced me that a snake on the ground, moving or resting, is not a sight that violently excites birds, as they are excited by the appearance of a fox, cat, weasel, hawk, or any other creature whose enmity is well known to them. I have frequently seen little birds running about and feeding on the ground within a few feet of a snake lying conspicuously in their sight; furthermore, I have been convinced on such occasions that the birds knew the snake was there, having observed them raise their heads at intervals, regard the reptile for a few moments attentively, then go on seeking food. This shows that birds do sometimes come near snakes and see them with little or no fear, but probably with some slight suspicion and a great deal of curiosity, on account of the singularity of their appearance, their resemblance to vegetable rather than to animal forms of life, and, above all, to their strange manner of progression. Now the bird, or lizard, or small mammal, thus brought by chance

near to a hungry, watchful snake, once it begins to
regard the snake curiously, is in imminent danger of
destruction in one of two ways, or by a combination
of both: in the first case it may be deluded as to
the distance of the suspicious-looking object and in
the end seized, just as the fly is seized by the *Salticus*
spider, before it can make its escape; secondly, it
may, while regarding its singular enemy, be thrown
into a trance or convulsive fit and so rendered powerless to escape, or it may even be moved to cast itself
into the open jaws of the snake. In either case, the
serpent's tongue would, I believe, play a very important part. In a case of the first kind the snake
would approach its intended victim so slowly and
continuously as almost to appear not to be moving;
still, in most cases the movement probably would
be detected but for the tongue, which attracts the
eye by its eccentric motions, its sudden successive appearances and disappearances; watching the tongue,
the long, sinuous body slowly gliding over the inter-
vening space would not be observed; only the
statuesque raised head and neck would be visible,
and these would appear not to move. The snake's
action in such a case would resemble the photogra-
pher's trick to make a restive child sit still while
its picture is being taken by directing its attention
to some curious object, or by causing a pocket-
handkerchief to flutter above the camera.

Snakes have been observed to steal upon their
victims in this quiet, subtle manner; the victim, bird
or lizard, has been observed to continue motionless

in a watchful attitude, as if ready to dart away, but still attentively regarding the gradually approaching head and flickering tongue; and in the end, by a sudden, quick-darting motion on the part of the snake, the capture has been effected. Cases of this description are usually set down to "fascination," which I think is a mistake.

Fascination is a fine old word, which has done good service and has had a long day and happily outlived its evil repute: but it had its faults at the best of times; it originally expressed things purely human, and therefore did not exactly fit things serpentine, and was, to some extent, misleading. What its future history—in science—will be cannot be guessed. In France it has been used to describe a mild form of hypnotism induced by the contemplation of a bright spot, and no doubt there would be a certain propriety in applying the word to the soothing somnolent effect produced on the human subject by the revolving mirror invented by Dr. Luys. But this is not the form we are concerned with. Fascination in serpent life is something very different; in the present state of knowledge on the subject the old word cannot be discarded. We are now in possession of a very large number of well-authenticated cases of undoubted fascination in which the victims are seen to act in a variety of ways, but all alike exhibit very keen distress. The animal that falls under the spell appears to be conscious of his loss of power, as in the case of the frog pursued by the ring-snake. He is thrown into violent convulsions, or trembles, or screams, or struggles to escape, and sometimes rushes in terror away only to return again, perhaps in the end to jump into the serpent's jaws. A brother of mine once observed a pipit running with flutterings round and round a coiled snake, uttering distressed chirps and cries; the snake, vibrating its tongue, moved its head round to follow the motions of the bird. This is a common form—the desire and vain striving to escape. But when an animal is seen to remain motionless, showing no signs of distress or fear, attentively regarding the gradually approaching snake, such a case cannot, I think, be safely set down to fascination, nor to anything more out of the common than curiosity, and, as in the case of the volatile, sprightly fly and terrestrial spider, to the illusion produced in the victim's mind that the suspicious-looking object is stationary.

Concerning the use, here suggested, of the tongue in fascination, I can scarcely expect that those whose knowledge of the snake is derived from books, from specimens in museums, and from seeing the animal alive in confinement, will regard it as anything more than an improbable supposition, unsupported by facts. But to those who have attentively observed the creature in a state of nature, and have been drawn to it by, and wondered at, its strangeness, the explanation, I venture to think, will not seem improbable. To weigh, count, measure, and dissect for purposes of identification, classification, and what not, and to search in bones and tissues for hidden affinities, it is necessary to see closely; but this close seeing would be out of place and a hindrance in other lines of inquiry. To know the creature, undivested of life or liberty or of anything belonging to it, it must be seen with an atmosphere, in the midst of the nature in which it harmoniously moves and has its being, and the image it casts on the observer's retina and mind must be identical with its image in the eye and mind of the other wild creatures that share the earth with it. It is not here maintained that the tongue is everything, nor that it is the principal agent in fascination, but only that it is a necessary part of the creature, and of the creature's strangeness, which is able to produce so great and wonderful an effect. The long, limbless body, lithely and mysteriously gliding on the surface; the glittering scales and curious mottlings, bright or lurid; the statuesque, arrowy head, sharp-cut and immovable; the round lidless eyes, fixed and brilliant; and the long, bifurcated tongue, shining black or crimson, with its fantastic flickering play before the close-shut, lipless mouth—that is the serpent, and probably no single detail in the fateful creature's appearance could be omitted and the effect of its presence on other animals be the same.

When, years ago, I had finished writing the above paper, which appeared later in the *Fortnightly Review*, I made the following entry in my diary, and reproduce it here just to show that I am not apt to set too high a value on my own theory.

This paper was not too long, but I'm glad it's finished and done with. Not because the subject didn't interest me—on the contrary, it had a tremendous attraction for me—but because, having written it, a difficulty has been removed, a pain relieved, a want satisfied.   True that I've only imagined this use for a serpent's tongue, and that it may not be the true use —if any use there be; but if we have a need to build, and there is any wind or cloud to build on, 'tis best to go on bravely with the building business.   Who cares if the structure is all to tumble down again?   Not I.   Nevertheless the mere building is a pleasure, and the completion of the structure a satisfaction in that it puts something where before there was nothing.   The speculative soul which is in man abhors the desert, vacant spaces and waters and islands of nothingness.   Thus, to illustrate this little thing by a big thing—the little flickering tongue of the serpent by something so big that it fills the entire universe—the existence of an ethereal medium is possibly no more than a figment of the mind, an invention to get us out of a difficulty, or a "purely hypothetical supposition," as was boldly said by one of our greatest physicists.   At all events, a lady lean and pale who came at our call, tottering forth wrapped in a gauzy veil—surely the most attenuated and shadowy of all the daughters of Old Father Speculation.   But having got her in our arms, thin and pale though she be, we imagine her beautiful and love her dearly, and rest satisfied with the breasts of her consolations, albeit they are of no more substance than thistledown.

CHAPTER XV

THE SERPENT'S STRANGENESS

THE following passages from the *Queen of the Air*, which refer to the serpent myth and the serpent's strange appearance and manner of progression, have, apart from their exceeding beauty, a very special bearing on the subject of this paper. And in quoting them I am only following Ruskin's own plan, when, in his lectures on natural history at Oxford, he considered in each case, first, what had been "beautifully thought about the creature." It would be hard, I imagine, to find a passage of greater beauty on this subject than Ruskin's own, unless it be that famous fragment concerning the divine nature of the serpent and the serpent tribe from Sanchoniathon the Phœnician, who flourished some thirty centuries ago. It is true that among the learned some hold that he never flourished at all, nor existed; but doctors disagree on that point; and, in any case, the fragment exists, and was most certainly written by someone.

Ruskin writes:

Next, in the serpent we approach the source of a group of myths, world-wide, founded on great and common human instincts. . . . There are such things as natural myths . . . the dark sayings of men may be difficult to read, and not always worth reading; but the dark sayings of nature will probably become clearer for the looking into, and will very certainly be worth reading. And, indeed, all guidance to the right sense of the human and variable myths will probably depend on our first getting at the sense of the natural and invariable ones. . . . Is there indeed no tongue, except the mute forked flash from its lips, in that running brook of horror on the ground? Why that horror? We all feel it, yet how imaginative it is, how disproportioned to the real strength of the creature! . . . But that horror is of the myth, not of the creature; . . . it is the strength of the base element that is so dreadful in the serpent; it is the omnipotence of the earth. . . . It is a divine hieroglyph of the demoniac power of the earth, of the entire earthly nature.

Of the animal's motions he says:

That rivulet of smooth silver — how does it flow, think you? It literally rows on the earth, with every scale for an oar; it bites the dust with the ridges of its body. Watch it when it moves slowly; a wave, but without wind! a current, but with no fall! all the body moving at the same instant, yet some of it to one side, some to another, and some forward, and the rest of the coil backwards; but all with the same calm will and equal way—no contraction, no extension; one soundless, causeless march of sequent rings, a spectral procession of spotted dust, with dissolution in its fangs, dislocation in its coils. Startle it: the winding stream will become a twisted arrow; the wave of poisoned life will lash through the grass like a cast lance.

He adds: "I cannot understand this forward motion of the snake," which is not strange, seeing that Solomon, the wise man, found in "the way of a serpent upon a rock" one of the three wonderful things that baffled his intellect. And before Solomon, the old Phœnician wrote that Taautus esteemed the serpent as the most inspired of all the reptiles, and of a fiery nature, inasmuch as it exhibits an incredible celerity, moving by its spirit without either hands or feet. Thanks to modern anatomists, this thing is no longer a puzzle to us; but with the mere mechanical question we are not concerned in this place, but only with the sense of wonder and mystery produced in the mind by the apparently "causeless march of sequent rings."

From English Coniston, where snakes are few and diminutive, let us go to the pine forest of the New World, where dwells the famous *Pituophis melanoleucus*, the serpent of the pines. This is the largest, most active and beautiful of the North American ophidians, attaining a length of ten to twelve feet, and arrayed in a "bright coat of soft creamy-white, upon which are laid, much in the Dolly Varden mode, shining blotches or mottlings, which beginning at the neck are of an intensely dark brown or chocolate colour, but which towards the tail lighten into a pale chestnut." A local Ruskin, the Rev. Samuel Lockwood, a lover of snakes, kept some of these reptiles in his house, and referring to their wonderful muscular feats, he writes as follows:

Owing to this command of the muscles the pine snake is capable of performing some evolutions which are not only beautiful, but so intricate and delicate as to make them seem imbued with the nature we call spiritual. I have often seen the *Pituophis*, spread out in loose coils with its head in the central one, wake up after a long repose and begin a movement in every curve, the entire body engaged in the mazy movements, with no going out or deviation from the complicated pattern marked on the floor. Observing this intricate harmoniousness of movement, I thought of the seer's vision of mystic wheels. Those revolving coils—" and their appearance and their work was as it were a wheel in the middle of a wheel." . . . The movements of a serpent are never started, rope-like, at one end, and then transmitted to the other; nor is the movement like the force-waves sent through a ribbon vibrating in the air. The movement consists of numberless units of individual activities, all regulated by and under control of one individual will that is felt in every curve and line. There is some likeness to the thousand personal activities of a regiment seen on their winding way. And all this perfection of control of so many complicated activities is true, whether the serpent, like an ogre, be crushing its victim's bones, or, as a limbless posturist, be going through its inimitable evolutions. In our thinking a serpent ranks as a paradox among animals. There is so much seeming contradiction. At one time encircling its prey as in iron bands; again assuming the immovable posturing of a statue; then melting into movements so intricate and delicate that the lithe limbless thing looks like gossamer incarnate. In this creature all the unities seem to be set aside. Such weakness and such strength; such gentleness and such vindictiveness; so much of beauty and yet so repulsive; fascination and terror: what need to wonder that, whether snake or python, the serpent should so figure in the myths of all ages and the literature of the whole world! Yes, in the best and worst thinkings of man!

In the literature of the whole world, true; but let no one run away with the idea that gems of this kind are to be picked up anywhere, and go out to seek for them, since for every one equalling these in lustre he will burden himself with many a bushel of common pebbles.

Lockwood called to mind the mystic wheels in Ezekiel's splendid imaginings—"for the spirit of the living creature was in the wheels." His lissom beautiful captive might also have been likened to Shelley's dream-serpent in the *Witch of Atlas*—

> In the flame
> Of its own volumes intervolved.

He had abundant reason to admire the creature's intricate and delicate movements when it appeared like "gossamer incarnate," after having witnessed its motions of another kind, and its deadly power. He had seen it lying extended, apparently asleep, on the floor of its box, when a rat, which had been placed with it, ran over it, but not quite over it, for, quick as lightning, it had wound itself round the rat's body, coil over coil, like hand grasping hand in squeezing a lemon, until the bones of the constricted animal cracked audibly; then it was dropped, dead and crushed and limp, on to the floor; and the serpent, having revenged the indignity, resumed its interrupted repose. With this lightning-like deadly quickness of motion and the melting mazy evolutions at the other times, he also contrasted its statue-like immobility, when, with head raised high and projecting forwards, it would actually remain for hours at a stretch, its brilliant eyes fixed on some object that had alarmed it or excited its curiosity.

This power of continuing motionless, with the lifted head projecting forwards, for an indefinite time, is one of the most wonderful of the serpent's muscular feats, and is of the highest importance to the animal both when fascinating its victim and when mimicking some inanimate object, as, for instance, the stem and bud of an aquatic plant; here it is only referred to on account of the effect it produces on the human mind, as enhancing the serpent's strangeness. In this attitude, with the round, unwinking eyes fixed on the beholder's face, the effect may be very curious and uncanny. Ernest Glanville, a South African writer, thus describes his own experience. When a boy he frequently went out into the bush in quest of game, and on one of these solitary excursions he sat down to rest in the shade of a willow on the bank of a shallow stream; sitting there, with cheek resting on his hand, he fell into a boyish reverie. After some time he became aware in a vague way that on the white sandy bottom of the stream there was stretched a long black line which had not been there at first. He continued for some time regarding it without recognising what it was; but all at once, with an inward shock, became fully conscious that he was looking at a large snake.

Presently, without apparent motion, so softly and silently was it done, the snake reared its head above the surface and held it there, erect and still, with gleaming eyes fixed on me in question of what I was. It flashed upon me then that it would be a good opportunity to test the power of the human eye on a snake, and I set myself the task of looking it down. It was a foolish effort. The bronze head and sinewy neck, about which the water flowed without a ripple, were as if carved in stone, and the cruel unwinking eyes, with the light coming and going in them, appeared to glow the brighter the longer I looked. Gradually there came over me a sensation of sickening fear, which, if I had yielded to it, would have left me powerless to move; but with a cry I leapt up, and, seizing a fallen willow branch, attacked the reptile with a species of fury. . . . Probably the idea of the Icanti originated in a similar experience of some native.

The Icanti, it must be explained, is a powerful and malignant being that takes the form of a great serpent, and lies at night in some deep dark pool; and should a man incautiously approach and look down into the water he would be held there by the power of the great gleaming eyes, and finally drawn down against his will, powerless and speechless, to disappear for ever in the black depths.

Not less strange than this statue-like immobility of the serpent, the effect of which is increased and made more mysterious by the flickering lambent tongue, suddenly appearing at intervals like lightning playing on the edge of an unmoving cloud, is that kind of progressive motion so even and slow as to be scarcely perceptible. But on this and other points relating to the serpent's strangeness I have spoken in the preceding chapter. Even in our conditions of self-absorption and aloofness—the mental habit of regarding nature as something outside of ourselves and interesting only to men of curious minds—this quality of the serpent is yet able to affect us powerfully. How great was its effect on the earlier races, and what great things resulted from it, when the floating scattered threads of all strange sensations and experiences, all unaccountable things, were gathered and woven into the many-coloured and quaintly figured cloth of religion, anthropology has for some time past been engaged in telling us.

We have seen in the history of palæontology that, when the fossil remains of some long-extinct animal have been discovered, in some district still perhaps inhabited by one or more representatives of archaic form, naturalists have concluded that the type was peculiar to the district; but subsequently fresh remains have been discovered in other widely separated districts, and then others, until it has been established that the type once supposed local has, at one time or another, ranged over a very large portion of the habitable globe. Something similar has been the case in the extension of the area over which evidences of serpent-worship have been brought to light by inquiries into the early history of mankind. It had existed in Phœnicia, India, Babylonia, and, in a mild form, in Greece and Italy in Europe; Persia was added, and, little by little, Cashmir, Cambodia, Thibet, China, Ceylon, the Kalmucks; in Lithuania it was universal; it was found in Madagascar and Abyssinia; the area over which it once flourished or still flourishes in Africa grows wider and wider, and promises to take in the entire continent; across the Atlantic it extended over a greater part of North, Central, and South America, and exists still among some tribes, as it still does in Egypt, India, and China. Meanwhile the area over which it once held sway in Europe has also been extended; among those who once regarded the serpent as a sacred animal we now include the Goths, British Celts, Scandinavians, Esthonians, and Finns. It would no longer be rash to say that in every part of the earth inhabited by the serpent this animal has at one time or other been reverenced by man.

Into the subject of serpent-worship, about which scores of books and hundreds of papers have been written, I do not wish to go one step further than I am compelled by my theme, which is, primarily, the serpent, and the effect on the human intelligence of its unique appearance and faculties. At the same time the two matters are so closely connected that we cannot treat of one without touching on the other. We find that the authorities are divided in their opinions as to the origin of this kind of worship, some holding that it had its rise in one centre—

Furgusson goes so far as to give the precise spot
—from which it spread to other regions and eventually over the earth; others, on the contrary, believe
that it sprang up spontaneously in many places and
at different periods.

The solution of this question is, I believe, to be
found in ourselves—in the effect of the serpent on
us. Much is to be gained by personal experience
and observation, and by close attention to our own
sensations. Just as the individual who has passed
the middle period of life, or attained to old age,
has outlived many conditions of mind and body so
different and distinct that when recalled they seem
to represent separate identities, and yet has preserved within himself something of them all—of
adolescence, of boyhood, even of childhood and
infancy—an ineradicable something corresponding to
the image, bright or dim, existing in his memory;
so do we inherit and retain something of our forgotten progenitors, the old emotions and obsolete
modes of thought of races that have preceded us by
centuries and by thousands of years.

In the next chapter, dealing with the subject of
man's irrational enmity to the serpent, there will be
more said on this subject; nevertheless, at the risk
of some overlapping, I must in this place dwell a
little on my own early experiences, which serve to
illustrate the familiar biological doctrine that the
ancient, outlived characters of the organism tend to
reappear for a season in its young. The mental
stripes on the human whelp are very perceptible.

From an æsthetic, that is, *our* æsthetic, point of view, there is not much to choose between an English infant, whether of aristocratic or plebeian descent, and a Maori, Patagonian, Japanese, or Greenland infant. The Greenland infant might be the fattest —I do not know. After the features and expression change, when infancy and early childhood is past, they are still alike in mind. The similarity of all children all the world over sometimes strikes us very forcibly. One day I stood watching a group of a dozen children playing in a small open green space in London; its openness to the sky and the green, elastic turf under their feet had suddenly made them mad with joy. Watching them I could not help laughing when all at once I remembered having once watched a group of children of about the same size as these on a spot of green turf in a distant region, playing the same rude game in the same way, with the same shrill, excited cries; and these were children of unadulterated savages—the nomad Tehuelches of Patagonia! In some savage tribes the adults are invariably of a gloomy, taciturn disposition—the "buoyant child surviving in the man" would be as astonishing a phenomenon to them as a fellow-creature with the melodious throat of a Rubini, or a pair of purple wings on his shoulders. The children of these people sit silent and unsmiling among their elders in the house, as if the burden of eternal care had been inherited by them from birth; but every day the grave young monkeys find a chance to steal off, and when they have got to some secluded spot in the woods, out of earshot of the village, a sudden transformation takes place: they are out of school, and as merry and shrill at their games and mock battles as any rough set of urchins just released from their lessons in our own land.

Many pages might be filled with similar instances. And when we consider what the law is, and that the period during which the human species has existed in any kind of civilisation, making its own conditions, is but a span compared with its long life of simple barbarism, it would be strange indeed if we did not find in the civilised child the psychological representative of primitive man. We do not look for the emotions and inherited or traditional habits proper to the adult. The higher mental faculties, which have had their growth in a developed social state, are latent in him. His senses and lower mental faculties are, on the contrary, at their best: in the acuteness of his senses, and the vividness and durability of the impressions made on him by external stimuli; in his nearness to or oneness with Nature, resulting from his mythical faculty, and in the quick response of the organism to every outward change, he is like the animals. His world is small, but the bright mirror of his mind has reflected it so clearly, with all it contains, from sun and stars and floating clouds above, to the floating motes in the beam, and the grass blades and fine grains of yellow sand he treads upon, that he knows it as intimately as if he had existed in it for a thousand years. And whatever is rare and strange, or outside of Nature's usual order, and opposed to his experience, affects him powerfully and excites the sense of mystery, which remains thereafter associated with the object. I remember that as a child, or small boy, I was affected in this way on seeing mushrooms growing in a chain of huge rings in a meadow; also by the sensitive-plant, when I saw it shrink and grow pale at the touch of my fingers. Other plants and flowers have affected me with a sense of mystery in the same way; and throughout the world, among inferior or savage races, plants of strange forms are often regarded with superstitious fear or veneration. Something of this—the mythical faculty of the primitive man and of the child—remains in all of us, even the most intellectual. There is a story told of an atheist who, coming from an orchid show, said that he had been converted to belief in the existence of a devil. A feeling, about which he probably knew little, was father to the witticism.

To pass from plants to animals. As a child I was powerfully moved at my first meeting with a large owl. I was exploring a dimly lighted loft in a barn, when, peering into an empty cask, I met its eyes fixed on mine—a strange monster of a bird with fluffed, tawny plumage, barred and spotted with black, and a circular, pale-coloured face, and set in it a pair of great luminous yellow eyes! My nerves tingled and my hair stood up as if I had received an electric shock. Recalling this experience, the vividness of the image printed on my mind, and the sense of mystery so long afterwards associated with this bird, it does not seem strange that among all races in all parts of the globe it should have been regarded as something more than a bird, and supernatural—a wise being, something evil and ghostly, a messenger from spirit-land, and prophet of death and disaster; a little sister or some other relation of the devil; and finally the devil himself; also, as in Samoa, a god incarnate. Its voice, as well as its strange appearance, had doubtless much to do with the owl's supernatural reputation. The owl is first, but only one, of a legion of feathered demons, ghosts, witches, and other unearthly beings, usually nocturnal birds with cries and notes that resemble the human voice expressing physical agony, incurable grief, despair and frenzy, always with something aerial and ventriloquial in it, heightening its mysterious and terrible character; and the birds that emit these sounds are of many families—night-jars, herons, rails, curlews, grebes, loons, and others.

But great as the owl is among birds that have been regarded as supernatural, or in league with the unseen powers, it has never risen to the height of the serpent in this respect: it had only its strange appearance, silent flight, and weird voice; the serpent had many and more impressive qualities. First and foremost is the strength and lastingness of the impression produced by its strangeness, and its beautiful, infinitely varied, and, to the unscientific mind, causeless motions; its spectre-like silence and subtlety; its infinite patience and watchfulness, and its power to continue with raised head and neck rigid

as if frozen to stone for a long period; and its wonderful quietude when lying day after day in sun or
shade on the same spot, as if in a deep perpetual
sleep, yet eternally awake, with open brilliant eyes
fixed on whosoever regards it. A sense of mystery
becomes inseparably associated with its appearance;
and when habitually regarded with such a feeling,
other qualities and faculties possessed by it would
seem in harmony with this strangeness, and outside
of the common order of nature: — its periodical
renewal of youth; the power of existing without
aliment and with no sensible diminution of vigour
for an indefinite time; the faculty of fascination—a
miraculous power over the ordinary lower animals;
and the deadliness which its venom and the lightning-like swiftness of its stroke give it, and which
is never exercised against man except in revenge for
an insult or injury. To this inoffensiveness of the
lethal serpent, together with its habit of attaching
itself to human habitations, about which it glides in
a ghostly manner, may be traced the notion of its
friendliness and guardianship and of its supernatural
power and wisdom; the belief that it was a re-
incarnation of a dead man's soul, a messenger from
the gods, and, finally, the Agathodæmon of so many
lands and so many races of men.

The serpent's strangeness and serpent-worship are
thus seen as cause and effect. Now, there is another
effect, or another subject, so mixed up with the one
I have been considering that this paper might appear
incomplete without some notice of it—I refer to the

widely prevalent belief in the existence of serpents of vast size and supernatural powers; in many cases the dæmons or guardian spirits of rivers, lakes, and mountains. Given the profound veneration for the natural serpent, and the mental condition in which the mythical faculty is very strong, men would scarcely fail to see such monsters in certain aspects of nature coinciding with certain mental moods; and that which any person saw, and gave an account of, as he would have done of a singular tree, rock, or cloud which he had seen, the others would believe in; and believing, they would expect to see it also; and with this expectation exciting them, when the right mood and aspect came they probably would see it.

Even to our purged and purified vision nature is full of suggestions of the serpent—that is, to those who are familiar with the serpent's form and have been strongly impressed with its strangeness. Ruskin has called the serpent a "living wave," and compares it in motion to a "wave without wind." In many of its aspects the sea is serpent-like; never more so than when the tide rises on a calm day, when wave succeeds to wave, lifting itself up serpentwise, gliding noiselessly and mysteriously shorewards, to break in foam on the low beach and withdraw with a prolonged hissing sound to the deep. Again, he has compared the serpent in motion to a "current without a fall." Before I had read Ruskin, or knew his name, the swift current of a shallow stream had reminded me on numberless occasions of a serpent in rapid motion. When rushing away at its greatest speed, the creature, as one looks down on it, changes its appearance from a narrow body moving in a sinuous line to a broad straight band, the outward and inward curves of the body appearing as curved lines on its surface, and the spots and blotches of colour forming the pattern as shorter lines. The shallow pebbly current shows a similar pattern on its swiftly moving surface, the ripples appearing as light and dark slanting lines that intersect, cross, and mingle with each other.

Viewed from an elevation, all rivers winding through the lower levels, glistening amidst the greens and greys and browns of earth, suggest the serpent form and appear like endless serpents lying across the world. Probably it is this configuration and shining quality of rivers, as well as the even, noiseless motion of flowing water, which has given rise to the belief among many savage tribes of huge water-serpents, like that of the stupendous Mother of the Waters, supposed to lie extended at the bottom of the Amazon, Orinoco, and other great rivers of tropical South America. The river boa of these regions is probably the largest existing serpent on the globe, but it is a small creature to the fabled monster that rests beneath the flood—so small comparatively that it might well be regarded as one of the unseen monster's newly born young.

There is also something in the hypnotic effect produced by deep clear water when gazed on steadily and for a long time which may have given rise to the African superstition of the Icanti already mentioned.

Among some North American tribes there also existed a belief in a serpent of enormous size that reposed at the bottom of some river or lake, and once every year rose to the surface showing a shining splendid stone on his head.

The mountains, too, have their serpent-shaped guardians: thus, it was believed by the neighbouring tribes that a huge camoodi, or boa, rested its league-long coils on the flat top of the table mountain of Roraima in Venezuela. Doubtless a serpent of cloud and mist; of the white vapour that, forming at the summit, dropped down in a long coil, or crept earthwards along the deep fissures that score the precipitous sides.

Other beliefs of this kind might be adduced, and other resemblances to the serpent's form and motion in nature traced, but enough on this point has been said. If it is due to these resemblances that the savage is disposed to see the life and intelligent spirit he attributes to nature, and to all natural objects, take the serpent form, may we not believe that the serpent-myths of the earlier civilised races originated in the same way? Doubtless in many cases, with the development of the reasoning powers and the decay of the mythical faculty, the fable would be somewhat changed in form and embellished, and perhaps come at last to be regarded as merely symbolical. But symbolism does not exist among barbarians and savages: it comes in only when the intellect has progressed sufficiently far to become enamoured of subtleties. When the savage Shawnees heard the hissing of a great snake in the thunder, and saw in the lightning a fiery serpent descending to the earth, the beings they heard and saw were real—as real as the rattlesnake. The same may be said of the monster serpent with a precious stone for a crown of the Iroquois and Algonquins; and of the mighty Onnient, the serpent of the Hurons, bearing a horn on its head with which it was able to pierce through rocks and hills.

Greater than these (as gods are greater than heroes) were some of the serpents of old, and they also had a vastly greater influence on human destiny; but in their origins they were probably the same— merely the strange births of the mythical faculty and the lawless imagination of the primitive mind: the Mexican Cihua Cohuatl, "the woman of the serpent," and mother of the human race; and the serpent of the Edda that encircled the world; and Persian Ahriman, "the old serpent having two feet," who seduced Mechia and Mechiana, the first man and woman; and, most awful of all, Aphôphis, "the destroyer, the enemy of the gods, and devourer of the souls of men; dweller in that mysterious ocean upon which the Boris, or boat of the sun, was navigated by the gods through the hours of day and night, in the celestial region."

CHAPTER XVI

THE BRUISED SERPENT

SOME hold that our abhorrence of the serpent tribe, the undiscriminating feeling which involves the innocent with the harmful, is instinctive in man. Many primitive, purely animal promptings and impulses survive in us, of which, they argue, this may be one. It is common knowledge that the sight of a serpent affects many persons, especially Europeans, in a sudden violent manner, with a tremor and tingling of the nerves, like a million messages of startling import flying from the centre of intelligence to all outlying parts of the bodily kingdom; and these sensations of alarm, horror, and disgust are, in most cases, accompanied or instantly followed by an access of fury, a powerful impulse to crush the offensive reptile to death. The commonness of the feeling and its violence, so utterly out of proportion to the danger to be apprehended, do certainly give it the appearance of a true instinctive impulse; nevertheless, such appearance may be deceptive. Fear, however it may originate, is of all emotions the least rational; and the actions of a person greatly excited by it will most nearly resemble those of the lower animals.

Darwin, on the slightest evidence, affirms that

monkeys display an instinctive or inherited fear of snakes. There are many who would think any further inquiry into the matter superfluous; for, they would argue, if monkeys fear snakes in that way, then assuredly we, developed monkeys, must regard them with a feeling identical in character and origin. To be able thus to skim with the swallow's grace and celerity over dark and possibly unfathomable questions is a very engaging accomplishment, and apparently a very popular one. What is done with ease will always be done with pleasure; and what can be easier or more agreeable than to argue in this fashion: "Fear of snakes is merely another example of historical memory, recalling a time when man, like his earliest ancestors, the anthropoid apes, was sylvan and solitary; a mighty climber of trees whose fingers were frequently bitten by bird-nesting colubers, and who was occasionally swallowed entire by colossal serpents of arboreal habits."

The instinctive fear of enemies, although plainly traceable in insects, with some other creatures low in the organic scale, is exceedingly rare among the higher vertebrates; so rare indeed as to incline anyone who has made a real study of their actions to doubt its existence. It is certain that zoological writers are in the habit of confusing instinctive or inherited with traditional fear, the last being the fear of an enemy which the young learn from their parents or other adults they associate with. Fear is contagious; the alarm of the adults communicates itself to the young, with the result that the object that excited it remains thereafter one of terror. Not only in this matter of snakes and monkeys, but with regard to other creatures, Darwin lays it down that in the higher vertebrates the habit of fear of any particular enemy quickly becomes instinctive; and this false inference has been accepted without question by Herbert Spencer, who was obliged to study animal habits in books, and was consequently to some extent at the mercy of those who wrote them.

It is frequently stated in narratives of travel in the less settled portions of North America that all domestic animals, excepting the pig, have an instinctive dread of the rattlesnake; that they know its whirring sound, and are also able to smell it at some distance, and instantly come to a dead halt, trembling with agitation. The fear is a fact; but why *instinctive*? Some time ago, while reading over again a very delightful book of travels, I came to a passage descriptive of the acute sense of smell and sagacity of the native horse; and the writer, as an instance in point, related that frequently, when riding at a swift pace across country on a dark night, over ground made dangerous by numerous concealed burrows, his beast had swerved aside suddenly, *as if he had trod on a snake*. His sense of smell had warned him in time of some grass-covered kennel in the way. But that image of the snake, introduced to give a more vivid idea of the animal's action in swerving aside, was false; and because of its falseness and the want of observation it betrayed, the charm of the passage was sensibly diminished. For not once or twice, but many scores of times it has happened to me, in that very country so graphically described in the book, while travelling at a swinging gallop in the bright daylight, that my horse has trodden on a basking serpent and has swerved not at all, nor appeared conscious of a living, fleshy thing that yielded to his unshod hoof. Passing on, I have thrown back a glance to see my victim writhing on the ground, and hoped that it was bruised only, not broken or fatally injured, like the serpent of the Roman poet's simile, over which the brazen chariot wheel has passed. Yet if the rider saw it—saw it, I mean, before the accident, although too late for any merciful action—the horse must have seen it. The reason he did not swerve was because serpents are very abundant in that country, in the proportion of about thirty harmless individuals to one that is venomous; consequently it is a rare thing for a horse to be bitten; and the serpentine form is familiar to and excites no fear in him. He saw the reptile lying just in his way, motionless in the sunlight, "lit with colour like a rock with flowers," and it caused no emotion, and was no more to him than the yellow and purple blossoms he trampled upon at every yard.

It is not the same in the western prairies of North America. Venomous serpents are relatively more abundant there, and grow larger, and their bite is more dangerous. The horse learns to fear them, especially the rattlesnake, on account of its greater power, its sluggish habits and warning faculties. The sound of the rattle calls up the familiar ophidian

image to his mind; and when the rattle has failed
to sound, the smell will often serve as a warning;
which is not strange when we consider that even
man, with his feeble olfactory sense, is sometimes
able to discover the presence of a rattlesnake, even
at a distance of several feet, by means of its powerful musky effluvium. The snake-eating savages of
Queensland track their game by the slight scent it
leaves on the ground in travelling, which is quite
imperceptible to Europeans. In the same way the
horse is said to smell wolves, and to exhibit instinctive terror when they are still at a distance and
invisible. The terror is not instinctive. The horses
of the white settlers on some frontier lands, exposed
to frequent attacks from savages, smell the coming
enemy, and fly in panic before he makes his appearance; yet when horses are taken from the savages
and used by the whites, these too after a time learn
to show terror at the smell of their former masters.
Their terror is derived from the horses of the whites.
The hunter Selous, as a result of ten years of observation while engaged in the pursuit of big game in
the heart of Africa, affirms that the horse has no
instinctive fear of the lion; if he has never been
mauled or attacked by them, nor associated with
horses that have learnt from experience or tradition
to dread them, he exhibits no more fear of lions
than of zebras and camelopards. The fact is, the
horse fears in different regions the lion, wolf, puma,
red-skin, and rattlesnake, just as the burnt child
dreads the fire.

But here is an incident, say the believers in Darwin's notion, which proves that the fear of certain animals is instinctive in the horse. A certain big-game hunter brought home a lion's hide, rolled up before it was properly dried, and wrapped up in canvas. It was opened in the stable where there were several horses, and the covering was no sooner removed and the hide peeled open than the horses were thrown into a panic. The true explanation is that horses are terrified at any strange *animal* smell, and a powerful smell from the hide of any animal unknown to them would have had the same effect. That fear of a strange animal smell is probably an instinct, but it may not be. In a state of nature the horse learns from experience that certain smells indicate danger, and in Patagonia and on the pampas, when he flies in terror from the scent of a puma which is imperceptible to a man, he pays not the slightest attention to the two most powerful mammalian stenches in the world—that of the skunk, and that of the pampas male deer, *Cervus campestris*. Experience has taught him—or it has come down to him as a tradition—that these most violent odours emanate from animals that cannot harm him.

So much for this view. On the other hand, our enmity to the serpent, which often exists together with a mythic and anthropomorphic belief in the serpent's enmity to us, might be regarded as purely traditional, having its origin in the Scriptural narrative of man's disobedience and explusion from Paradise. Whether we believe with theologians that

our great spiritual enemy was the real tempter, who
merely made use of the serpent's form as a convenient disguise in which to approach the woman,
or take without gloss the simple story as it stands
in Genesis, which only says that the serpent was the
most subtle of all things made and the sole cause
of our undoing, the result for the creature is equally
disastrous. A mark is set upon him: "Because thou
hast done this thing thou art cursed above all cattle,
and above every beast of the field; upon thy belly
shalt thou go, and dust shalt thou eat all the days of
thy life: and I will place enmity between thy seed
and her seed; and it shall bruise thy head, and thou
shalt bruise its heel." This prophecy, so far as it
tells against the creature, has been literally fulfilled.

The Satanic theory concerning snakes—that "destructive delusion" which, Sir Thomas Browne
shrewdly remarks, "hath much enlarged the opinion
of their mischief"—makes it necessary for the theo-
logian to believe not only that the serpent of Paradise
before its degradation walked erect on two legs, as
the Fathers taught—some going so far as to give it
a beautiful head as well as a ready tongue—but also
that after the devil had cast aside the temporary
coil something of his demoniac spirit remained thereafter in it, to be transmitted by inheritance, like a
variation in structure or a new instinct, to its re-
motest descendants. There is the further objection,
although not an important one, that it would be un-
just to afflict the serpent so grievously for a crime of
which it had only been made the involuntary agent.

Believers in an instinct in man inimical to the serpent might still argue that the Scriptural curse only goes to show that this reptile was already held in general abhorrence—that, in fact, the feeling suggested the fable. That the fable had some such origin is probable, but we are just as far from an instinct as ever. The general feeling of mankind, or, at any rate, of the leading men during the earliest civilised periods of which we have any knowledge, was one of veneration, even of love, for the serpent. The Jews alone were placed by their monotheistic doctrine in direct antagonism to all nature-worship and idolatry. In their leaders—prophets and priests—the hatred of the heathen and of heathen modes of thought was kept alive, and constantly fanned into a fierce flame by the prevalent tendency in the common people to revert to the surrounding older and lower forms of religion, which were more in harmony with their mental condition. The proudest boast of their highest intellects was that they had never bowed in reverence or kissed their hand to anything in nature. In such circumstances it was unavoidable that the specific object—rock, or tree, or animal—singled out for worship, or for superstitious veneration, should to some extent become involved in the feeling first excited against the worshipper. If the Jews hated the serpent with a peculiarly bitter hatred, it was doubtless because all others looked on it as a sacred animal, an incarnation of the Deity. The chosen people had also been its worshippers at an earlier period, as the Bible shows, and while hating it, they still retained the old belief, intimately connected with serpent-worship everywhere, in the creature's preternatural subtlety and wisdom. The priests of other Eastern nations introduced it into their sacred rites and mysteries; the Jewish priests introduced it historically into the Garden of Eden to account for man's transgression and fall. "Be ye wise as serpents," was a saying of the deepest significance. In Europe men were anciently taught by the Druids to venerate the adder; the Jews— or Jewish books—taught them to abhor it. To my way of thinking, neither blessing nor banning came by instinct.

Veneration of the serpent still survives in a great part of the world, as in Hindustan and other parts of Asia. It is strong in Madagascar, and flourishes more or less throughout Africa. It lingers in North America, and is strong in some places where the serpents, used in religious serpent dances, unlike those of Madagascar, are venomous, and it has not yet wholly died out in Europe. The Finns have a great regard for the adder.

It may be added here that there are many authenticated instances of children becoming attached to snakes and making pets of them. The solution of a question of this kind is sometimes to be found in the child-mind. My experience is that when young children see this creature, its strange appearance and manner of progression, so unlike those of other animals known to them, affect them with amazement and a sense of mystery, and that they fear it just as they would fear any other strange thing. Monkeys are doubtless affected in much the same way, although, in a state of nature, where they inhabit forests abounding with the larger constrictors and venomous tree-snakes, it is highly probable that they also possess a traditional fear of the serpent form. It would be strange if they did not. The experiment of presenting a caged monkey with a serpent carefully wrapped up in paper and watching his behaviour when he gravely opens the parcel, expecting to find nothing more wonderful than the familiar sponge-cake or succulent banana—well, such an experiment has been recorded in half a hundred important scientific works, and out of respect to one's masters one should endeavour not to smile when reading it.

A third view might be taken, which would account for our feeling towards the serpent without either instinct or tradition. Extreme fear of all ophidians may simply result from a vague knowledge of the fact that some kinds are venomous, that in some rare cases death follows swiftly on their bite, and that, not being sufficiently intelligent to distinguish the noxious from the innocuous—at all events while under the domination of a sudden violent emotion —we destroy them all alike, thus adopting Herod's rough-and-ready method of ridding his city of one inconvenient babe by a general massacre of innocents.

It might be objected that in Europe, where animosity to the serpent is greatest, death from snake-bite is hardly to be feared, that Fontana's six thousand

experiments with the viper, showing how small is the
amount of venom possessed by this species, how
rarely it has the power to destroy human life, have
been before the world for a century. And although
it must be admitted that Fontana's work is not in
the hand of every peasant, the fact remains that
death from snake-bite is a rare thing in Europe,
probably not more than one person losing his life
from this cause for every two hundred and fifty who
perish by hydrophobia, of all forms of death the
most terrible. Yet while the sight of a snake excites
in a majority of persons the most violent emotions,
dogs are universal favourites, and we have them
always with us and make pets of them, in spite of
the knowledge that they may at any time become
rabid and inflict that unspeakable dreadful suffering
and destruction on us. This leads to the following
question: Is it not at least probable that our excessive fear of the serpent, so unworthy of us as
rational beings and the cause of so much unnecessary
cruelty, is, partly at all events, a result of our superstitious fear of sudden death? For there exists, we
know, an exceedingly widespread delusion that the
bite of a venomous serpent must kill, and kill quickly.
Compared with such ophidian monarchs as the bush-
master, fer-de-lance, hamadryad, and ticpolonga, the
viper of Europe—the poor viper of many experiments and much, not too readable, literature—may
be regarded as almost harmless, at all events not
much more harmful than the hornet. Nevertheless,
in this cold northern world, even as in other worlds

where nature elaborates more potent juices, the delusion prevails, and may be taken in account here, although its origin cannot now be discussed.

Against sudden death we are taught to pray from infancy, and those who believe that their chances of a happy immortality are enormously increased when death comes slowly, approaching them, as it were, visibly, so that the soul has ample time to make its peace with an incensed Deity, have not far to look for the cause of the feeling. It is true that death from hydrophobia is very horrible, and, comparatively, of frequent occurrence, but it does not find its victim wholly unprepared. After being bitten he has had time to reflect on the possible, even probable, consequence, and to make due preparation for the end; and even at the last, although tortured to frenzy at intervals by strange unhuman agonies, however clouded with apprehensions his intellect may be, it is not altogether darkened and unconscious of approaching dissolution. We know that men in other times have had no such fear of sudden death, that among the most advanced of the ancients some even regarded death from lightning-stroke as a signal mark of Heaven's favour. We, on the contrary, greatly fear the lightning, seldom as it hurts; and the serpent and the lightning are objects of terror to us in about the same degree, and perhaps for the same reason.

Thus any view which we may take of this widespread and irrational feeling is at once found to be so complicated with other feelings and matters affecting us that no convincing solution seems possible. Perhaps it would be as well to regard it as a compound of various elements: traditional feeling having its origin in the Hebrew narrative of man's fall from innocency and happiness; our ignorance concerning serpents and the amount of injury they are able to do us; and, lastly, our superstitious dread of swift and unexpected death. Sticklers for the simple—and to my mind erroneous—theory that a primitive instinct is under it all, may throw in something of that element if they like—a small residuum existing in races that emerged in comparatively recent times from barbarism, but which has been eliminated from a long-civilised people like the Hindoos.

For my own part I am inclined to believe that we regard serpents with a destructive hatred purely and simply because we are so taught from childhood. A tradition may be handed down without writing, or even articulate speech. We have not altogether ceased to be "lower animals" ourselves. Show a child by your gestures and actions that a thing is fearful to you, and he will fear it, that you hate it, and he will catch your hatred. So far back as memory carries me I find the snake, in its unwarrantable intrusion on the scene, ever associated with loud exclamations of astonishment and rage, with a hurried search for those primitive weapons always lying ready to hand, sticks and stones, then the onset and triumphant crushing of that wonderfully fashioned vertebra in its scaly vari-coloured mantle, coiling and writhing for a few moments under the cruel rain of blows, appealing not with voice but with agonised yet ever graceful action for mercy to the merciless; and finally, the pæan of victory from the slayer, lifting his face still aglow with righteous wrath, a little St. George in his own estimation; for has he not rid the earth of another monster, one of that demoniac brood that was cursed of old, and this without injury to his sacred heel?

CHAPTER XVII

PREAMBLE

AMONG the thousand and one projects I have entertained at various times was one for a work on snakes, with the good though somewhat ambitious title of "The Book of the Serpent." This was not to be the work of one who must write a book about something, but a work on a subject which had long had a peculiar fascination for the author, which for years had cried to be written, and finally had to be written.

As it was a work requiring a great deal of research, it would take a long time to write, long years, in fact, since it would have to be done at odd times, when hours or days or weeks could be spared from the hard business of manufacturing mere bread-and-cheese books. Collecting material would have to be a slow process, involving the perusal or consultation of a thousand volumes, and probably ten thousand periodicals and annals and proceedings and journals of many natural history societies, great and small, of many countries. And all this research, with the classification and indexing of notes, would be exceeded by the task of selection to follow—selection and compression—since "The Book of the Serpent" would be in one volume and not in half a dozen. And after selection, or let us say deglutition, there would ensue the dilatory process of digestion and assimilation. If properly assimilated, the personal impressions of a hundred independent observers, field-naturalists and travellers, and of a hundred independent students of ophiology, would be fused, as it were, and run into one along with the author's personal observations and his deductions.

Now, even if all this could have been done, and the best form hit upon, and the work eloquently written, it would still fall far short of the ideal "Book of the Serpent" on account of insufficient knowledge of a particular kind—I don't mean anatomy. And had I been a person of means I should, before beginning my work—getting a pale, wan face through poring over miserable books—have gone away on a five or ten years' serpent quest to get that particular kind of knowledge by becoming acquainted personally with all the most distinguished ophidians on the globe. The first sight of a thing, the shock of emotion, the vivid and ineffaceable image registered in the brain, is worth more than all the knowledge acquired by reading, and this applies to the serpent above all creatures. There is indeed but little difference between this creature dead and in confinement. It was the serpent in motion on the rock that was a wonder and mystery to the wisest man. In one of my snake-books by a French naturalist in the West Indies there is an account of a fer-de-lance which he kept confined in order to study its habits. He watched it hour after hour, day after day, lying prone on the floor of its cage as if asleep or stupefied, until he was sick and tired of seeing it in that dull, dead-alive state, and in his disgust he threw open the door to let it go free. He watched it. Slowly the head turned, and slowly, slowly it began to move towards the open door, and so dragged itself out, then over the space of bare ground towards the bushes and trees beyond. But once well out in the open air its motions and aspect began to change. The long, straightened-out, dull-coloured, dragging body was smitten with a sudden new life and became sinuous in form; its slow motion grew swift, and from a dragging became a gliding motion: the dangerous head with its flickering tongue lifted itself high up, the stony eyes shone, and all along the body the scales sparkled like wind-crinkled water in the sun: watching it, he was thrilled at the sight and amazed at this wonderful change in its appearance.

And that is how I, too, would have liked to see the fer-de-lance in its dreadful beauty and power; the cribo too, that gives it battle, and conquers and devours it in spite of its poison fangs; also its noble relations, the rattlesnakes and pit-vipers, led by the Surucurú, the serpent monarch of the West; and the constricting anacondas, with the greatest of them all, the giant Camudi, "mother of the waters"; also the bull snake and the black snake, and that brilliant deadly harlequin, the coral snake. These all are in the New World, and I should then go to the Old in quest of blue sea-snakes and wonderful viridescent tree-snakes, and many historic serpents—the ticpolonga, the hooded cobras, and their king and slayer, the awful hamadryad.

A beautiful dream all this, like that of the poor little pale-faced quill-driver at his desk, summing up columns of figures, who falls to thinking what his life would be with ten thousand a year. All the thorny and stony and sandy wilderness, the dark Amazonian and Arawhimi forests, the mighty rivers to be ascended three thousand miles from the sea to their source, the great mountain-chains to be passed, Alps and Andes, and Himalayas and the Mountains of the Moon, the entire globe to be explored in quest of serpents, from the hot tropical jungles and malarious marshes to the desolate windy roof of the world —all would have to be sought in the British Museum and one or two other dim stuffy libraries, where a man sits in a chair all day and all the year round with a pile of books before him.

Alas! in such conditions, without the necessary precious personal knowledge so much desired, "The Book of the Serpent" would never be written. So I said and repeated, yet still went on with the preliminary work, and after two or three years, finding that so far as material went I had got almost more than I could manage, I thought I would begin to try my hand at writing a few chapters, each dealing with some special aspect of or question relating to the serpent, and about a dozen were written, but left in the rough, unfinished, as all would eventually have to go back into the melting-pot once more. By-and-by I took up and finished three or four of these tentative chapters just to see how they would look in print; these appeared in three or four monthly reviews and are all that is left of my ambitious book.

It could not be done, because, as I tried to make myself believe, it was too long a task for one who had to make a living by writing, but a still small voice told me that I was deceiving myself, that if I had just gone on, slowly, slowly, like the released fer-de-lance, until I had got out into the open air and sunshine—until I had a full mind and full command of my subject—I too might have gone on to a triumphant end. No, it was not because the task was too long; the secret and real reason was a discouraging thought which need not be given here, since it is stated in the paper to follow. There's nothing more to say about it except that I now make a present of the title—"The Book of the Serpent"—to any person who would like to use it, and I only ask that it be not given to a handbook on snakes, nor to a monograph—God deliver us! as Huxley said. Or if he did not use that particular expression he protested against the multiplication of such works, and even feared that we should all be buried alive under them —the ponderous tomes which nobody reads, elephantine bodies without souls; or shall we say, carcasses, dressed and placed in their canvas coverings on shelves in the cold storage of the zoological libraries.

As to the paper which follows, it was never intended to use it as it stands for the book. It is nothing but a little exercise, and merely touches the fringe of a subject for a great book—not an anthology (Heaven save us!), but a history and review of the literature of the serpent from Ruskin back to Sanchoniathon, and I now also generously give away this title of "The Serpent in Literature."

When the snakists of the British Museum or other biological workshop have quite done with their snake, have pulled it out of its jar and popped it in again to their hearts' content; weighed, measured, counted ribs and scales, identified its species, sub-species, and variety; and have duly put it all down in a book, made a fresh label, perhaps written a paper—when all is finished, something remains to be said; something about the snake; the creature that was not a spiral-shaped, rigid, cylindrical piece of clay-coloured gutta-percha, no longer capable of exciting strange emotions in us—the unsightly dropped coil of a spirit that was fiery and cold. Where shall that something be found? Not assuredly in the paper the snakist has written, nor in the monographs and natural histories; where then?—since in the absence of the mysterious creature itself it might be interesting to read it.

It is true that in spite of a great deal of bruising by Christian heels the serpent still survives in this country, although it can hardly be said to flourish. Sometimes, walking by a hedge-side, a slight rustling sound and movement of the grass betrays the presence of the common or ring snake; then, if chance favours and eyes are sharp, a glimpse may be had of the shy creature, gliding with swift sinuous motions out of harm's way. Or on the dry open common one may all at once catch sight of a strip of coppery-red or dull brown colour with a curious black mark on it—an adder lying at ease in the warm sunshine! Not sleeping, but awake; a little startled at the muffled thunder of approaching foot-falls, with crackling of dead leaves and sticks, as of a coming conflagration; then, perhaps, the appearance of a shape, looming vast and cloudlike on its dim circumscribed field of vision; but at the same time lethargic, disinclined to move, heavy with a meal it will never digest, or big with young that, jarred with their parent, have some vague sense of peril within the living prison from which they will never issue.

Or a strange thing may be seen—a cluster of hibernating adders, unearthed by workmen in the winter time when engaged in quarrying stone or grubbing up an old stump. Still more wonderful it is to witness a knot or twined mass of adders, not self-buried, semi-torpid, and of the temperature of the cold ground, but hot-blooded in the hot sun, active, hissing, swinging their tails. In a remote corner of this island there exists an extensive boggy heath where adders are still abundant, and grow black as the stagnant rushy pools, and the slime under the turf, which invites the foot with its velvety appearance, but is dangerous to tread upon. In this snaky heath-land, in the warm season, when the frenzy takes them, twenty or thirty or more adders are sometimes found twined together; they are discovered perhaps by some solitary pedestrian, cautiously picking his way, gun in hand, and the sight amazes and sends a sharp electric shock along his spinal cord. All at once he remembers his gun and discharges it into the middle of the living mass, to boast thereafter to the very end of his life of how he killed a score of adders at one shot.

To witness this strange thing, and experience the peculiar sensation it gives, it is necessary to go far and to spend much time in seeking and waiting and watching. A bright spring morning in England no longer "craves wary walking," as in the days of Elizabeth. Practically the serpent hardly exists for us, so seldom do we see it, so completely has it dropped out of our consciousness. But if we have known the creature, at home or abroad, and wish in reading to recover the impression of a sweet summer-hot Nature that invites our caresses, always with a subtle serpent somewhere concealed in the folds of her garments, we must go to literature rather than to science. The poet has the secret, not the naturalist. A book or an article about snakes moves us not at all—not in the way we should like to be moved—because, to begin with, there is too much of the snake in it. Nature does not teem with snakes; furthermore, we are not familiar with these creatures, and do not handle and examine them as a game-dealer handles dead rabbits. A rare and solitary being, the sharp effect it produces on the mind is in a measure due to its rarity—to its appearance being unexpected

—to surprise and the shortness of the time during which it is visible. It is not seen distinctly as in a museum or laboratory, dead on a table, but in an atmosphere and surroundings that take something from and add something to it; seen at first as a chance disposition of dead leaves or twigs or pebbles on the ground—a handful of Nature's mottled riff-raff blown or thrown fortuitously together so as to form a peculiar pattern; all at once, as by a flash, it is seen to be no dead leaves or twigs or grass, but a living active coil, a serpent lifting its flat arrowy head, vibrating a glistening forked tongue, hissing with dangerous fury; and in another moment it has vanished into the thicket, and is nothing but a memory—merely a thread of brilliant colour woven into the ever-changing vari-coloured embroidery of Nature's mantle, seen vividly for an instant, then changing to dull grey and fading from sight.

It is because the poet does not see his subject apart from its surroundings, deprived of its atmosphere—a mere fragment of beggarly matter—does not see it too well, with all the details which become visible only after a minute and, therefore, cold examination, but as a part of the picture, a light that quivers and quickly passes, that we, through him, are able to see it too, and to experience the old mysterious sensations, restored by his magic touch. For the poet is emotional, and in a few verses, even in one verse, in a single well-chosen epithet, he can vividly recall a forgotten picture to the mind and restore a lost emotion.

Matthew Arnold probably knew very little about the serpent scientifically; but in his solitary walks and communings with Nature he, no doubt, became acquainted with our two common ophidians, and was familiar with the sight of the adder, bright and glistening in its renewed garment, reposing peacefully in the spring sunshine; seeing it thus, the strange remoteness and quietude of its silent life probably moved him and sank deeply into his mind. This is not the first and most common feeling of the serpent-seer—the feeling which Matthew Arnold himself describes in a ringing couplet:

> Hast thou so rare a poison?—let me be
> Keener to slay thee lest thou poison me.

When no such wildly improbable contingency is feared as that the small drop of rare poison in the creature's tooth may presently be injected into the beholder's veins to darken his life; when the fear is slight and momentary, and passing away gives place to other sensations, he is impressed by its wonderful quietude, and is not for the moment without the ancient belief in its everlastingness and supernatural character; and, if curiosity be too great, if the leaf-crackling and gravel-crunching footsteps approach too near, to rouse and send it into hiding, something of compunction is felt, as if an indignity had been offered:

> O thoughtless, why did I
> Thus violate thy slumberous solitude?

In those who have experienced such a feeling as this at sight of the basking serpent it is most powerfully recalled by his extremely beautiful "Cadmus and Harmonia":

> Two bright and aged snakes,
> Who once were Cadmus and Harmonia,
> Bask in the glens and on the warm sea-shore,
> In breathless quiet after all their ills;
> Nor do they see their country, nor the place
> Where the Sphinx lived among the frowning hills,
> Nor the unhappy palace of their race,
> Nor Thebes, nor the Ismenus any more.
>
> There those two live, far in the Illyrian brakes!
> They had stayed long enough to see
> In Thebes the billows of calamity
> Over their own dear children rolled,
> Curse upon curse, pang upon pang,
> For years, they sitting helpless in their home,
> A grey old man and woman.
>
> .   .   .   .
>
> Therefore they did not end their days
> In sight of blood; but were rapt, far away,
> To where the west wind plays,
> And murmurs of the Adriatic come
> To those untrodden mountain lawns; and there
> Placed safely in changed forms, the pair
> Wholly forget their first sad life, and home,
> And all that Theban woe, and stray
> For ever through the glens, placid and dumb.

How the immemorial fable—the vain and faded imaginings of thousands of years ago—is freshened into life by the poet's genius, and the heart stirred as by a drama of the day we live in! But here we are concerned with the serpentine nature rather than with the human tragedy, and to those who are familiar with the serpent, and have been profoundly impressed by it, there is a rare beauty and truth in that picture of its breathless quiet, its endless placid dumb existence amid the flowery brakes.

But the first and chief quality of the snake—the sensation it excites in us—is its *snakiness*, our best word for a feeling compounded of many elements, not readily analysable, which has in it something of fear and something of the sense of mystery. I doubt if there exists in our literature, verse or prose, anything that revives this feeling so strongly as Dr. Gordon Hake's ballad of the dying serpent-charmer. "The snake-charmer is a bad naturalist," says Sir Joseph Fayrer, himself a prince among ophiologists; it may be so, and perhaps he charms all the better for it, and it is certainly not a lamentable thing, since it detracts not from the merit of the poem, that Dr. Hake is a bad naturalist, even as Shakespeare and Browning and Tennyson were, and draws his snake badly, with venomous stinging tongue, and flaming eyes that fascinate at too great a distance. Fables notwithstanding, he has with the poet's insight, in a moment of rare inspiration, captured the very illusive spirit of Nature, to make it pervade and glorify his picture. The sunny, brilliant, declining day, the joyous wild melody of birds, the low whispering wind, the cool greenness of earth, where

> The pool is bright with glossy dyes
> And cast-up bubbles of decay:

and everywhere, hidden in grass and brake, released at length from the spell that made them powerless, coming ever nearer and nearer, yet as though they came not, the subtle, silent, watchful snakes. Strangely real and vivid is the picture conjured up; the everlasting life and gladness at

the surface, the underlying mystery and melancholy — the failing power of the old man and
vanishing incantation; the tremendous retribution
of Nature, her ministers of vengeance ever imperceptibly gliding nearer.

Yet where his soul is he must go,

albeit now only to be mocked on the scene of his
old beloved triumphs:

For all that live in brake and bough—
All know the brand is on his brow.

Even dying he cannot stay away; the fascination
of the lost power is too strong on him; even dying
he rises and goes forth, creeping from tree to tree,
to the familiar sunlit green spot of earth, where

Bewildered at the pool he lies,
And sees as through a serpent's eyes;

his tawny, trembling hand still fingering, his feeble
lips still quivering, on the useless flute. He cannot
draw the old potent music from it:

The witching air
That tamed the snake, decoyed the bird,
Worried the she-wolf from her lair.

It is all fantasy, a mere juggling arrangement of
brain-distorted fact and ancient fiction; the essence
of it has no existence in nature and the soul for the
good naturalist, who dwells in a glass house full of
intense light without shadow; but the naturalists
are not a numerous people, and for all others the
effect is like that which nature itself produces on our
twilight intellect. It is snaky in the extreme; reading

it we are actually there in the bright smiling sunshine; ours is the failing spirit of the worn-out old
man, striving to drown the hissing sounds of death
in our ears, as of a serpent that hisses. But the
lost virtue cannot be recovered; our eyes too

> are swimming in a mist
> That films the earth like serpent's breath;

and the shadows of the waving boughs on the sward
appear like hollow, cast-off coils rolled before the
wind; fixed, lidless eyes are watching us from the
brake; everywhere about us serpents lie matted on
the ground.

If serpents were not so rare, so small, so elusive,
in *our* brakes we should no doubt have had other
poems as good as this about them and the strange
feelings they wake. As it is, the poet, although he
has the secret of seeing rightly, is in most cases
compelled to write (or sing) of something he does
not know personally. He cannot go to the wilds
of Guiana for the bush-master, nor to the Far East
in search of the hamadryad. Even the poor little
native adder as a rule succeeds in escaping his observation. He must go to books for his serpent or else
evolve it out of his inner consciousness. He is
dependent on the natural historians, from Pliny
onwards, or to the writer of fairy-tales: a Countess
d'Aulnoy, for example, or Meredith, in *The Shaving
of Shagpat*, or Keats his Lamia, an amazing creature,
bright and cirque-couchant, vermilion-spotted and
yellow and green and blue; also striped like a zebra,
freckled like a pard, eyed like a peacock, and barred

with crimson and full of silver moons. Lamia may be beautiful and may please the fancy with her many brilliant colours, her moons, stars, and what not, and she may even move us with a sense of the supernatural, but it is not the same kind of feeling as that experienced when we *see* a serpent. That comes of the mythical faculty in us, and the poet who would reproduce it must himself go to the serpent, even as the Druids did for their sacred nadder-stone.

In prose literature the best presentation of serpent life known to me is that of Oliver Wendell Holmes: and being the best, in fiction at all events, I am tempted to write of it at some length.

Now, very curiously, although, as we have just seen, the incorrect drawing takes nothing from the charm and, in one sense, from the truth of Dr. Hake's picture, we no sooner turn to *Elsie Venner* than we find ourselves crossing over to the side of the good naturalist, with apologies for having insulted him, to ask the loan of his fierce light—for this occasion only. Ordinarily in considering an excellent romance, we are rightly careless about the small inaccuracies with regard to matters of fact which may appear in it; for the writer who is able to produce a work of art must not and cannot be a specialist or a microscopist, but one who views nature as the ordinary man does, at a distance and as a whole, with the vision common to all men, and the artist's insight added. Dr. Holmes's work is an exception; since it is a work of art of some excellence, yet cannot be read in this tolerant spirit; we distinctly refuse to overlook its distortions of fact and false inferences in the province of zoology; and the author has only himself to blame for this uncomfortable temper of mind in his reader.

The story of the New England serpent-girl is in its essence a romance; the author thought proper to cast it in the form of a realistic novel, and to make the teller of the story a clear-headed, calm, critical onlooker of mature age, one of the highest attainments in biological science who is nothing if not philosophical.

How strange that this superior person should select and greatly exaggerate for the purposes of his narrative one of the stupid prejudices and superstitions of the vulgar he is supposed to despise! Like the vulgar who are without light he hates a snake, and it is to him, as to the meanest peasant, typical of the spirit of evil and a thing accurst. This unphilosophical temper (the superstitious belief in the serpent's enmity to man), with perhaps too great a love of the picturesque, have inspired some of the passages in the book which make the snakist smile. Let me quote one, in which the hero's encounter with a huge *Crotalus* in a mountain cave is described.

His look was met by the glitter of two diamond eyes, small, sharp, cold, shining out of the darkness, but gliding with a smooth and steady motion towards the light, and himself. He stood fixed, struck dumb, staring back into them with dilating pupils and sudden numbness of fear that cannot move, as in a terror of dreams. The two sparks of fire came forward until they grew to circles of flame, and all at once lifted themselves up in angry surprise. Then for the first time trilled in Mr.

Barnard's ears the dreadful sound which nothing that breathes, be it man or brute, can hear unmoved—the loud, long stinging whir, as the huge thick-bodied reptile shook his many-jointed rattle, and adjusted his loops for the fatal stroke. His eyes were drawn as with magnets towards the circle of flame. His ears rung as in the overture to the swooning dream of chloroform.

And so on, until Elsie appears on the scene and rescues the too easily fascinated schoolmaster.

The writing is fine, but to admire it one must be unconscious of its exaggeration; or, in other words, ignorant of the serpent as it is in nature. Even worse than the exaggerations are the half-poetic, half-scientific tirades against the creature's ugliness and malignity.

It was surely one of destiny's strange pranks to bestow such a subject on the "Autocrat of the Breakfast Table," and, it may be added, to put it in him to treat it from the scientific standpoint. I cannot but wish that this conception had been Hawthorne's; for though Hawthorne wrote no verse, he had in large measure the poetic spirit to which such a subject appeals most powerfully. Possibly it would have inspired him to something beyond his greatest achievement. Certainly not in *The Scarlet Letter*, *The House of the Seven Gables*, nor in any of his numerous shorter tales did he possess a theme so admirably suited to his sombre and beautiful genius as the tragedy of Elsie Venner. Furthermore, the exaggerations and inaccuracies which are unpardonable in Holmes would not have appeared as blemishes in Hawthorne; for he would have viewed the animal world and the peculiar facts of the case — the intervolved human and serpentine nature of the heroine—from the standpoint of the ordinary man who is not an ophiologist; the true and the false about the serpent would have been blended in his tale as they exist blended in the popular imagination, and the illusion would have been more perfect and the effect greater.

Elsie's biographer appears to have found his stock of materials bearing on the main point too slender for his purpose, and to fill out his work he is obliged to be very discursive. Meanwhile, the reader's interest in the chief figure is so intense that in following it the best breakfast-table talk comes in as a mere impertinence. There is no other interest; among the other personages of the story Elsie appears like a living palpitating being among shadows. One finds it difficult to recall the names of the scholarly father in his library; the good hero and his ladylove; the pale schoolmistress, and the melodramatic villain on his black horse, to say nothing of the vulgar villagers and the farmer, some of them supposed to be comic. If we except the rattlesnake mountain, and the old nurse with her animal-like affection and fidelity, there is no atmosphere, or, if an atmosphere, one which is certainly wrong and produces a sense of incongruity. A better artist— Hawthorne, to wit—would have used the painful mystery of Elsie's life, and the vague sense of some nameless impending horror, not merely to put sombre patches here and there on an otherwise sunny landscape, but to give a tone to the whole picture, and the effect would have been more harmonious. This inability of the author to mix and shade his colours shows itself in the passages descriptive of Elsie herself; he insists a great deal too much on her ophidian, or crotaline, characteristics—her stillness and silence and sinuous motions; her bizarre taste in barred gowns; her drowsy condition in cold weather, with intensity of life and activity during the solstitial heats—even her dangerous impulse to strike with her teeth when angered. These traits require to be touched upon very lightly indeed; as it is, the profound pity and love, with a mixture of horror which was the effect sought, come too near to repulsion. While on this point it may be mentioned that the author frequently speaks of the slight sibilation in Elsie's speech—a strange blunder for the man of science to fall into, since he does not make Elsie like any snake, or like snakes in general, but like the *Crotalus durissus* only, the New England rattlesnake, which does not hiss, like some other venomous serpents that are not provided with an instrument of sound in their tails.

After all is said, the conception of Elsie Venner is one so unique and wonderful, and so greatly moves our admiration and pity with her strange beauty, her inarticulate passion, her unspeakably sad destiny, that in spite of many and most serious faults the book must ever remain a classic in our literature, among romances a gem that has not its like, perennial in interest as Nature itself, and Nature's serpent.

If it had only been left for ever unfinished, or had ended differently! For it is impossible for one who admires it to pardon the pitifully commonplace and untrue *dénouement*. Never having read a review of the book I do not know what the professional critic or the fictionist would say on this point; he might say that the story could not properly have ended differently; that, from an artistic point of view, it was necessary that the girl should be made to outgrow the malign influence which she had so strangely inherited; that this was rightly brought about by making her fall in love with the good and handsome young schoolmaster—the effect of the love, or "dull ache of passion," being so great as to deliver and kill her at the same time.

If the interest of the story had all been in the dull and pious villagers, their loves and marriages and trivial affairs, then it would have seemed right that Elsie, who made them all so uncomfortable, should be sent from the village, which was no place for her, to Heaven by the shortest and most convenient route. Miserably weak is that dying scene with its pretty conventional pathos; the ending somewhat after the fashion set by Fouqué, which so many have followed since his time—the childish "Now-I-have-got-a-soul" transformation scene with which Fouqué himself spoilt one of the most beautiful things ever written. The end is not in harmony with the conception of Elsie, of a being in whom the human and serpentine natures were indissolubly joined; and no accident, not assuredly that "dull ache of passion," could have killed the one without destroying the other.

The author was himself conscious of the inadequacy of the reason he gave for the change and deliverance. He no doubt asked himself the following question: "Will the reader believe that a fit of dumb passion, however intense, was sufficient to cause one of Elsie's splendid physique and vitality to droop and wither into the grave like any frail consumptive schoolgirl who loves and whose love is not requited?" He recognises and is led to apologise for its weakness; and, finally, still unsatisfied, advances an alternative theory, which is subtle and physiological—a sop thrown to those among his readers who, unlike the proverbial ass engaged in chewing hay, meditate on what they are taking in. The alternative theory is, that an animal's life is of short duration compared with man's; that the serpent in Elsie, having arrived at the end of its natural term, died out of the human life with which it had been intervolved, leaving her still in the flower of youth and wholly human; but that this decay and death in her affected her with so great a shock that her own death followed immediately on her deliverance.

If the first explanation was weak the second will not bear looking at. Some animals have comparatively short lives, as, for instance, the earthworm, canary, dog, mouse, etc.; but the serpent is not of them; on the contrary, the not too numerous facts we possess which relate to the comparative longevity of animals give support to the universal belief that the reptilians—tortoise, lizard, and serpent—are extremely long-lived.

Now this fact—namely, that science and popular belief are at one in the matter—might very well have suggested to the author a more suitable ending to the story of Elsie than the one he made choice of. I will even be so venturesome as to say what that ending should be. Let us imagine the girl capable of love, even of "a dull ache of passion," doomed by the serpent-nature in her, which was physical if anything, to a prolonged existence, serpent-like in its changes, waxing and waning, imperceptibly becoming dim as with age in the wintry season, only to recover the old brilliant beauty and receive an access of strength in each recurring spring. Let us imagine that the fame of one so strange in life and history and of so excellent an appearance was bruited far and wide, that many a man who sought her village merely to gratify an idle curiosity loved and remained to woo, but feared at the last and left her with a wound in his heart. Finally, let us imagine that as her relatives and friends, and all who had known her intimately, stricken with years and worn with grief, faded one by one into the tomb, she grew more lonely and apart from her fellow-creatures, less human in her life and pursuits; joy and sorrow and all human failings touching her only in a faint vague way, like the memories of her childhood, of her lost kindred, and of her passion. And after long years, during which she has been a wonder and mystery to the villagers, on one of her solitary rambles on the

mountain occurs the catastrophe which the author
has described—the fall of the huge overhanging ledge
of rock under which the serpent brood had their
shelter—burying her for ever with her ophidian
relations, and thus bringing to an end the strange
story of "Elsie Venner Infelix."

CHAPTER XVIII

WASPS

ONE rough day in early autumn I paused in my walk in a Surrey orchard to watch a curious scene in insect life—a pretty little insect comedy I might have called it had it not brought back to remembrance old days when my mind was clouded with doubts, and the ways of certain insects, especially of wasps, were much in my thoughts. For we live through and forget many a tempest that shakes us; but long afterwards a very little thing—the scent of a flower, the cry of a wild bird, even the sight of an insect—may serve to bring it vividly back and to revive a feeling that seemed dead and gone.

In the orchard there was an old pear-tree which produced very large late pears, and among the fruit the September wind had shaken down that morning there was one over-ripe in which the wasps had eaten a deep cup-shaped cavity. Inside the cavity six or seven wasps were revelling in the sweet juice, lying flat and motionless, crowded together. Outside the cavity, on the pear, thirty or forty blue-bottle flies had congregated, and were hungry for the juice, but apparently afraid to begin feeding on it; they were standing round in a compact crowd, the hindmost pressing on and crowding over the others: but

198

still, despite the pressure, the foremost row of flies refused to advance beyond the rim of the eaten-out part. From time to time one of a more venturesome spirit would put out his proboscis and begin sucking at the edge; the slight tentative movement would instantly be detected by a wasp, and he would turn quickly round to face the presumptuous fly, lifting his wings in a threatening manner, and the fly would take his proboscis off the rim of the cup. Occasionally hunger would overcome their fear; a general movement of the flies would take place, and several would begin sucking at the same time; then the wasp, seeming to think that more than a mere menacing look or gesture was required in such a case, would start up with an angry buzz, and away the whole crowd of flies would go to whirl round and round in a little blue cloud with a loud, excited hum, only to settle again in a few moments on the big yellow pear and begin crowding round the pit as before.

Never once during the time I spent observing them did the guardian wasp relax his vigilance. When he put his head down to suck with the others his eyes still appeared able to reflect every movement in the surrounding crowd of flies into his little spiteful brain. They could crawl round and crawl round as much as they liked on the very rim, but let one begin to suck and he was up in arms in a moment.

The question that occurred to me was: How much of all this behaviour could be set down to instinct and how much to intelligence and temper?

The wasp certainly has a waspish disposition, a quick resentment, and is most spiteful and tyrannical towards other inoffensive insects. He is a slayer and devourer of them, too, as well as a feeder with them on nectar and sweet juices; but when he kills, and when the solitary wasp paralyses spiders, caterpillars, and various insects and stores them in cells to provide a horrid food for the grubs which will eventually hatch from the still undeposited eggs, the wasp then acts automatically, or by instinct, and is driven, as it were, by an extraneous force. In a case like the one of the wasp's behaviour on the pear, and in innumerable other cases which one may read of or see for himself, there appears to be a good deal of the element of mind. Doubtless it exists in all insects, but differs in degree; and some orders appear to be more intelligent than others. Thus, any person accustomed to watch insects closely and note their little acts would probably say that there is less mind in the beetles and more in the Hymenoptera than in other insects; also that in the last-named order the wasps rank highest.

The scene in the orchard also served to remind me of a host of wasps, greatly varying in size, colour, and habits, although in their tyrannical temper very much alike, which I had been accustomed to observe in boyhood and youth in a distant region. They attracted me more, perhaps, than any other insects on account of their singular and brilliant coloration and their formidable character. They were beautiful but painful creatures; the pain they caused me was first bodily, when I interfered in their concerns or handled them carelessly, and was soon over; later it was mental and more enduring.

To the very young colour is undoubtedly the most attractive quality in nature, and these insects were enamelled in colours that made them the rivals of butterflies and shining metallic beetles. There were wasps with black and yellow rings and with black and scarlet rings; wasps of a uniform golden brown; others like our demoiselle dragon-fly that looked as if fresh from a bath of splendid metallic blue; others with steel-blue bodies and bright red wings; others with crimson bodies, yellow head and legs, and bright blue wings; others black and gold, with pink head and legs; and so on through scores and hundreds of species "as Nature list to play with her little ones," until one marvelled at so great a variety, so many singular and beautiful contrasts, produced by half a dozen brilliant colours.

It was when I began to find out the ways of wasps with other insects on which they nourish their young that my pleasure in them became mixed with pain. For they did not, like spiders, ants, dragon-flies, tiger-beetles, and other rapacious kinds, kill their prey at once, but paralysed it by stinging its nerve centres to make it incapable of resistance, and stored it in a closed cell, so that the grub to be hatched by-and-by should have fresh meat to feed on—not fresh-killed but live meat.

Thus the old vexed question—How reconcile these facts with the idea of a beneficent Being who designed it all?—did not come to me from reading, nor from teachers, since I had none, but was thrust upon me by nature itself. In spite, however, of its having come in that sharp way, I, like many another, succeeded in putting the painful question from me and keeping to the old traditions. The noise of the battle of Evolution, which had been going on for years, hardly reached me; it was but a faintly heard murmur, as of storms immeasurably far away "on alien shores." This could not last.

One day an elder brother, on his return from travel in distant lands, put a copy of the famous *Origin of Species* in my hands and advised me to read it. When I had done so, he asked me what I thought of it. "It's false!" I exclaimed in a passion, and he laughed, little knowing how important a matter this was to me, and told me I could have the book if I liked. I took it without thanks and read it again and thought a good deal about it, and was nevertheless able to resist its teachings for years, solely because I could not endure to part with a philosophy of life, if I may so describe it, which could not logically be held, if Darwin was right, and without which life would not be worth having. So I thought at the time; it is a most common delusion of the human mind, for we see that the good which is so much to us is taken forcibly away, and that we get over our loss and go on very much as before.

It is curious to see now that Darwin himself gave the first comfort to those who, convinced against their will, were anxious to discover some way of

escape which would not involve the total abandon-
ment of their cherished beliefs. At all events, he
suggested the idea, which religious minds were quick
to seize upon, that the new explanation of the origin
of the innumerable forms of life which people the
earth from one or a few primordial organisms afforded
us a nobler conception of the creative mind than the
traditional one. It does not bear examination,
probably it originated in the author's kindly and
compassionate feelings rather than in his reasoning
faculties; but it gave temporary relief and served its
purpose. Indeed, to some, to very many perhaps,
it still serves as a refuge—this poor, hastily made
straw shelter, which lets in the rain and wind, but
seems better to them than no shelter at all.

But of the intentionally consoling passages in the
book, the most impressive to me was that in which
he refers to instincts and adaptation such as those
of the wasp, which writers on natural history subjects
are accustomed to describe, in a way that seems
quite just and natural, as *diabolical*. That, for
example, of the young cuckoo ejecting its foster-
brothers from the nest; of slave-making ants, and
of the larvæ of the Ichneumonidæ feeding on the
live tissues of the caterpillars in whose bodies they
have been hatched. He said that it was not perhaps
a logical conclusion, but it seemed to him more
satisfactory to regard such things "not as specially
endowed or created instincts, but as small conse-
quences of one general law"—the law of variation
and the survival of the fittest.

CHAPTER XIX

BEAUTIFUL HAWK-MOTHS

IN the late summer I often walk by flowery places of an evening, or at some late hour by moonlight, in the hope of seeing that rare nightwanderer, the death's-head moth; but the hope is now an old one, so worn and faded that it is hardly more than the memory of a hope. Why, I have asked myself times without number, am I so luckless in my quest of an insect which is not only a large object to catch the eye but has a voice, or sound, as well to attract a seeker's attention? On consulting others on this point, some of them lepidopterists and diligent collectors, they have assured me that they have never once had a glimpse of the living free *Acherontia atropos* going about on his flowery business.

A few years ago, while on a ramble in a southern county, I heard of a gentleman in the neighbourhood who had a taste for adders and death's-head moths and was accustomed to collect and keep them in considerable numbers in his house. My own partiality for adders induced me to call on him, and we exchanged experiences and had some pleasant talk about these shy, beautiful and (to us) harmless creatures. I am speaking of adders now; I had not yet heard of his predilection for the great moth; when he spoke of this second favourite I begged him to show me a specimen or two. Turning to his wife, who was present and shared his queer tastes, he told her to go and get me some. She left the room, and returned by-and-by with a large cardboard box, such as milliners and dressmakers use; removing the lid, she raised it above my head and emptied the contents over me—a shower of living, shivering, fluttering, squeaking or creaking death's-head moths! In a moment they were all over me, from my head right down to my feet, not attempting to fly, but running, quivering, and shaking their wings, so that I had a bath and feast of them.

At that moment it mattered not that I was a stranger there, in the library or study of a country house, with those two looking on and laughing at my plight. It is what we feel that matters: I might have been standing in some wilderness never trodden by human foot, myself an unhuman solitary, and merely by willing it I had drawn those beautiful beings of the dark to me, charming them as with a flowery fragrance from their secret hiding-places in a dim world of leaves to gather upon and cover me over with their downy, trembling, mottled grey and rich yellow velvet wings.

Even this fascinating experience did not wholly satisfy me: nothing, I said, would satisfy me short of seeing the undomesticated moth living his proper life in the open air. He smiled and shook his head. Useless to look for such a thing! *He* had never seen it and didn't believe that I ever would; he couldn't say why. He got his moths by paying sixpence apiece for the chrysalids to workmen in the potato fields and rearing them himself; in this way he obtained as many as he wanted—sixty or seventy or eighty every year.

I can only hope that time will prove him wrong, and I go on as before haunting the flowery places in the last light of day and when the moon shines.

Another surprisingly beautiful moth which, they say, is as rarely seen as the *Acherontia* is the crimson underwing. Once only have I been able to observe this lovely moth flying about—and it was in a room! I was staying with friends at the Anglers' Inn at Bransbury on the Test when one evening, after the lamps were lit, the moth appeared in our sitting-room and remained two days and nights with us in spite of our kind persecutions and artful plans for his expulsion. It was early September, with mild sunny days and misty or wet nights, and in the evening, when the room was very warm, we would throw the windows and doors open, thinking of the delicious relief it would be for our prisoner to pass out of that superheated atmosphere, that painful brightness, into his own wide, wet world, its darkness and silence and fragrance, and a mysterious signal wafted to him from a distance out of clouds of whispering leaves, from one there waiting for him. Then with fans and hats and folded newspapers we would try to fan him out, but it only made him wild—wild as a newly caught linnet in a cage; he

would dart hither and thither about the room, now
among us, now over our heads, still refusing to go
out. We didn't want him to go, so that after religi-
ously doing our best for him we were pleased to
have him stay. We even tried to make him happy
as our guest by offering him honey and golden-syrup
and placing flowers in vases all about the room, but
he would accept nothing from us.

At rest on a wall or curtain he appeared as a grey
triangular patch, ornamented, when viewed closely,
with mottlings of a dusky hue; but on lifting his
fore-wings, the lovely crimson colour of the under-
wings was displayed. No crimson flower, no sea-shell,
no sunset cloud, can show a hue to compare in loveliness with it. Another hidden beauty was revealed
when the lamps were lighted to start him flying up
and down the room over our heads, always keeping
close to the low ceiling. He then had a surprisingly
bird-like appearance, and the under-surface of the
bird-shaped body being pure white and downy he
was like a miniature martin with crimson on the
wings. He was then at his best, our "elf-darling";
no one dared touch him even with a finger-tip lest
that exquisitely delicate down should be injured.
I have frequently had humming-birds blunder into
a room where I sat and fly round seeking an exit,
but never one of these, for all the glittering scale-
like feathers, seemed so perfectly beautiful as our
dark crimson underwing.

On the third evening, to our regret, we succeeded
in getting him to fly out.

Now, we asked, what had the books-about-moths-makers to tell us concerning this particular elf-darling? I proceeded to get out my work on Butterflies and Moths—one recently published. It gave a description of the insect—colour and measurements; then, under the heading of "general remarks," came the following: "This moth will never be seen, but by judicious sugaring as many as half a dozen specimens may be obtained in a single night." That was all! It was a shock to us, and we wondered whether any of our naturalists had tried the plan of "judicious sugaring" to obtain a few specimens of that rarer, more elusive creature, the fairy, before its final extinction in Britain.

The memory of those two evenings with a crimson underwing brings to mind just now yet another enchanting evening I spent in the valley of the Wiltshire Avon. It was June, just before hay-cutting, and for most of the time, until the last faint underglow had faded and the stars were out, I was standing motionless, knee-deep in the plumy seeded grasses, watching the ghost-moths, as I had never seen them before, in scores and in hundreds, dimly visible in their whiteness all over the dusky meadow, engaged in their quaint, beautiful, rhythmic love-dance. It was the wide silent night and the moths' strange motions and whiteness in the dark that gave it a magic on that occasion. Seen by daylight or lamplight it is Lord de Tabley's "owl-white moth with mealy wings," or one of them, and nothing more.

Moths are mostly haunters of the twilight and

the dark, but we have one of the larger and highly distinguished species, the humming-bird hawk-moth, which flies abroad by day, even during the hottest seasons, and visits our gardens in the full blaze of noon. It has no glory of colour like the crimson underwing and death's-head moth, nor ghostly white, yet it outshines all the others in beauty and in the sense of wonder and delight its appearance produces. Here I will quote part of a letter written to me some years ago by a lady who wanted to know if I could identify an insect she was particularly interested in, from her description. She had seen it when a child in the garden at her early home in Wiltshire, and never since, nor had she ever discovered what it was.

When I was a child [the letter says], I had a great fancy for a rare, strange, fascinating insect called by the children of my day the Merrylee-dance-a-pole. Only on the hottest and longest of summer days did the radiant being delight our eyes; to have seen it conferred high honour and distinction on the fortunate beholder. We regarded it with mingled awe and joy, and followed its erratic and rapid flight with ecstasy. It was soft and warm and brown, fluffy and golden, too, and created in our infantile minds an indescribable impression of glory, brilliance, aloofness, elusiveness. We thought it a being from some other world, and during each of its frequent sudden disappearances among the flowering bushes we held our breath, fearing it would return no more, but had flown right through the blossoming screen and back to the sun and stars. To me it was an apparition of inexpressible delight, and I longed to be a Merrylee-dance-a-pole myself to fly to unheard-of, unthought-of, undreamed-of beautiful flowery lands.

A descriptive passage, this, by one who is not a literary person, a student of expression anxiously seeking after the "explicit word," yet an expression rare and beautiful as the thing described: one reads it with a quickened pulse. Who should dream of finding its like anywhere in the thousand books of British Butterflies and Moths which our exceedingly industrious lepidopterists have produced during the last six or seven decades? Yet these same thousand volumes were written less for the scientific student of entomology than for the general reader, or for every person who on seeing a white admiral or a privet moth wants to know what it is and goes to a book to find out all about it. These writers all fail in the very thing which one would imagine to be most important in books intended for such a purpose—the power to convey to the reader's mind a vivid image of the thing described. One would like to know what the professional entomologist or writer of books about moths would say of the passage I have quoted from a letter asking for information about an insect. Probably he would say that the lady wrote more from the heart than the head, that writing so she is rhapsodical and as inaccurate as one would expect her to be, although one is able to identify her Merrylee-dance-a-pole as the *Macroglossa stellatarum*.

It would be perfectly true—she is inaccurate, yet succeeds in producing the effect aimed at while the accurate writers fail. She succeeds because she saw the object as a child, emotionally, and after thirty years was still able to recover the precise feeling experienced then and to convey to another the image in her mind. We may say that impressions are vivid and live vividly in the mind, even to the end of life, in those alone in whom something that is of the child survives in the adult — the measureless delight in all this visible world, experienced every day by the millions of children happily born outside the city's gates, but so rarely expressed in literature, as Traherne, let us say, expressed it; and, with the delight, the sense of wonder in all life, which is akin to, if not one with, the mythical faculty, and if experienced in a high degree is a sense of the supernatural in all natural things. We may say, in fact, that unless the soul goes out to meet what we see we do not see it; nothing do we see, not a beetle, not a blade of grass.

CHAPTER XX

W E read in the books of the astounding strength and energy of this creature that "swims in the earth," as they say, just as a diving auk, guillemot, or puffin does in the water. The energy of a squirrel that runs up a very tall tree-trunk, darts along a far-reaching horizontal branch, flings himself from the end of it to the branch of another tree, and is a hundred feet high and away before you can finish speaking a sentence of twenty words, is nothing to compare with the feats of the mole underground. But, being out of sight, he is out of mind, on which account his most remarkable qualities are not properly appreciated. He is also a small beast—no bigger than a lady's gloved hand —consequently his strength, like that of the beetle, does not matter to us. It would matter a great deal if moles grew to the size of cows and bulls. In or under London they would excavate numberless tunnels which would serve as subways for the foot-passengers and for the tubular railways. This would be an advantage, but as a set-off they would, in throwing up their hills, cause a considerable amount of damage. A mole of that size would easily overturn the Royal Exchange, and even Westminster Palace would be tumbled down, burying our congregated law-givers in its ruins.

The life of the mole is an amazingly strenuous one; his appetite surpasses that of any other creature of land or sea, and he does not "eat to burstness" only because his digestion is just as powerful and rapid in its action as his digging muscles. He feeds like a Gargantua, and having dug out and devoured his dinner, he digs again to where a spring exists, and refreshes himself with copious draughts of cold water.

The west-country field labourer, who gets through his two or three gallons of cider at a sitting, is a poor drinker in comparison. After digging and eating and drinking, he goes to sleep, and so soundly does he sleep that you could not wake him by beating drums and firing guns off over his head. Out of this condition he comes very suddenly, like a giant refreshed, and goes furiously to work again at his digging.

If by chance you catch a mole above ground and seize him with your hand you find him a difficult creature to hold. The prickly hedgehog and slippery snake or eel are more easy to manage. You are puzzled by finding that you cannot keep your grip on him, and, if you are a novice, he will probably slip back through his skin until his head is in your hand, and then, when half a dozen of his needle-like teeth are deep in your flesh, you will be glad to drop him.

He is not, when caught, a submissive creature, nor has he a friendly or social disposition: in the rutting season the males have the most savage battles; the floors and walls of the tunnels are washed with blood, and he that falls is worried to death, and his corpse devoured by the victor.

But the mole is seldom seen out of doors, so to speak, taking his walks abroad; when he is striking out in shallow runs in hot pursuit of earthworms and throwing up little hills at short intervals you can often see him when he comes to the surface; he just shows you his back for a few moments; then, having pushed up the loose soil, sinks below again. Now it once happened that a mole showing himself, or his back, to me in this way, taught me something about the creature which I did not know, not having found it in the books. It was on a bright March morning, and I was seated on a stump in a beech wood near the village of Ockley, in Surrey. The ground all about me was covered with a deep carpet of dead leaves, glowing gold and red and russet in the sunlight, when presently, attracted by a rustling among the leaves, I saw that they were being thrust up by some creature under them. It was not the small animal I was listening and watching for just then—the shrew who comes out to sun himself—but a mole throwing up a hill at that spot within a yard of my foot. By-and-by his velvety-black back became visible, and made in its setting of red and yellow leaves a prettily coloured picture. Presently he disappeared, then quickly rose again with more earth; but the leaves evidently annoyed him, and to rid himself of them he suddenly began agitating his body in an astonishing way, for while the movement lasted he looked like a black ball spinning round so rapidly as to give it the misty appearance of a revolving wheel or the wings of a hovering hawk-moth. This swift motion on his part set the leaves flying, and mole and dust and dancing leaves together formed a little whirlwind or mael-strom. When it was over the leaves settled again on the mound, and twice again the extraordinary performance was repeated, and the little animal being then almost above the ground I foolishly put out my hand to pick him up, and before I could properly grasp him he was gone.

The spinning or revolving motion was an illusion of the sight produced by the exceedingly rapid motions of the skin while the animal was stationary, and the deluding motions were effected by means of what the anatomists call the "twitching muscle," which is possessed in some degree by most, if not by all, mammalians. We see it every day in our domestic animals, especially in the dog when he shakes himself after a swim; and if he has shaggy hair and it is full of water he throws it off so violently that it fills the air with a dense spray for several feet around him. He could not do this by merely shaking or rocking his whole body from side to side; he does rock his body too, but at the same time he gives the rapid vibratory motion to the whole skin which discharges the wet. So it is with the horse when he shakes off the wet or the dust after rolling.

But in the horse the twitching power does not extend, or is not uniformly powerful, over the whole surface; it is feeble on the hind quarters, and we can only suppose that in the horse, and other large mammalians, the chief use of the twitching act is to shake off dust, flies, and other tormenting insects, and that growth of the hairy tail in the horse, used to switch insects off, has made the twitching power less useful on this portion of the body. In other words, when this highly specialised tail had fully taken this office or function on itself it caused the decay of the twitching muscle through disuse in those parts of his body.

We see, too, that the muscle has its greatest power in that part of the body which is just out of reach of the tail, and is also more difficult for the animal to reach with his mouth—that is to say, his back over the shoulders. A man riding bare-back can feel it powerfully when the horse shakes himself. "It is like riding on an earthquake," I heard a man say once; to me, with no experience of earthquakes, the sensation was like that of an electric shock.

In man we can imagine the loss of the twitching power has had a twofold cause: first the hands, which, like the beak in birds, can reach to pretty well any part of the body, and, secondly, the custom of wearing clothes, which protect the skin and make the twitching unnecessary.

The twitching power survives only in the face, and is almost confined to the forehead: but even there it is, with its slow up-and-down motion, a poor faculty compared with the rapid shaking or trembling motion other mammals are capable of, which they are able to confine to the exact spot on which an insect has alighted. In a few persons the power extends over the scalp, and I have heard of a man who could cause his hat to fall off, not with shaking his head, but simply by working the muscles of his forehead and scalp. Altogether, we may say that the faculty is weakest in man—that he is at one end of the pole, and the mole is at the other. The mole exists in the earth, moving in and covered with the dust he creates in digging, and he no doubt frees himself from it by means of his twitching muscle a hundred times a day.

That this wonderful muscle can do anything more to increase his happiness I doubt, and this I say, because it is told in the sacred writings of the East that Buddha changed himself into a hare and jumped into a fire to roast himself to provide a meal for a hungry beggar, and that before jumping in, he— Buddha as a hare—shook himself three times so that none of the insects in his fur should perish with him.

I don't believe it! My Ockley mole has proved to me that insect parasites cannot be got rid of in that way. The hare's twitching muscle is not more powerful than that of the generality of animals. I have seen him make the water fly like a mist out of his fur, but the dog can do it nearly as well. In the mole the movement is more sustained and, I imagine, more rapid, yet the fleas must be able to keep their hold on him since we always find him much infested by them.

CHAPTER XXI

A FRIENDLY RAT

MOST of our animals, also many creeping things, such as our "wilde wormes in woods," common toads, natterjacks, newts, and lizards, and stranger still, many insects, have been tamed and kept as pets.

Badgers, otters, foxes, hares, and voles are easily dealt with; but that any person should desire to fondle so prickly a creature as a hedgehog, or so diabolical a mammalian as the bloodthirsty, flat-headed little weasel, seems very odd. Spiders, too, are uncomfortable pets; you can't caress them as you could a dormouse; the most you can do is to provide your spider with a clear glass bottle to live in, and teach him to come out in response to a musical sound, drawn from a banjo or fiddle, to take a fly from your fingers and go back again to its bottle.

An acquaintance of the writer is partial to adders as pets, and he handles them as freely as the schoolboy does his innocuous ring-snake; Mr. Benjamin Kidd once gave us a delightful account of his pet humble-bees, who used to fly about his room, and come at call to be fed, and who manifested an almost painful interest in his coat buttons, examining them every day as if anxious to find out their true significance. Then there was my old friend, Miss Hopley, the writer on reptiles, who died recently, aged ninety-nine years, who tamed newts, but whose favourite pet was a slow-worm. She was never tired of expatiating on its lovable qualities. One finds Viscount Grey's pet squirrels more engaging, for these are wild squirrels in a wood in Northumberland, who quickly find out when he is at home and make their way to the house, scale the walls, and invade the library; then, jumping upon his writing-table, are rewarded with nuts, which they take from his hand. Another Northumbrian friend of the writer keeps, or kept, a pet cormorant, and finds him no less greedy in the domestic than in the wild state. After catching and swallowing fish all the morning in a neighbouring river, he wings his way home at meal-times, screaming to be fed, and ready to devour all the meat and pudding he can get.

The list of strange creatures might be extended indefinitely, even fishes included; but who has ever heard of a tame pet rat? Not the small white, pink-eyed variety, artificially bred, which one may buy at any dealers, but a common brown rat, *Mus decumanus*, one of the commonest wild animals in England and certainly the most disliked. Yet this wonder has been witnessed recently in the village of Lelant, in West Cornwall. Here is the strange story, which is rather sad and at the same time a little funny.

This was not a case of "wild nature won by kindness"; the rat simply thrust itself and its friendship on the woman of the cottage: and she, being childless and much alone in her kitchen and living-room, was not displeased at its visits: on the contrary, she fed it; in return the rat grew more and more friendly and familiar towards her, and the more familiar it grew, the more she liked the rat. The trouble was, she possessed a cat, a nice, gentle animal not often at home, but it was dreadful to think of what might happen at any moment should pussy walk in when her visitor was with her. Then, one day, pussy did walk in when the rat was present, purring loudly, her tail held stiffly up, showing that she was in her usual sweet temper. On catching sight of the rat, she appeared to know intuitively that it was there as a privileged guest, while the rat on its part seemed to know, also by intuition, that it had nothing to fear. At all events these two quickly became friends and were evidently pleased to be together, as they now spent most of the time in the room, and would drink milk from the same saucer, and sleep bunched up together, and were extremely intimate.

By-and-by the rat began to busy herself making a nest in a corner of the kitchen under a cupboard, and it became evident that there would soon be an increase in the rat population. She now spent her time running about and gathering little straws, feathers, string, and anything of the kind she could pick up, also stealing or begging for strips of cotton, or bits of wool and thread from the work-basket. Now it happened that her friend was one of those cats with huge tufts of soft hair on the two sides of her face; a cat of that type, which is not uncommon, has a quaint resemblance to a mid-Victorian gentleman with a pair of magnificent side-whiskers of a silky softness covering both cheeks and flowing down like a double beard. The rat suddenly discovered that this hair was just what she wanted to add a cushion-like lining to her nest, so that her naked pink little ratlings should be born into the softest of all possible worlds. At once she started plucking out the hairs, and the cat, taking it for a new kind of game, but a little too rough to please her, tried for a while to keep her head out of reach and to throw the rat off. But she wouldn't be thrown off, and as she persisted in flying back and jumping at the cat's face and plucking the hairs, the cat quite lost her temper and administered a blow with her claws unsheathed.

The rat fled to her refuge to lick her wounds, and was no doubt as much astonished at the sudden change in her friend's disposition as the cat had been at the rat's new way of showing her playfulness. The result was that when, after attending to her scratches, she started upon her task of gathering soft materials, she left the cat severely alone. They were no longer friends; they simply ignored one another's presence in the room. The little ones, numbering about a dozen, presently came to light and were quietly removed by the woman's husband, who didn't mind his missis keeping a rat, but drew the line at one.

The rat quickly recovered from her loss and was the same nice affectionate little thing she had always been to her mistress; then a fresh wonder came to light—cat and rat were fast friends once more! This happy state of things lasted a few weeks; but, as we know, the rat was married, though her lord and master never appeared on the scene, indeed, he was not wanted; and very soon it became plain to see that more little rats were coming. The rat is an exceedingly prolific creature; she can give a month's start to a rabbit and beat her at the end by about forty points.

Then came the building of the nest in the same old corner, and when it got to the last stage and the rat was busily running about in search of soft materials for the lining, she once more made the discovery that those beautiful tufts of hair on her friend's face were just what she wanted, and once more she set vigorously to work pulling the hairs out. Again, as on the former occasion, the cat tried to keep her friend off, hitting her right and left with her soft pads, and spitting a little, just to show that she didn't like it. But the rat was determined to have the hairs, and the more she was thrown off the more bent was she on getting them, until the breaking-point was reached and puss, in a sudden rage, let fly, dealing blow after blow with lightning rapidity and with all the claws out. The rat, shrieking with pain and terror, rushed out of the room and was never seen again, to the lasting grief of her mistress. But its memory will long remain like a fragrance in the cottage—perhaps the only cottage in all this land where kindly feelings for the rat are cherished.

CHAPTER XXII

THE LITTLE RED DOG

SAUNTERING along a lane-like road between Charterhouse Hinton and Woolverton, in the West Country, I spied a small red dog trotting along some distance behind me. He was in the middle of the road, but seeing that he was observed he sheered off to the other side, and when nearly abreast of me paused suspiciously, sniffed the air to get the exact smell, then made a dash past, and after going about twenty or thirty yards full speed, dropped once more into his travelling trot, to vanish from sight at the next bend in the road.

Though alone, I laughed, for he was a very old acquaintance of mine. I knew him well, although he did not know me, and regarding me as a stranger he very naturally associated my appearance with that well-aimed stone or half-brick which had doubtless registered an impression on his small brain. I knew him because he is a common type, widely distributed on the earth; I doubt if there are many countries where you will not meet him—a degenerate or dwarf variety of the universal cur, smaller than a fox-terrier and shorter-legged; the low stature, long body, small ears, and blunt nose giving him a somewhat stoaty or even reptilian appearance among the canines. His red colour is, indeed, the commonest hue of the common dog, or cur, wherever found. It is rarely a bright red, like that of the Irish setter, or any pleasing shade of red, as in the dingo, the fox, and the South American maned wolf; it is dull, often inclining to yellow, sometimes mixed with grey as in the jackal, sometimes with a dash of ginger in it. The unbeautiful yellowish-red is the prevailing hue of the pariah dog. At all events that is the impression one gets from the few of the numberless travellers in the East who have condescended to tell us anything about this low-down animal.

Where the cur or pariah flourishes, there you are sure to find the small red dog, and perhaps wonder at his ability to maintain his existence. He is certainly placed at a great disadvantage. If he finds or steals a bone, the first big dog he meets will say to him, "Drop it!" And he will drop it at once, knowing very well that if he refuses to do so it will be taken from him, and his own poor little bones perhaps get crunched in the process. As compensation he has, I fancy, a somewhat quicker intelligence, a subtler cunning. His brains weigh less by a great deal than those of the bulldog or a big cur, but—like ladies' brains compared with men's—they are of a finer quality.

When I encountered this animal in the quiet Somerset road, and laughed to see him and exclaimed mentally, "There he goes, the same old little red dog, suspicious and sneaky as ever, and very brisk and busy although his years must be

well-nigh as many as my own," I was thinking of
the far past, and the sight of him brought back a
memory of one of the first of the small red dogs
I have known intimately. I was a boy then, and
my home was in the pampas of Buenos Ayres. I
had a young sister, a bright, lively girl, and I remember that a poor native woman who lived in a
smoky hovel a few miles away was fond of her, and
that she came one day with a present for her—
something precious wrapped up in a shawl—a little
red pup, one of a litter which her own beloved dog
had brought forth. My sister accepted the present
joyfully, for though we possessed fourteen or fifteen
dogs at the time, these all belonged to the house;
they were everybody's and nobody's in particular,
and she was delighted to have one that would be
her very own. It grew into a common red dog, rather
better-looking than most of its kind, having a bushier
tail, longer and brighter-coloured hair, and a somewhat foxy head and face. In spite of these good
points, we boys never tired of laughing at her little
Reddie, as he was called, and his intense devotion
to his young mistress and faith in her power to
protect him only made him seem more ludicrous.
When we all walked together on the grass plain,
my brother and I used to think it great fun to
separate Reddie from his mistress by making a
sudden dash, and then hunt him over the turf.
Away he would go, performing a wide circuit, then,
doubling back, would fly to her for safety. She,
stooping and holding out her hands to him, would

wait his coming, and at the end, with one flying leap, he would land himself in her arms, almost capsizing her with the force of the impact, and from that refuge look back reproachfully at us.

The cunning little ways of the small red dog were learned later when I came to know him in the city of Buenos Ayres. Loitering at the waterside one day, I became aware of an animal of this kind following me, and no sooner did he catch my eye than he came up, wagging, wriggling, and grinning, smiling, so to speak, all over his body; and I, thinking he had lost home and friends and touched by his appeal, allowed him to follow me through the streets to the house of relations where I was staying. I told them I intended keeping the outcast awhile to see what could be done with him. My friends did not welcome him warmly, and they even made some disparaging remarks about little red dogs in general; but they gave him his dinner—a big plateful of meat—which he devoured greedily, and then, very much at home, he stretched himself out on the hearth-rug and went fast asleep. When he woke an hour later he jumped up and ran to the hall, and, finding the street-door closed, made a great row, howling and scratching at the panels. I hurried out and opened the door, and out and off he went, without so much as a thank-you. He had found a fool and had succeeded in getting something out of him, and his business with me was ended. There was no hesitation; he was going straight home, and knew his way quite well.

Years afterwards it was a surprise to me to find

that the little red dog was an inhabitant of London. There was no muzzling order then, in the 'seventies, and quite a common sight was the independent dog, usually a cur, roaming the streets in search of stray scraps of food. He shared the sparrows' broken bread; he turned over the rubbish heaps left by the road-sweepers; he sniffed about areas, on the look-out for an open dust-bin; and he hung persistently about the butcher's shop, where a jealous eye was kept on his movements. These dogs doubtless had owners, who paid the yearly tax; but it is probable that in most cases they found for themselves. Probably, too, the adventurous life of the streets, where carrion was not too plentiful, had the effect of sharpening their wits. Here, at all events, I was witness of an action on the part of a small red dog which fairly astonished me; that confidence trick the little Argentine beast had practised on me was nothing to it.

In Regent Street, of all places, one bright winter morning, I caught sight of a dog lying on the pavement close to the wall, hungrily gnawing at a big beef bone which he had stolen or picked out of a neighbouring dust-hole. He was a miserable-looking object, a sort of lurcher, of a dirty red colour, with ribs showing like the bars of a gridiron through his mangy side. Even in those pre-muzzling days, when we still had the pariah, it was a little strange to see him gnawing his bone at that spot, just by Peter Robinson's, where the broad pavement was full of shopping ladies; and I stood still to watch him.

Presently a small red dog came trotting along the pavement from the direction of the Circus, and catching sight of the mangy lurcher with the bone he was instantly struck motionless, and crouching low as if to make a dash at the other, his tail stiff, his hair bristling, he continued gazing for some moments; and then, just when I thought the rush and struggle was about to take place, up jumped this little red cur and rushed back towards the Circus, uttering a succession of excited shrieky barks. The contagion was irresistible. Off went the lurcher, furiously barking too, and quickly overtaking the small dog dashed on and away to the middle of the Circus to see what all the noise was about. It was something tremendously important to dogs in general, no doubt. But the little red dog, the little liar, had no sooner been overtaken and passed by the other, than back he ran, and picking up the bone, made off with it in the opposite direction. Very soon the lurcher returned and appeared astonished and puzzled at the disappearance of his bone. There I left him, still looking for it and sniffing at the open shop doors. He perhaps thought in his simplicity that some kind lady had picked it up and left it with one of the shopmen to be claimed by its rightful owner.

I had heard of such actions on the part of dogs before, but always with a smile; for we know the people who tell this kind of story—the dog-worshippers, or canophilists as they are sometimes called, a people weak in their intellectuals, and as a rule unveracious, although probably not consciously so. But now I had myself witnessed this thing, which, when read, will perhaps cause others to smile in their turn.

But what is one to say of such an action? Just now we are all of us, philosophers included, in a muddle over the questions of mind and intellect in the lower animals, and just how much of each element goes to the composition of any one act; but probably most persons would say at once that the action of the little red dog in Regent Street was purely intelligent. I am not sure. The swiftness, smoothness, and certainty with which the whole thing was carried out gave it the appearance of a series of automatic movements rather than a reasoned act which had never been rehearsed.

Recently during my country rambles I have been on the look-out for the small red dog, and have met with several interesting examples in the southern counties. One, in Hampshire, moved me to laughter like that small animal at Charterhouse Hinton.

This was at Sway, a village near Lymington. A boy, mounted on a creaking old bike, was driving some cows to the common, and had the greatest difficulty in keeping on while following behind the lazy beasts on a rough track among the furze bushes; and behind the boy at a distance of ten yards trotted the little red dog, tongue out, looking as happy and proud as possible. As I passed him he looked back at me as if to make sure that I had seen him and noted that he formed part of that important procession. On another day I went to the village and renewed my acquaintance with the little fellow and heard his history. Everybody praised him for his affectionate disposition and his value as a watch-dog by night, and I was told that his mother, now dead, had been greatly prized, and was the smallest red dog ever seen in that part of Hampshire.

Some day one of the thousand writers on "man's friend" will conceive the happy idea of a chapter or two on *the* dog—the universal cur—and he will then perhaps find it necessary to go abroad to study this well-marked dwarf variety, for with us he has fallen on evil days. There is no doubt that the muzzling order profoundly affected the character of our dog population, since it went far towards the destruction of the cur and of mongrels—the races already imperilled by the extraordinary predominance of the fox-terrier. The change was most marked in the metropolis, and after Mr. Long's campaign I came to the conclusion that here at all events the little red dog had been extirpated. He, with other varieties of the cur, was the dog of the poor, and when the muzzle deprived him of the power to fend for himself, he became a burden to his master. But I was mistaken; he is still with us, even here in London, though now very rare.

CHAPTER XX

THE subject of this paper, for which I am unable to find a properly descriptive title, will be certain changes noticeable during recent years in the dogs of the Metropolis, and, in a less degree, of the country generally. At the same time there has been an improvement in the character of the dog population, due mainly to the weeding out of the baser breeds, but this matter does not concern us here; the change with which I propose to deal is in the temper and, as to one particular, the habits of the animal. This was the result of the famous (it used to be called the infamous) muzzling order of 1897, which restrained dogs throughout the country from following their ancient custom of quarrelling with and biting one another for the unprecedented period of two and a half years. Nine hundred days and over may not seem too long a period of restraint in the case of a being whose natural term runs to threescore years and ten, but in poor Tatters' or Towzer's brief existence of a dozen summers it is the equivalent of more than twenty years in the life of the human animal.

As a naturalist I was interested in the muzzling

order, and after noting its effects my interest in the subject has continued ever since. It should also, I imagine, be a matter of interest and importance to all who have a special regard for the dog or who are "devoted to dogs," who regard them as the "friends of man," even holding with the canophilists of the old Youatt period of the last century that the dog was specially created to fill the place of man's servant and companion. Strange to say, I have not yet met with any person of the dog-loving kind who has himself noticed any change in the temper or habits of the dog during the last fourteen or fifteen years or has any knowledge of it. One can only suppose—and this applies not only to those who cherish a peculiar affection for the dog, but to the numerous body of London naturalists as well— that the change was unmarked on account of the very long period during which the order was in force, when dogs were deprived of the power to bite, so that when the release came the former condition of things in the animal world was no longer distinctly remembered. It was doubtless assumed that, the muzzle once removed, all things were exactly as they had been before: if a few remembered and noticed the change, they failed to record it—at all events I have seen nothing about it in print. Circumstances made it impossible for me not to notice the immediate effect of the order, and at the end of the time to forget the state of things as they existed before its imposition.

I was probably more confined to London during

the years 1897–9 than most persons who are keenly
interested in animal life, and being so confined, I
was compelled to gratify my taste or passion by
paying a great deal of attention to the only animals
that there are to observe in our streets, the dog
being the most important. I also took notes of
what I observed—my way of remembering not to
forget; and, refreshing my mind by returning to
them, I am able to recover a distinct picture of the
state of things in the pre-muzzling times. It is a
very different state from that of to-day. One thing
that was a cause of surprise to me in those days
was the large number of dogs, mostly mongrels and
curs, to be seen roaming masterless about the streets.
These I classed as pariahs, although they all, no
doubt, had their homes in mean streets and courts,
just as the ownerless pariah dogs in Eastern towns
have their homes—their yard or pavement or spot
of waste ground where they live and bask in the sun
when not roaming in quest of food and adventures.
Many of these London pariahs were wretched-looking
objects, full of sores and old scars, some like skeletons
and others with half their hair off from mange and
other skin diseases. They were to be seen all over
London, always hunting for food, hanging about
areas, like the bone- and bottle-buyers, looking for
an open dust-bin where something might be found to
comfort their stomachs. They also haunted butchers'
shops, where the butcher kept a jealous eye on their
movements and sent them away with a kick and
a curse whenever he got the chance. Most, if not

all, of these poor dogs had owners who gave them shelter but no food or very little, and probably in most cases succeeded in evading the licence duty. There is no doubt that in the past the dog population of London was always largely composed of animals of this kind—"curs of low degree," and a great variety of mongrels, mostly living on their wits. An account of the dogs of London of two or three or four centuries ago would have an extraordinary interest for us now, but, unfortunately, no person took the pains to write it. Caius, our oldest writer on dogs, says of "curres of the mungrel and rascall sort"—the very animals we want to know about: "Of such dogs as keep not their kind, of such as are mingled out of sundry sortes not imitating the conditions of some one certaine Spece, because they resemble no notable shape, nor exercise any worthy property of the true, perfect, and gentle kind, it is not necesarye that I write any more of them, but to banish them as unprofitable implements out of the boundes of my Booke." It is regrettable that he did "banish" them, as he appears to have been something of an observer on his own account. Had he given us a few pages on the life and habits of the "rascall sort" of animal, his *Booke of Englishe Dogges*, which after so many centuries is still occasionally reprinted, would have been as valuable to us now as Turner's on British birds (1544) and Willughby's half a century later on the same subject, and as Gould's brilliant essay on the habits of British ants—which, by the way, has never been reprinted—and as Gilbert White's classic, which came later in the eighteenth century. That the bond uniting man and dog in all instances when the poor brute was obliged to fend for himself in the inhospitable streets of London was an exceedingly frail one was plainly seen when the muzzling order of 1897 was made. An extraordinary number of apparently ownerless dogs, unmuzzled and collarless, were found roaming about the streets and taken by hundreds every week to the lethal chamber. In thirty months the dog population of the metropolis had decreased by about one hundred thousand. The mongrels and dogs of the "rascall sort" had all but vanished, and this was how the improvement in the character of the dog population mentioned before came about immediately. But a far more important change had been going on at the same time—the change in the temper of our dogs; and it may here be well to remark that this change in disposition was not the result of the weeding-out process I have described. The better breeds are not more amiable than the curs of low degree. The man who has made a friend and companion of the cur will tell you that he is as nice-tempered, affectionate, faithful, and intelligent as the nobler kinds, the dogs of "notable shape."

Let us now go back to the muzzling time of 1897-9, and I will give here the substance of the notes I made at the time. They have among my notes on many subjects a peculiar interest to me as a naturalist because in the comments I made at the time I ventured to make a prediction which has not been fulfilled. I was astonished and delighted to find that (on this one occasion) I had proved a false prophet.

The dog-muzzling question (I wrote) does not interest me personally, since I keep no dog, nor love to see so intelligent and serviceable a beast degraded to the position of a mere pet or plaything —a creature that has lost or been robbed of its true place in the scheme of things. Looking at the matter from the outside, simply as a student of the ways of animals, I am surprised at the outcry made against Mr. Long's order, especially here in London, where there is so great a multitude of quite useless animals. No doubt a large majority of the dogs of the metropolis are household pets, pure and simple, living indoors in the same rooms as their owners, in spite of their inconvenient instincts. On this subject I have had my say in an article on "The Great Dog Superstition," for which I have been well abused; the only instinct of the dog with which I am concerned at present is that of pugnacity. This is, like his love of certain smells disgusting to us, part and parcel of his being, so that for a dog to be perfectly gentle and without the temper that barks and bites must be taken as evidence of its decadence —not of the individual but of the race or breed or variety. Whether this fact is known or only dimly surmised by dog-lovers, more especially by those who set the fashion in dogs, we see that in recent years there has been a distinct reaction against the more degenerate kinds [1]—those in whose natures the jackal and wild-dog writing has quite or all but faded out —the numerous small toy terriers; the Italian greyhound, shivering like an aspen leaf; the drawing-room pug, ugliest of man's (the breeder's) many inventions; the pathetic Blenheim and King Charles spaniels, the Maltese, the Pomeranian, and all the others that have, so to speak, rubbed themselves out by acquiring a white liver to please their owners' fantastic tastes. A more vigorous beast is now in favour, and one of the most popular is undoubtedly the fox-terrier. This is assuredly the doggiest dog we possess, the most aggressive, born to trouble as the sparks fly upward. From my own point of view it is only right that fox-terriers and all other good fighters should have liberty to go out daily into the streets in their thousands in search of shindies, to strive with and worry one another to their hearts' content; then to skulk home, smelling abominably of carrion and carnage, and, hiding under their master's sofa, or other dark place, to spend the time licking their wounds until they are well again and ready to go out in search of fresh adventures. For God hath made them so.

But this is by no means the view of the gentle ladies and mild-tempered gentlemen who own them,

[1] Alas! since these notes were made, fourteen years ago, there has been a recrudescence of the purely woman's drawing-room pet dog. The wretched griffon, looking like a mean cheap copy of the little Yorkshire—one of the few small pet animals which has not wholly lost its soul—appears to have vanished. But the country has now been flooded with the Pekinese, and one is made to loathe it from the constant sight of it in every drawing-room and railway carriage and motor-car and omnibus, clasped in a woman's arms.

nor, I dare say, of any canophilist, whether the
owner of a dog or not.   What these people want
is that their canine friends shall have the same
liberty enjoyed by themselves to make use of our
streets and parks without risk of injury or insult;
that they shall be free to notice or not the saluta-
tions and advances of others of their kind; to
graciously accept or contemptuously refuse, with
nose in air, according to the mood they may happen
to be in or to the state of their digestive organs,
an invitation to a game of romps.   This liberty and
safety they do now undoubtedly enjoy, thanks to
the much-abused muzzling order.

It is true that to the canine mind this may not
be an ideal liberty: "For on a knight that hath
neither hardihood nor valour in himself, may not
another knight that hath more force in him reasonably prove his mettle; for many a time have I
heard say that one is better than other."   These
words, spoken by the Best Knight in the World,
exactly fit the case of the fox-terrier, or any other
vigorous variety whose one desire when he goes out
into the world is reasonably to prove his mettle.
'Tis an ancient and noble principle of action, con-
ceivably advantageous in certain circumstances; but
in the conditions in which we human beings find
ourselves placed it is not tolerated, and the valour
and hardihood of our Percivals may no longer shine
in the dark forests of this modern world.

Is it, then, so monstrous a thing, so great a tyranny,
that the same restraint which has this long time been

put upon the best and brightest of our own kind should now, for the public good, be imposed on our four-footed companions and servants! True, we think solely of ourselves when we impose the restraint, but incidentally (and entirely apart from the question of rabies) we are at the same time giving the greatest protection to the dogs themselves. Furthermore—and here we come to the point which mainly concerns us—the reflex effect of the muzzle on the dogs themselves may now be seen to be purely beneficial. Confining ourselves to London, the change in the animals' disposition, or at all events behaviour, has been very remarkable. It has forcibly reminded me of the change of temper I have witnessed in a rude, semi-barbarous community when someone in authority has issued an order that at all festivals and other public gatherings every man shall yield up his weapons—knives, pistols, iron-handled whips, etc.—to some person appointed to receive them, or be turned back from the gates. The result of such a general disarmament has been an all-round improvement in temper, a disposition of the people to mix freely instead of separating into well-defined groups, each with some famous fighting-man, wearing a knife as long as a sword, for its centre; also instead of wild and whirling words, dust raised, and blood shed, great moderation in language, good humour, and reasonableness in argument.

In the same way we may see that our dogs grow less and less quarrelsome as they become more conscious of their powerlessness to inflict injury. Their confidence, and with it their friendliness towards one another, increases; the most masterful or truculent cease from bullying, the timid outgrow their timidity, and in their new-found glad courage dare to challenge the fiercest among them to a circular race and rough-and-tumble on the grass.

Now all this, from the point of view of those who make toys of sentient and intelligent beings, is or should be considered pure gain. Moreover, this undoubted improvement could not have come about if the muzzle had been the painful instrument that some dog-owners believe or say. It seems to me that those who cry out against torturing our dogs, as they put it, do not love their pets wisely and are bad observers. Undoubtedly every restraint is in some degree disagreeable, but it is only when an animal has been deprived of the power to exercise his first faculties and obey his most importunate impulses that the restraint can properly be described as painful. Take the case of a chained dog; he is miserable, as anyone may see since there are many dogs in that condition, because eternally conscious of the restraint; and the perpetual craving for liberty, like that of the healthy energetic man immured in a cell, rises to positive torture. Again, we know that smell is the most important sense of the dog, that it is as much to him as vision to the bird; consequently, to deprive him of the use of this all-important faculty by, let us say, plugging up his nostrils, or by destroying the olfactory nerve in some devilish way known to the vivisectors, would be to make him perfectly miserable, just as the destruction of its sense of sight would make a bird miserable. By comparison the restraint of the muzzle is very slight indeed: smell, hearing, vision are unaffected, and there is no interference with free locomotion; indeed, so slight is the restraint that after a while the animal is for the most part unconscious of it except when the impulse to bite or to swallow a luscious bit of carrion is excited.

We frequently see or hear of dogs that joyfully run off to fetch their muzzles when they are called to go out for a walk, or even before they are called if they but see any preparations being made for a walk: no person will contend that these are made unhappy by the muzzle, or that they deliberately weigh two evils in their mind and make choice of the lesser. The most that may be said is that these muzzle-fetchers are exceptions, though they may be somewhat numerous. For how otherwise can the fact be explained that some dogs, however ready and anxious to go for a walk they may be, will, on catching sight of the muzzle, turn away with tail between their legs and the expression of a dog that has been kicked or unjustly rebuked? My experience is that this attitude towards the muzzle of some dogs, which was quite common in the early muzzling days, is now rare and is dying out. The explanation, I think, is that as the muzzle is at first keenly felt as a restraint, imposed for no cause that the dog sees, it is in fact taken as a punishment, and resented as much as an undeserved blow or angry word would be. Everyone who observes dogs must be familiar with the fact that they do very often experience the feeling of injury and resentment towards their human masters and companions. As a rule this feeling vanishes with the exciting cause; unfortunately, in some cases the sight of the muzzle becomes associated with the feeling and is slow to disappear.

But if dogs still exist in this city of dogs that show any sign of such a feeling when a muzzle is held up before them, we can see that even in these super-sensitive ones it vanishes the instant they are out of doors. Again, let any person watch the scores and hundreds of dogs that disport themselves in our grassy parks on any fine day, and he will quickly be convinced that not only are they happy but that they are far happier than any company of unmuzzled dogs thrown casually together. They are happier, madly happy, because they know—this knowledge having now filtered down into their souls —that it is perfectly safe for them to associate with their fellows, to be hail-fellow-well-met with all the dogs in the place, from the tiniest trembling lap-dog to the burliest and most truculent-looking bull-dog and the most gigantic St. Bernard or Danish boarhound. It is for us a happiness to see their confidence, their mad games, the way they all chase and tumble over one another, pretending to be furious and fighting a grand battle.

I do not say that there is any radical or any permanent change in the dog's character. Like other beasts, he is morally and mentally non-progressive;

that which the uninformed canophilist takes as progression is merely decadence. Remove the muzzle, and in a short time the habit which the muzzle has bred will fade away and the old bickerings and bullyings and blood-sheddings begin afresh. As it is, some dogs refuse to let their fighting temper rust in spite of the muzzle.

In Hyde Park some time ago I witnessed a sublime but bloodless battle between a Danish boarhound and a bull-dog. Neither of them lost consciousness of the muzzle which prevented them from "washing" their teeth in one another's blood; they simply dashed themselves against each other, then drew back and dashed together again and again, with such fury that they would, no doubt, have succeeded in injuring each other had not their owners, assisted by several persons who were looking on, succeeded in drawing them apart.

One more instance of many which I have observed during the last two years. This is of a rather large and exceptionally powerful fox-terrier, who when out for a walk keeps a very sharp look-out for other dogs, and the instant he spies one not bigger than himself charges him furiously and with the impact hurls him to the ground, and, leaving him there, he dashes on in search of a fresh victim.

These are, however, exceptions, few individuals having intelligence enough to find out a new way of inflicting injury. As a rule the dog of ineradicably savage temper looks at his fellows as if saying "Oh, for five minutes with this cursed muzzle off!" And the others, seeing his terrible aspect, are glad that the muzzle is on—a *blessed* muzzle it is to them; and if they only knew what the doggie people were saying in the papers and could express their views on the subject, many of them would be heard to cry out, "Save us from our friends!"

The muzzling order had thus appeared to me as a sort of Golden Age of the metropolitan dogs—and cats, for these too had incidentally been affected and strangely altered in their habits. And here I must say that all I wrote in my note-book about the dogs during and just after the muzzling period has been compressed into as short a space as possible, and all I wrote about the cats (as indirectly affected by the order) has been left out for want of space to deal with the entire subject in a single chapter.

When dog-owners were rejoicing to hear that the Board of Agriculture had come to the conclusion that rabies had been completely stamped out, and were eagerly looking forward to the day when they would be allowed to remove the hated muzzle from their pets, the prospect did not seem a very pleasant one to me and to many others who kept no pets. I was prepared once more for the old familiar but unforgotten spectacle of a big dog-fight in the streets producing a joyful excitement in a crowd, quickly sprung out of the stones of the pavement as it were, of loafers and wastrels of all kinds—keen sportsmen every one of them—a spectacle which was witnessed every day by any person who took a walk in London before the muzzling time. These scenes would be

common again: in one day the dogs' (and cats')
dream of perpetual peace would be ended, and all
canines of a lofty spirit would go forth again like the
good Arthurian knight and the Zulu warrior to wash
his long-unused weapons in an adversary's blood.
But I was wrong. A habit had been formed in those
two and a half years of restraint which did not lose
its power at once: the something new which had
come into the dog's heart still held him. But it
would not, it could not, hold him long.
Days followed and nothing happened—the Golden
Age was still on. I walked the streets and watched
and waited; then, when nearly a week had elapsed,
I witnessed a fine old-fashioned dog-fight, with two
dogs in a tangle on the ground biting and tearing
each other with incredible fury and with all the
growls and shrieks and other warlike noises appropriate to the occasion. From all parts around the
"wond'ring neighbours ran" to look on, even as in
former times down to the blessed year 1897.
"Just as I thought!" I exclaimed, and heartily
wished that the president of the Board of Agriculture
had made the muzzling order a perpetual one.
Other days and weeks followed and I witnessed
no serious quarrel, and later it was so rare to see a
dog-fight in the streets and parks, fights which one
used to witness every day, that I began to think
the new pacific habit had got a tighter grip on the
animal than I could have believed. It would, I
thought, perhaps take them two or three months to
outgrow it and go back to their true natures.

I was wrong again: not months only but years have gone by—fourteen to fifteen years—and the beneficent change which had been wrought in those thirty months of restraint about which so great a pother was made at the time by dog-owners has continued to the present time. We may say that in more senses than one the dogs (and cats) of the London of to-day are not the same beings we were familiar with in the pre-muzzling days. The object of that order we have seen was gained in the brief period of thirty months. Hydrophobia for the first time in the annals of England had ceased to exist, and so long as the quarantine law is faithfully observed will perhaps never return. Rabies broke out again in this country in 1917, its first appearance since 1897, owing to some person having succeeded in eluding the quarantine order and bringing an infected dog to Plymouth. From that centre it spread to other parts of Devon and to Cornwall, and despite the prompt action of the authorities in imposing a new muzzling order in these two counties, the infection has spread to other parts of the country, and new muzzling orders are being issued just now—April 1919. Up till the year of 1897 the average number of persons who perished annually as the result of a dog-bite was twenty-nine. "Well, that's not many in a population of forty millions," cried the canophilists; but for twenty-nine who actually died of dog-madness, the most horrible shape in which death can appear to a human being, there were hundreds, and probably thousands, every year who lived for weeks and months in a constant state of apprehension lest some slight bite or abrasion received from the tooth of an angry or playful dog should result in that frightful malady.

This was unquestionably a great, a very great gain; but Mr. Long had builded better than he knew, and I am not sure that the accidental result, the change in the dog's habits in one particular, will not be regarded as the most important gain by those who are fond of dogs and by all who recognise that, in spite of some disgusting instincts which can't be changed, the dog is and probably always will be with us — our one and only four-footed associate.

CHAPTER XXIV

THE GREAT DOG-SUPERSTITION

NO person can give a careful and loving study to animal life for a long period without meeting with species exhibiting aptitudes of which a great deal might be made in a domestic state, and which, together with their beauty and cleanly habits, seem specially to fit them for companionship with man in a greater degree than those which we now possess. For it is an undoubted fact that some animals are more intelligent than others, slight differences in this respect being perceptible even among the species of a single group or genus. We measure the animal mind by ours; and looking down from the summit of our mountain the earth beneath us at first seems level; but it is not quite level, as we are able to see by regarding it attentively. Even more important are the differences in temper, ranging from the morose and truculent to the placable and sweet; more important, because compared with this diversity in disposition that which we find in intelligence is not great. There are also animals solitary by nature, and almost or quite incapable of any attachment excepting that of the sexes; while others are gregarious or social, and able to form attachments not only among themselves, but also with those of other species, and, when domesticated, with man. There is a third matter, which is doubtless the most important of all, to be considered when weighing the comparative advantages of different kinds, namely, the habits, or instincts, which change so slowly that they are practically immutable, even in altered conditions, and which, in the domesticated or pet animal, according to their character, may prove a source of pleasure and profit to man, or, on the contrary, a perpetual annoyance and trouble. When our progenitors far back in time tamed the animals we now possess, it cannot be supposed that they expended much thought on such considerations as these: probably chance determined everything for them, and they took and tamed the animals which came first to hand, or which promised to be most useful to them, either as food or in assisting them to procure food. If they were barbarians they would think little of beauty, little of the small differences in intelligence, and of the much greater differences in disposition, and, naturally, nothing at all about certain instincts in some animals which would become increasingly repugnant to man in a civilised state.

We have the dog so constantly with us; the grand result of centuries of artificial selection and training is so patent to every one, that we have actually come to look on this animal as by nature superior in mental endowment, genial qualities, and general adaptiveness to all others. Yet the qualities which make the dog valuable to us now formed no part of its original character; it is valuable chiefly for its various instinctive tendencies, and these are a later growth and purely the result of individual spontaneous variations, and of man's unconscious selection. The dog's affection for his master—the anxiety to be constantly with and to be noticed and caressed by him, the impatience at his absence and grief at his loss, and the courage to defend him and his house and his belongings from strangers—this affection of which we are accustomed to think so highly, regarding it as something unique in Nature, is in reality a very small and a very low thing; and by low is here meant common in the animal world, for it exists in a great many, probably in a large majority, of mammalian brains in every order and every family. Nor is it confined to mammalians. The duck does not occupy a distinguished place in the scale of being, and the lame duck that attached itself to Mr. Caxton, and affectionately followed him up and down in his walk, might seem an exceptionally gifted bird to those who know little of animal life. It is of course here assumed that Bulwer did not invent the lame duck: a peacock or bird of paradise, with all its organs complete, would have suited his fancy better. Probably the incident—for such incidents are very common—was told to him as true, and thinking that it would give a touch of reality and homely pathos to the description of Mr. Caxton's mild and lovable character he introduced it into his novel. A friend of the writer owned a duck far more worthy of admiration than Bulwer's immortal bird. This was

not a domestic duck, but a teal, which he brought
down with his gun slightly wounded in the wing,
and feeling all at once a strange compassion for it,
he tied it up in a handkerchief and carried it to his
home in the suburbs of a large town. The captive
was turned into a courtyard and its wants attended
to; it soon grew accustomed to its new mode of
existence, and furthermore became strongly attached
to all the members of the family, seeking for them in
the rooms when it felt lonely, and always exhibiting
distress of mind and anger in the presence of strangers.
When a cat or dog was fondled in its presence it
would run to the spot, administer a few vindictive
blows to the animal with its soft bill, and solicit a
caress for itself. The most curious thing in its history
was that it took a special liking to its captor, and
singled him out for its most marked attentions. When
he went away to business in the morning the teal
would accompany him to the street door to see him
off, returning afterwards contentedly to the yard;
and in the afternoon it would again repair to the
door, always left open, and standing composedly on
the middle of the step wait its master's return—for
this teal took count of time. If, while it stood there
watching the road, a stranger came in, it would open
its beak and hiss and strike at his legs, showing as
much suspicion and "sense of proprietorship" as a
dog does when it barks and snaps at a visitor. Its
owner's arrival would be greeted with demonstrations
of affection and joy, and following him into the
house it would spend an hour or two very happily

if allowed to sit on his feet, or nestling close against them on the hearth-rug.

The behaviour of this poor teal might seem a very great thing, but it amounts to very little after all; the memory that all animals have, and perhaps a little judgment—the "small dose of reason" which Huber found that even insects possessed—and attachment to the beings it was accustomed to see and associate with, and who attended to all its wants and gently caressed it. In the matter of the affections it has no advantage even over Darwin's celebrated snail. No doubt the self-sacrificing snail proved too much for Darwin's argument, as Professor Mivart has pointed out; fortunately the case of the teal, which can be substantiated, does not prove too much for the argument contained in this article. To be astonished at the display of such faculties and affections in a bird so low down in the scale would show ignorance of Nature. And there is no doubt that most men are very ignorant about her; so ignorant that if the teal had the place in our life which belongs to the dog, and had been with us for centuries, a companion and pet in our houses to the exclusion of other kinds, we should now believe that it surpassed all other creatures in human-like feelings; our periodicals would teem with anecdotes of its marvellous intelligence; innumerable books would be written on the subject, and the psychological biologists would put it next to man in their systems, one step below him on the throne of life, and far above the general herd of animals.

It is a fact, that might well stagger belief in the dog's superior intellect, that mammalians so low down as rats and mice when properly treated and trained make attached and intelligent pets; and that a mouse, or a sparrow, or a snake, or even a creature so small and far down in the organic scale as a flea may be taught, without very great difficulty, to perform tricks which, if performed by a dog, would be pronounced very clever indeed. Most people who witness the pretty performances of small mammals, birds and insects—which are usually up to the level of the dog's performances seen at the music-halls—probably think, if they think anything at all about the matter, that the exhibitor in such cases is the possessor of a mysterious kind of talent by means of which he is able to make these small creatures come for a few moments out of the instinctive groove they move in to do the things he wishes, much as little toy ducks and swans, which are hollow inside, are made to swim round in a basin of water after a stick of loadstone; only in the case of the exhibitor of animals the loadstone is hidden from the spectators. His trick, or mysterious talent, consists in the knowledge that the animal he wishes to train is not a little hollow duck or automaton, but that it has faculties corresponding to the lower psychical faculties in man, and that by the exercise of considerable patience it may be made, when the stimulus is applied, to repeat again and again a few actions in the same order. The question which concerns us to know is, Has the dose of reason or have these lower psychical faculties in the dog been so greatly developed during its long companionship with man as to raise it a great deal nearer to man's level, and place a great gulf between its mind and that of the pig or the crow? The gulf exists only in our imagination, and the "development" is a fairy-tale, of which Science was probably not the original author, but which she has thought proper to include, somewhat amplified and with new illustrations, in the recent editions of her collected works. The dog, taken directly from a wild life, if taken young, will be tame and understand and obey his master—numerous instances are on record—and if patiently trained will perform tricks just as wonderful as those that were related to an astonished audience at the late meeting of the British Association by a well-known writer and authority on zoological science. And in the mammalian division there are hundreds of species, some higher, some lower than the dog, which may be taught the same things, or other things equally wonderful. These greatly vaunted performances of the dog only prove that its mind is, and ever will be, what it was when, thousands of years ago, some compassionate woman took the pup her owner threw into her arms, and reared it, suckling it perhaps at her own breast; and when in after days it followed at the heels of its savage master and astonished him by assisting in the capture of his quarry.

It is not, then, the dog's intelligence, which is less than that of many other species, and is non-progressive in spite of all that training and selection can do, which makes it valuable to us. Nor has it any advantage over other species in those qualities of affection, fidelity, and good temper about which we hear so much rapturous language; for these things are lower down than reason and exist throughout the mammalian world, in animals high and low, little and big, from the harvest mouse to the hippopotamus. The dog is more valuable to us than other species because we have got him. We inherited him and were thereby saved a large amount of trouble. He is tame; the others are wild. His intellect is small and stationary, but his structure is variable, and, more important still, so are his instincts; or perhaps it would be more correct to say that new propensities, which often prove hereditary, and which by selection and training may be fixed and strengthened until they are made to resemble instincts, are of frequent occurrence in him. The more or less settled propensities in our domestic animals, originating in the domestic state, are no doubt in one sense instincts, since they are of the nature of instinct and its beginnings; but the difference between them and the true natural instinct, which has had incalculable time to crystallise in, is greater than can be expressed. The last is the rock and eternal; the others are snow-flakes, formed in a moment, that settle and show white, and even before our sight is withdrawn melt away and vanish. This same variability, or habit of varying, is in some vague way taken as a proof of versatility; hence one reason of the popular notion that the dog is so vastly superior to other four-footed creatures. If a dog could be taught to turn a spit, find truffles, save a man from drowning or from perishing in a snow-drift, point out a partridge, retrieve a wounded duck, kill twenty rats in as many seconds, and herd a flock of sheep, then it would indeed be an animal to marvel at. These are special instincts or incipient instincts, and to bestow such epithets as "generous" and "noble" on a dog for pulling a drowning man out of the water, or scratching him out of a snow-drift, is fully as irrational as it would be to call the swallow and cuckoo intrepid explorers of the Dark Continent, or to praise the hive-bees of the working caste for their chastity, loyalty, and patriotism, and for their profound knowledge of chemistry and the higher mathematics, as shown in their works. Cross the dogs and these various propensities, which being useful to man and not to the animals themselves are preserved artificially, fade away and disappear, and from moving artificially apart in twenty different grooves the animals all revert to the one old simple groove in which they were first found by man. This much may then be said in favour of the dog: he is plastic. The plasticity is probably due to domestication, to the variety of conditions to which he is subjected as man's companion in all regions of the globe, the selection which separates and preserves new varieties as they arise, and the crossing again of widely separated breeds. That he is plastic must be our excuse for determining to make the most we can of him to the complete exclusion of all other species, which might or might not prove plastic in the same degree. The fowl and pigeon are plastic, while the goose, guinea-fowl, pheasant, and peacock vary little or not at all. Nature may have better things than the dog, but we cannot guess her secrets, and to find them out by experiment would take a very long time. A bird in the hand, any bird, even a cock-sparrow, is better than all the birds of paradise that are in the bush. The other animals will serve us for sport while they last; and when they are gone we of this age shall be gone too, and deaf to whatever unkind things our posterity may say of us. The dog is with us, esteemed above all brutes, our favourite, and we shall give him no cause for jealousy.

If we had him not, if we had never had him or had forgotten his memory, and were to go out again to select a friend and companion from the beasts of the field, the wild dog would be passed by without a thought. There is nothing in him to attract, but on the contrary much to repel. In a state of nature he is an animal of disgusting habits, with a vulture-like preference for dead and decomposing meat. Cowardly he also is, yet when unopposed displays a bloodthirstiness almost without a parallel among true beasts of prey. Nor does he possess any compensating beauty or sagacity, and compared with many carnivores he is neither sharp-sighted nor fleet of foot. Some keen genealogist might be tempted to ask, Which wild dog is here meant? He may follow his fancy and choose his own wild dog—jackal, dhole, baunsuah, wolf; or take them all, and even include the coyote, as Darwin did. The multiple origin of the domestic dog is by no means an improbable theory; but it is also highly probable that the jackal had by far the largest share in his parentage. There are also reasons for believing that most of the wild dogs, including the dingo, have sprung from tame breeds; and, as a fact, the wild dogs with which the writer is most familiar are known to be the descendants of domestic animals which ran away from their masters and adopted a feral life.

Out of this same coarse material man, unconsciously imitating Nature's method, has fashioned his favourite; or rather, since the dog has become so divergent in his keeping, his large group of favourites, with their various forms and propensities. Only now, too late by some thousands of years, he is able to see that it was a mistake to go so low in the first place, to have contentedly taken base metal, dull-witted barbarian that he was, when he might just as well have taken gold. For the baseness of the metal shows in spite of much polishing to make it shine. Polishing powders we have, but not the powders of projection; and the dog, with all his new propensities, remains mentally a jackal, above some mammalians and below others; nor can he outlive ancient, obscene instincts which become increasingly offensive as civilisation raises and refines his master man.

How did our belief in the mental superiority of this animal come to exist? Doubtless it came about through our intimacy with the dog, in the fields where he helped us, and in our houses where we made a pet of him, together with our ignorance of the true character of other animals. All animals were to us simply "brutes that perish," and "natural brute beasts made to be taken and destroyed," with no faculties at all resembling ours; and when it was discovered that the dog could be made to understand many things, and that he had some feelings in common with us, and was capable of great affection, which sometimes caused him to pine at his master's loss, and in some instances even to die of grief; and that in all these things he was, or seemed to be, widely separated from other domestic brutes, the notion grew up that he was essentially different, an animal set apart for man's benefit, and, finally, that he had been specially created for such an object. Thus, Youatt says, "The dog, next to the human being, ranks highest in intelligence, and was evidently designed to be the companion and friend of man"; and in another place he says that it is highly probable that he descended from no such inferior and worthless animal as the jackal or wolf, but was originally created, somewhat as we now find him— the associate and friend of man.

This was not so very hard to believe in the pre-Darwinian days, since domesticated dogs, and even some of the breeds which we now possess, were known to have existed between three and four thousand years ago, while the world was only supposed to have existed about six thousand years. It seems probable that this curious superstition of the dog's special creation grew up gradually and only became popular in very recent times. It was gladly seized on by the poets, who made as much out of it as they had formerly done out of the melody of the dying swan; and the artists were not slow in following their example. A dog may be choked with pudding, but the human mind greedily gulped down as much of this mawkish dog-sentiment as any person, with misdirected talents, chose to manufacture for it.

Before proceeding with the story of our dog-superstition, I will here interpose a remark anent that which obtains in the other half, or more than half, of the world—the East. "The people of the East," says Youatt, "have a strange superstition with regard to the dog." Strange indeed, almost incredible to our properly enlightened Western minds! We, who in a manner despise these "people of the East," and object to many of their habits with regard to personal cleanliness, and so on, to be told that our friend and associate the dog, our pet who shares our living and sleeping rooms, and is caressed with our hands and lips, is an unclean beast and unfit to be touched by man! And so we find that the East is East, and the West is West, with regard to this as well as to most things, and that there are two great dog-superstitions. And now to proceed with the story of the one which is ours.

In due time the evolutionists came, teaching that the earth is old, that all the living things on it are the descendants of one or of a very few primordial forms, and as a consequence of such teaching the

special creation of the dog was no longer tenable.
How then came the dog-superstition—the belief in
its superiority—to survive so rude a shock? For
the evolutionists taught that all the brutes possess,
potentially and in germ, all the faculties found in
man, and the conclusion seems unavoidable that
there must be a correspondence in the physical and
psychical development, and that the root of the
higher mental and moral powers must exist in the
animals of the highest grades; that the mammal
must be more rational than the bird, and the bird
than the reptile, and the reptile than the fish; and
that the hyena, civet, and mongoose are nearer to
us than the dog, the cats above the mongoose, and
the monkeys higher still. Why then was not the
dog relegated to a lower place? Dr. Lauder Lindsay
has given the reason: "The mental scale—the scale
of intellectual and moral development—is not quite
synonymous with the zoological scale. The most
intellectual and moral animals are not necessarily
those nearest to man in the classification commonly
adopted by zoologists." Furthermore it has been
assumed that contact with man has had the effect of
enlarging the dog's mind, and making him, beyond all
other animals, intellectual, moral, and even religious.

It ought to be a great comfort to those who devote
themselves to canine pets, and to canophilists generally, to know that the philosophers are at one with
them. To some others it will perhaps add a new terror
to existence if students of dog-psychology generally
should feel themselves tempted to imitate a recent

illustrious example, and go about the country lecturing on the marvellous development of mind in their respective pets. Leibnitz once gave an account of a dog that talked; and quite recently a writer in a London journal related how, in a sheltered spot among the rocks on a lonely Scotch moor, he stumbled on an old shepherd playing whist with his collie. Nothing approaching to these cases in dramatic interest can be looked for in the apprehended discourses. The animal to be described will as a rule be of a quiet, thoughtful character proper in a philosopher's dog; not fond of display or much given to wild flights of imagination. He will only show that he possesses that faculty when asleep and barking at the heels of a dream-hare. He will show a deep affection for his master, like the teal spoken of in this article; also a strong sense of proprietorship, again like the teal and like the tame snake described by White of Selborne—a display of intellect which strangely simulates an instinct common to all creatures. And he will also show an intelligent curiosity, and examine things to find out what they are, and prove himself a very agreeable companion; as much so as Mr. Benjamin Kidd's pet humble-bee. Moreover he will be accomplished enough to sit up and beg, retrieve a walking-stick from the Serpentine, close an open door, etc.; and besides these ordinary things he will do things extraordinary, such as picking up numbered or lettered cards, red, blue, and yellow, at his master's bidding; in fact such tricks as a pig will perform without being very learned, not a Porson of its kind, but only possessing the ordinary porcine abilities. In conclusion the lecturer will bring up the savage, not in person, but a savage evolved from his inner consciousness, and compare its understanding with that of the dog, or of his dog, and the poor savage will have very much the worst of it.

We have come to the end of the dog's mind, and have arrived at that other question to which allusion has been made. The dog has a body as well as a soul, senses, appetites, and instincts, and it is worth while inquiring whether contact with man has had the same ameliorating effect on these as it is supposed to have had on his psychical faculties. In other words, he has ceased to be a jackal. For if a negative answer must be given, it follows that, however fit to be the servant, the dog is scarcely fit to be the intimate associate and friend of man; for friendship implies a similarity in habits, if nothing more, and man is not by nature an unclean animal.

Dr. Romanes, in his work on *Mental Evolution in Animals*, speaks of what he calls unpleasant survivals in the dog, such as burying food until it becomes offensive before eating it, turning round and round on the hearth-rug before lying down, rolling in filth, etc., etc., and he says that they have remained unaffected by contact with man because these instincts being neither useful nor harmful have never been either cultivated or repressed. From which it may be inferred that in his opinion these disagreeable habits may be got rid of in time. But why does he call them survivals? If the action, so frequently observed in the dog, of turning round several times before lying down, is correctly ascribed to an ancient habit in the wild animal of treading down the grass to make a bed to sleep on, it is rightly called a survival, and is a habit neither useful nor harmful in the domesticated state, which has never been either cultivated or repressed, and will in time disappear. Thus far it is easy to agree with Dr. Romanes. The other offensive instinct of the dog, of which burying meat to make it putrid, rolling in filth, etc., etc., are different manifestations, is not a survival, in the sense in which zoologists use that word, any more than the desire of the well-fed cat for the canary, and of the hen-hatched ducklings for the pond, are survivals. These are important instincts which have never ceased to operate. The dog is a flesh-eater with a preference for carrion, and his senses of taste and smell are correlated, and carrion attracts him just as fruit attracts the frugivorous bat. Man's smelling sense and the dog's do not correspond; they are inverted, and what is delightful to one is disgusting to the other. "A cur's tail may be warmed and pressed and bound round with ligatures, and after twelve years of labour bestowed on it, it will retain its original form," is an Oriental saying. In like manner the dog may be shut up in an atmosphere of opoponax and frangipani for twelve hundred years and he will love the smell of carrion still. When the dog runs frisking and barking, he expresses gladness; and he expresses a still greater degree of gladness by madly rolling, feet up, on the grass, uttering a continuous purring growl. The discovery of a carrion smell on the grass will always cause the dog to behave in this way. It is the something wanting still in the life of enforced separation from the odours that delight him; and when he unexpectedly discovers a thing of this kind his joy is uncontrolled. His sense of smell is much keener than ours; it is probably more to him than sight is to us; he lives in it, and the odours that are agreeable to him afford him the highest pleasure of which he is capable. We can do much with a dog, but there is a limit to what we can do; we can no more alter the character of his sense of smell than we can alter the colour of his blood.

"The dog is a worshipper of man," says Dr. Lauder Lindsay, "and is, or may be, made in the image of the being he worships." That refers merely to the animal's intellectual and moral nature; or, in other words, it is the fashionable "inverted or biological anthropomorphism" of the day, of which we shall all probably be heartily ashamed by-and-by; just now we are concerned with a more important matter, to wit, the dog's nose. Its character may be seen even in the most artificial breeds, that is to say, in those which have most widely diverged from the parent-form and are entirely dependent on us, such as pugs and toy-terriers. The pampered lap-dog in the midst of his comforts has one great thorn in his side, one perpetual misery to endure, in the perfumes which please his mistress. He too is a little

Venetian in his way, but his way is not hers. The camphor-wood chest in her room is an offence to him, the case of glass-stoppered scents an abomination. All fragrant flowers are as asafœtida to his exquisite nostrils, and his face is turned aside in very ill-concealed disgust from the sandal-wood box or fan. It is warm and soft on her lap, but an incurable grief to be so near her pocket-handkerchief, saturated with nasty white-rose or lavender. If she must perfume herself with flowery essences he would prefer an essential oil expressed from the gorgeous *Rafflesia arnoldi* of the Bornean forest, or even from the humble carrion-flower which blossoms nearer home.

The moral of all this is, that while the dog has become far too useful for us to think of parting with it—useful in a thousand ways, and likely to be useful in a thousand more, as new breeds arise with modified forms and with new unimagined propensities—it would be a blessed thing, both for man and dog, to draw the line at useful animals, to put and keep them in their place, which is not in the house, and value them at their proper worth, as we do our horses, pigs, cows, goats, sheep, and rabbits.

But there is a place in the human heart, the female heart especially, which would be vacant without an animal to love and fondle, a desire to have some furred creature for a friend—not a feathered creature, albeit feathered pets are common enough, because, owing to the bird's organisation, to be handled is often painful and injurious to it, and in any case it deranges the feathers; and this love is unsatisfied and feels itself defrauded of its due unless it can be expressed in the legitimate mammalian way, which is to have contact with its object, to touch with the fingers and caress. Fortunately such a feeling or instinct can be amply gratified without the dog; there are scores, perhaps hundreds, of species incomparably before this animal in all estimable qualities, which can be touched with hand and lips without defilement. Only a few need be mentioned in this place.

One of the first animals worthy of so high a distinction, which would occur to many travelled men, is the marmoset: a fairy monkey in its smallness and extreme beauty, clothed in long soft hair with a lustre as of spun silk; in manners pleasantly tricksy, but not scatter-brained and wildly capricious like its larger irresponsible relations, which is an advantage. No visitor to the Brazils can have failed to be charmed with these small animals, which are frequently kept as pets by ladies, and among pets they are surpassed by none in attachment to their mistress.

A nobler animal, capable of endearing itself to man as well as woman, is the lemur, of which there are several very beautiful species. Strong, agile, swift and graceful in action as the monkey, to which it is related, but with an even, placid disposition; monkey-like in form, but without the monkey's angularities and that appearance of spareness which reminds one of a naked, half-starved Hindoo, he has a better-proportioned figure for beauty, and his dark, richly coloured coat of woolly fur gives a pleasing roundness to his form. Moreover, he has not got the monkey's pathetic old man's withered countenance, but a sharp, somewhat vulpine face, black as ebony, a suitable setting for his chief glory—the luminous eyes, of every shining yellow colour seen in gold, topaz, and cat's-eye. "Night wood-ghost," the natives name it on account of its brilliant eyes which shine by night, and its motions in the trees, swift and noiseless as the flight of an owl. He is of ancient lineage, one of Nature's aristocrats; a child of the savage forest, as you can see in the flashing hostile orbs, and in the combined ease and power of its motions; yet withal of a sweet and placable temper.

Even among the small-brained rodents we should not look in vain for favourites; and foremost in attractiveness are perhaps the squirrels, inhabiting all climates. Blithe-hearted as birds and as volatile in disposition, almost aerial in their habits, and in some tropical, richly coloured forms resembling cuckoos and other long-tailed, graceful avians, as they run leaping from branch to branch among the trees; what animation and marvellous swiftness of motion they display, what an endless variety of pretty whimsical attitudes and gestures! "All the motions of a squirrel imply spectators as much as those of a dancing-girl," says Thoreau. They are easily tamed, coming at call to be fed from the hand; how strange it seems that they are not domestic, and found at every house in town and country where there are trees! Their unfailing spirits and fantastic performances would have a wholesome effect on our too sombre minds, and in cities like London would bring us a thought of the alert life and eternal gladness of Nature.

For those who would prefer a more terrestrial rodent, yet one more daintily fashioned than the rough-cast rabbit and guinea-pig, there are others. For a large animal the beautiful Patagonian dolichotis, like no other mammalián in its form, double the size of the hare, and a docile pet when tamed; and for a small one the charming lagidium or Andean vizcacha, with rabbit-like ears, long tail, arched like a squirrel's, the fur blue-grey in colour above, and beneath golden yellow. And the chinchilla, white and pale grey, with round leaf-like ears, and soft dove's eyes—a rare and delicate creature. There is in this small mountain troglodyte something poetic, tender, flower-like—a mammalian *edelweiss*. Poor little hunted chinchilla, did the Incas of old love you more than we do now, who love you only dead? For you were also of the great mountains, where Viracocha sat on his throne of snow, and the coming sun-god first touched your stony dwelling-places with rose and amber flame; and perhaps they regarded you as an animal sacred to the Immortals. If so, then you have indeed lost your friends, for we have no such fancies, and spare not.

It is a great descent, in more senses than one, to the prairie marmot—from the mountain to the plain, and from the beautiful to the grotesque; yet this dweller on the flat earth, gross in form and drab in colour, is a great pleasure-giver. He tickles the sense of the ludicrous, and it is good to laugh. His staring eyes, spasmodic gestures, and barking exclamations are almost painful, they are so genuine; for what an unearthly-looking monster one must seem to him! He is a gnome who has somehow stumbled out of his subterranean abode, and, like the young mole in Lessing's fable, is overwhelmed with astonishment at everything he sees in this upper world. Then there is the agouti, with pointed head, beautifully arched back, and legs slender, proportionally, as the gazelle's; its resemblance in form to the small musk-deer has been remarked—a rodent moulded in the great Artist-Mother's happiest mood. The colour of its coat, relieved only by its pink ears and a broad shining black stripe on the back, is red Venetian gold, the hue which the old Italian masters gave to the tresses of their angelic women. A mild-tempered animal, which may be taken from its native woods and made tame in a few days. Many of the smaller rodents might also be mentioned, such as the quaint, bird-like jerboa, and the variegated loucheres; and so on down even to the minute harvest-mouse. Forms and sizes to suit all tastes; for why should we all have alike? Let fashion in pets go out with the canines.

To go back to the other extreme, from low to high, there are the wild cats inhabiting all desert places on the globe. Tigers and leopards made small; clouded, or with a clear golden ground-colour, pale or red gold or grey, and black-striped, barred zebra-like, or spotted, or with the colours disposed in strange patterns, beautifully harmonious. As in the lemurs, and surpassing them, here are brilliant luminous eyes and great strength of sinew; but these are not of peace: the serpent-like silence of the movements and fateful stillness of the lithe form, and the round watchful orbs that seem like the two fiery gems set in a carved figure of rich stone—these betray the deadly purpose. Yet their hearts may also be conquered with kindness. The domestic cat is a proof of it; she is found in most houses, and whether we make a pet of her or not, long familiarity has given her a place in our affections. But when we go from home and visit regions infinitely richer in life than our own, it surprises and offends us to meet with the same cat still; for it looks as if man had failed, in the midst of so much variety, to find anything better or equally good. Nature abhors monotony; why should we force it on her to our own disadvantage?

Here then we have a few mammalian forms gathered at random from several widely separated families, each as it were the final and highest effort of Nature in one particular direction—"the bright consummate flower" in a group, the other members of which seem by comparison coarse and unfinished. We boast to be lovers of the beautiful, and it is here in its highest form. Birds may be said to have a greater beauty, but it is different in kind; and they are winged and far from us. They are of the sky and their forms are aerial; and their aerial nature is not in touch with ours. For the mammalians we, who are also mammals and bound to earth, have a greater sympathy, and their beauty has for us a more enduring charm. If it is out of our sight and far removed from most of us, and growing farther year by year, we have only ourselves to blame. For how rich are the mountains and forests and desert places of the earth, where we sometimes go to slay Nature's untamed beautiful children, assisted in our task by that servant and friend that is so worthy of us! And on the other hand, how poor are our houses and villages and cities! The dog is there, inherited from barbarous progenitors, who tamed him not to be a pet or friend, but to assist them in their quest for flesh, and for other purposes; to be a scavenger, as he still is in Eastern countries, or, as in the case of the ancient Hyrcanians, to devour the corpses of their dead. He is there, but his title is bad; why should we suffer him? We may wash him daily with many waters, but the jackal taint remains. That which Nature has made unclean let it be unclean still, for we cannot make it different. Her lustral water which purifies for ever is a secret to our chemistry. Or if not altogether a secret, if, as some imagine, the ingredients may be dimly guessed, they are too slow for us in their working. Man's years are limited and his purposes change. Nature has all time for her processes; "the eternal years of God are hers." Moreover, there is nothing we can desire and not find in her garden, which has infinite variety. Why should we cherish a carrion-flower and wear it in our bosoms while carelessly trampling on so many bright and beautiful blooms? It is a pity to trample on them, since the effect of so destructive a habit is to make them rare; and "rarity," as certain of our great naturalists have told us, "is the precursor to extinction." And perhaps by-and-by, blaming ourselves for the past, we shall be diligently seeking everywhere for them, anxious to find and to bring them into our houses, where, after long companionship with the dog, they will serve to sweeten our imaginations and be a joy for ever.

NOTE.—I had pronounced the foregoing old magazine article unusable, partly because of the manner of it, its carefulness, and partly because it was somewhat polemical and touched on questions which are not natural history, pure and simple. Now at the last moment I have resolved to put it in—just for fun.

It appeared anonymously ages ago in *Macmillan's Magazine*, then edited by Mowbray Morris, who wrote to me that my article had given him a painful shock, that it would hurt and disgust many readers of the Magazine, and, finally, that all I and others like me could say in derogation of the dog would have no effect on those who loved and esteemed that friend of man at its proper worth.

"All right," I replied, "Send me back the MS. Of course you mustn't let anything appear in your magazine to hurt the feelings of these dear people."

No, he wouldn't, he said. He had accepted the article and would print it. And in due time print it he did.

Just then a lady named Frances Power Cobbe, whom I greatly esteemed and admired for her courage in combating one of the most horrible forms of cruelty practised on animals, had a book in the press entitled *The Friend of Man and his Friends, the Poets*. Reading my unsigned paper in the Magazine, she picked up her pen in a noble rage to add some words to her Introduction, in which she hurled at me certain sayings of Schopenhauer describing man as a very contemptible creature when compared with the dog, and also saying that the writer of the article was " worse than a vivisectionist."

This struck me as a bit thick, seeing that a vivisectionist had always been to her the most damnable being in the universe.

One or two of my friends, who knew I had written the article, then remonstrated with the lady for using such expressions of one who, though tactless and somewhat brutal, was also a lover of all the creatures, and didn't like to hear so much praise of the dog at the expense of the other animals. The result was that she smoothed her ruffled plumes and sent her regrets and a promise to excise the obnoxious passage in her preface in the next edition.

Of course it doesn't matter two straws whether she ever had the opportunity of doing so or not: the best part of the story is still to come—the funny part, and a wise word which, though laughingly spoken, may yet do good.

The lady's book in the meantime had fallen by chance into the hands of Andrew Lang, and as it was just the sort of thing to delight him, he made it the subject of one of his most charmingly amusing leaders in the *Daily News* of that time. In this article, after the usual pleasant word for the book and its author, he deals with the subject of the dog and man's feeling for it in ancient and modern times, and of the great length to which it has been carried recently, and concludes with a passage which I must quote in full, as I don't think this article ever reappeared among his *Lost Leaders*, and it is worth preserving for the sake of its Andrew Langishness, as well as of its moral. After quoting some of the most notable sayings in praise of the dog, he concludes:

"There is perhaps some slight danger of reaction against all this, and Miss Cobbe seems to have anticipated it in a sharp attack on a writer hostile to dogs. This writer, as though in his turn anticipating the coming worship of the dog, has expressed himself with considerable force against the 'great dog superstition,' and has gone so far as to characterise the dog's affection, devotion, and courage in defence of his master as a ' very small and very low thing.' It is easy to imagine how Miss Cobbe characterises *him*. Warned by this example, we shall take care not to say that, nowadays perhaps, the dog is too much with us in literature. It may be thought—we do not say it is our opinion —that the dog's worst peril awaits him at the moment of his highest fortune, when he has become the pet and protégé of women. Women may spoil him, so the cynic might say—if a cynic could be expected to say anything unkind on such a subject—as they spoil all their favourites. Under their enervating patronage he may gradually lose some of his most cherished qualities, until he whines with the poet, ' What is it, in this world of ours, that makes it fatal to be loved ? ' For fatal it would be if the dog were gradually evolved into a thing of tricks, a suppliant of sugar at afternoon tea, a pert assailant only of the people who never mean to rob the house, or a being deaf to the cry of 'rats,' but fiercely active in the pursuit of a worsted ball—a fine-coated dandy with his initials embroidered on his back. His affection, his fidelity, his reasoning power are very good things, but it is not all a blessing for him that they are finding their way into literature. For literature never can take a thing simply for what it is worth. The plain-dealing dog must be distinctly bored by the ever-growing obligation to live up to the anecdotes of him in the philosophic journals. These anecdotes are not told for his sake; they are told to save the self-respect of people who want an idol, and who are distorting him into a figure of pure convention for their domestic altars. He is now expected to discriminate between relations and mere friends of the house; to wag his tail at 'God save the Queen'; to count up to five in chips of firewood, and to seven in mutton bones; to howl for all deaths in the family above the degree of second cousin; to post letters, and refuse them when they have been insufficiently stamped; and last and most intolerable, to show a tender solicitude when the tabby is out of sorts. He will do these things when they are required of him, for he is the most good-natured and obliging fellow in the world, but it ought never to be forgotten that he hates to do them, and that all he really cares for is his daily dinner, his run, his rat, and his occasional caress. He is not in the least concerned about the friendship of the poets, and the attempt to live up to their interest in him is playing havoc with his sincerity, and making him only less of a *névrose* than the quite unnecessary cat. His earlier difficulty with the Egyptians is a warning that ought to serve for all time. If he ate up Apis it was but as a rough and ready way of inviting the worshippers of Apis to leave him alone."

CHAPTER XXV

MY FRIEND THE PIG

IS there a man among us who on running through a list of his friends is unable to say that there is one among them who is a perfect pig? I think not; and if any reader says that he has no such an one for the simple reason that he would not and could not make a friend of a perfect pig, I shall maintain that he is mistaken, that if he goes over the list a second time and a little more carefully, he will find in it not only a pig, but a sheep, a cow, a fox, a cat, a stoat. and even a perfect toad.

But all this is a question I am not concerned with, seeing that the pig I wish to write about is a real one—a four-footed beast with parted hoofs. I have a friendly feeling towards pigs generally, and consider them the most intelligent of beasts, not excepting the elephant and the anthropoid ape—the dog is not to be mentioned in this connection. I also like his disposition and attitude towards all other creatures, especially man. He is not suspicious, or shrinkingly submissive, like horses, cattle, and sheep; nor an impudent devil-may-care like the goat; nor hostile like the goose; nor condescending like the cat; nor a flattering parasite like the dog. He views us from a totally different, a sort of democratic, standpoint as fellow-citizens and brothers, and takes it for granted,

or grunted, that we understand his language, and
without servility or insolence he has a natural,
pleasant, camerados-all or hail-fellow-well-met air
with us. It may come as a shock to some of my readers
when I add that I like him, too, in the form of
rashers on the breakfast-table; and this I say with
a purpose on account of much wild and idle talk one
hears on this question even from one's dearest friends
—the insincere horror expressed and denunciation of
the revolting custom of eating our fellow-mortals.
The other day a lady of my acquaintance told me
that she went to call on some people who lived a
good distance from her house, and was obliged to
stay to luncheon. This consisted mainly of roast
pork, and as if that was not enough, her host, when
helping her, actually asked if she was fond of a
dreadful thing called the crackling!

It is a common pose; but it is also something
more, since we find it mostly in persons who are
frequently in bad health and are restricted to a low
diet; naturally at such times vegetarianism appeals
to them. As their health improves they think less
of their fellow-mortals. A little chicken broth is
found uplifting; then follows the inevitable sole, then
calves' brains, then a sweetbread, then a partridge,
and so on, progressively, until they are once more
able to enjoy their salmon or turbot, veal and lamb
cutlets, fat capons, turkeys and geese, sirloins of
beef, and, finally, roast pig. That's the limit; we
have outgrown cannibalism, and are not keen about

haggis, though it is still eaten by the wild tribes inhabiting the northern portion of our island. All this should serve to teach vegetarians not to be in a hurry. Thoreau's "handful of rice" is not sufficient for us, and not good enough yet. It will take long years and centuries of years before the wolf with blood on his iron jaws can be changed into the white innocent lamb that nourishes itself on grass.

Let us now return to my friend the pig. He inhabited a stye at the far end of the back garden of a cottage or small farmhouse in a lonely little village in the Wiltshire downs where I was staying. Close to the stye was a gate opening into a long green field, shut in by high hedges, where two or three horses and four or five cows were usually grazing. These beasts, not knowing my sentiments, looked askance at me and moved away when I first began to visit them, but when they made the discovery that I generally had apples and lumps of sugar in my coat pockets they all at once became excessively friendly and followed me about, and would put their heads in my way to be scratched, and licked my hands with their rough tongues to show that they liked me. Every time I visited the cows and horses I had to pause beside the pig-pen to open the gate into the field; and invariably the pig would get up and coming towards me salute me with a friendly grunt. And I would pretend not to hear or see, for it made me sick to look at his pen in which he stood belly-deep in the fetid mire, and it made me ashamed to think that so intelligent and good-tempered an animal, so profitable to man, should be kept in such abominable conditions. Oh, poor beast, excuse me, but I'm in a hurry and have no time to return your greeting or even to look at you!

In this village, as in most of the villages in all this agricultural and pastoral county of Wiltshire, there is a pig-club, and many of the cottagers keep a pig; they think and talk a great deal about their pigs, and have a grand pig-day gathering and dinner, with singing and even dancing to follow, once a year. And no wonder that this is so, considering what they get out of the pig; yet in any village you will find it kept in this same unspeakable condition. It is not from indolence nor because they take pleasure in seeing their pig unhappy before killing him or sending him away to be killed, but because they cherish the belief that the filthier the state in which they keep their pig the better the pork will be! I have met even large prosperous farmers, many of them, who cling to this delusion. One can imagine a conversation between one of these Wiltshire pig-keepers and a Danish farmer. "Yes," the visitor would say, "we too had the same notion at one time, and thought it right to keep our pigs as you do; but that was a long time back, when English and Danes were practically one people, seeing that Canute was king of both countries. We have since then adopted a different system; we now believe, and the results prove that we are in the right way, that it is best to consider the animal's nature and habits and wants, and to make the artificial conditions imposed on him as little oppressive as may be. It is true that in a state of nature the hog loves to go into pools and wallow in the mire, just as stags, buffaloes, and many other beasts do, especially in the dog-days when the flies are most troublesome. But the swine, like the stag, is a forest animal, and does not love filth for its own sake, nor to be left in a miry pen, and though not as fastidious as a cat about his coat, he is naturally as clean as any other forest creature."

Here I may add that in scores of cases when I have asked a cottager why he didn't keep a pig, his answer has been that he would gladly do so, but for the sanitary inspectors, who would soon order him to get rid of it, or remove it to a distance on account of the offensive smell. It is probable that if it could be got out of the cottager's mind that there must need be an offensive smell, the number of pigs fattened in the villages would be trebled.

I hope now after all these digressions I shall be able to go on with the history of my friend the pig. One morning as I passed the pen he grunted—spoke, I may say—in such a pleasant friendly way that I had to stop and return his greeting; then, taking an apple from my pocket, I placed it in his trough. He turned it over with his snout, then looked up and said something like "Thank you" in a series of gentle grunts. Then he bit off and ate a small piece, then another small bite, and eventually taking what was left in his mouth he finished eating it. After that he always expected me to stay a minute and speak to him when I went to the field; I knew it from his way of greeting me, and on such occasions I gave him an apple. But he never ate it greedily: he appeared more inclined to talk than to eat, until by degrees I came to understand what he was saying. What he said was that he appreciated my kind intentions in giving him apples. But, he went on, to tell the real truth, it is not a fruit I am particularly fond of. I am familiar with its taste as they sometimes give me apples, usually the small unripe or bad ones that fall from the trees. However, I don't actually dislike them. I get skim milk and am rather fond of it; then a bucket of mash, which is good enough for hunger; but what I enjoy most is a cabbage, only I don't get one very often now. I sometimes think that if they would let me out of this muddy pen to ramble like the sheep and other beasts in the field or on the downs I should be able to pick up a number of morsels which would taste better than anything they give me. Apart from the subject of food I hope you won't mind my telling you that I'm rather fond of being scratched on the back.

So I scratched him vigorously with my stick, and made him wriggle his body and wink and blink and smile delightedly all over his face. Then I said to myself: "Now what the juice can I do more to please him?" For though under sentence of death, he had done no wrong, but was a good, honest-hearted fellow-mortal, so that I felt bound to do something to make the miry remnant of his existence a little less miserable.

I think it was the word *juice* I had just used—
for that was how I pronounced it to make it less
like a swear-word—that gave me an inspiration. In
the garden, a few yards back from the pen, there
was a large clump of old elder-trees, now overloaded
with ripening fruit—the biggest clusters I had ever
seen. Going to the trees I selected and cut the finest
bunch I could find, as big round as my cap, and
weighing over a pound. This I deposited in his trough
and invited him to try it. He sniffed at it a little
doubtfully, and looked at me and made a remark or
two, then nibbled at the edge of the cluster, taking
a few berries into his mouth, and holding them some
time before he ventured to crush them. At length
he did venture, then looked at me again and made
more remarks, "Queer fruit this! Never tasted anything quite like it before, but I really can't say yet
whether I like it or not."

Then he took another bite, then more bites, looking up at me and saying something between the
bites, till, little by little, he had consumed the whole
bunch; then turning round, he went back to his bed
with a little grunt to say that I was now at liberty
to go on to the cows and horses.

However, on the following morning he hailed my
approach in such a lively manner, with such a note
of expectancy in his voice, that I concluded he had
been thinking a great deal about elder-berries, and
was anxious to have another go at them. Accordingly I cut him another bunch, which he quickly
consumed, making little exclamations the while—

" Thank you, thank you, very good — very good indeed!" It was a new sensation in his life, and made him very happy, and was almost as good as a day of liberty in the fields and meadows and on the open green downs.

From that time I visited him two or three times a day to give him huge clusters of elder-berries. There were plenty for the starlings as well; the clusters on those trees would have filled a cart.

Then one morning I heard an indignant scream from the garden, and peeping out saw my friend, the pig, bound hand and foot, being lifted by a dealer into his cart with the assistance of the farmer.

"Good-bye, old boy!" said I as the cart drove off; and I thought that by-and-by, in a month or two, if several persons discovered a peculiar and fascinating flavour in their morning rasher, it would be due to the elder-berries I had supplied to my friend the pig, which had gladdened his heart for a week or two before receiving his quietus.

CHAPTER XXVI

THE POTATO AT HOME AND IN ENGLAND

WHEN I was a small boy running about wild on the pampas, amazingly interested in everything and making wonderful discoveries every day, I was attracted by a small flower among the grasses—pale and meek-looking, with a yellow centre, petals faintly washed with purple, and a lovely scent. It charmed me with its gentle beauty and new fragrance, and surprised me with its resemblance, both in flower and leaf, to the potato-plant. On showing a spray to my parents, they told me that it *was* a potato-flower. This seemed incredible, since the potato was a big plant with large clusters of purplish flowers, almost scentless, and, furthermore, it was a *cultivated* plant. They explained that all cultivated plants were originally wild; that long cultivation had had the effect of changing their appearance and making them larger; that was how we had got our wheat, which came from a poor little grass with a seed scarcely bigger than a pin's head. Even the botanists had had great difficulty in identifying it as the original wheat-plant. Also our maize and huge pumpkins and water-melons, and all our vegetables and fruit. I then took a table-knife and went to look for a plant, and when I found one I dug down to a depth of six inches, and there sure enough was the tuber, attached to the root, but quite small—not bigger than a hazel-nut—perfectly round with a pimply skin, curiously light-coloured, almost pearly. A pretty little thing to add to my collection of curios, but all the same a potato. How strange!

From that time I began to take a new interest in the potato, and would listen eagerly when the subject of potatoes was discussed at table. When the potatoes were taken up about the beginning of December, and then the second crop in autumn— April or May—my father would tell the gardener to pick out a few of the biggest for him, and these, when washed and weighed, would be placed as ornaments on the dining-room mantelpiece, in a row of half a dozen. They were not pretty to look at, but they were astonishingly big when I put my small marble of a wild potato by the side of them. Then when some English neighbour, ten or twenty miles away, would ride over to see us and stay to lunch, my father would take up the potatoes one by one and hand them to him and say: "What do you think of this one? And of this one?" Then: "And of *this* one?" *This* one would be the biggest. Then he would add: "What does *your* biggest potato weigh?" And when the other replied: "Ten"—or perhaps twelve—"ounces," my father would laugh and say: "This one weighs fourteen ounces and a half; this fifteen and three-quarters; this one just turns the balance at sixteen, and *this* one seventeen ounces. What do you say to that?" The other would reply that he couldn't have believed it if he hadn't seen and handled the potato himself, and my father would be happy and triumphant.

Not only were the potatoes of that land as large as any in the world, but they were probably the best in the world to eat. They were beautifully white and mealy, with that crystalline sparkle of the properly cooked potato in them which one rarely sees in this country. Strange to say, our Spanish neighbours, even those who had a garden, did not grow or eat them; they were confined to the English settlers and a few foreigners of other nationalities.

Here I will venture to relate an incident which, though trivial, goes to show how little our native neighbours knew about the potato, which was so important to us; and that the same time it will serve to illustrate a trait common to the native of that land—the faculty of keeping his face.

A young girl of about twelve, the child of poor natives living in a small ranch a couple of miles from us, was invited by a little sister of mine to come and spend a day with her, to look at dolls and other treasures, eat peaches, and enjoy herself generally. We were a big family, but my sister's little guest, Juanita, took her place at table as if to the manner born. Lamb cutlets with a nice big potato on the plate were placed before her, also a cup of tea, for in those days tea was drunk at every meal. After a glance round to see how eating was managed in these novel conditions, she began on the cutlets, and presently my little sister, anxious to guide her, called attention to the untasted potato. She looked at it, hesitated a moment, then, taking it up in her fingers, dropped it into her tea-cup! The poor girl had never seen a boiled potato before and had never had a cup of tea, and had just made a guess at what she was expected to do. We youngsters exploded with laughter and our elders smiled, but the girl kept her balance—not a flush, not a change in her countenance.

"Oh, you must not do that!" cried my sister. "You must eat the potato with the cutlet on the plate, with salt on it."

And Juanita, turning towards her little hostess, replied in a quiet but firm tone: "I prefer to eat it this way." And in *this* way she did eat it, first mashing it up, stirring it about in the tea, making a sort of gruel of it, "not too thick and not too thin," then eating it with a spoon.

This singular presence of mind and faculty of keeping their dignity under difficulties is, I imagine, an instinct of all uncivilised people, and is in some curious way related to the instinct of self-preservation, as when they are brought face to face with a great danger and are perfectly cool where one would expect them to be in a state of confusion and panic.

Other memories connected with the potato come back to me. I had a small brother, and one day we were discussing that most important subject to small boys, the things we liked best to eat, when it occurred to us as very strange that certain articles of food were only eaten in combination with certain other things; some with salt, and others with sugar, and so on, and we agreed to try and discover a new and better way of combining different flavours. We started on our boiled eggs and ate them with sugar or treacle and cinnamon instead of salt, and found that it wasn't very nice. By-and-by we found that peaches cut up and eaten with cream and sugar tasted delicious. And after that we broke the peach-stones and made a mash of the kernels in a mortar and ate that with cream and sugar, and agreed that it was a great success. By-and-by one of our elders told us that the peculiar flavour of the peach-stone pip which delighted us and was so good with cream and sugar was due to the presence of prussic acid, and that if we went on with this dish it would certainly kill us all in a little while. That frightened us, and we started experimenting with the harmless potato. And here we met with our greatest success; let all gourmets make a note of it. Select a good-sized egg-shaped baked potato and place it in a small cup and treat it as you would an egg, cutting off the top. Then with your spoon break it up inside, pour in oil and vinegar, and add pepper and salt. A delightful combination! We tried to improve on it by substituting cream or butter for the oil, but it was the flavour of olive oil and vinegar combined with that of the potato which made it perfect.

Other experimenters may have discovered this way of eating a potato, but the only approach to it I have found in reading is contained in an anecdote

of Byron, at the time when he was the hero of
London society. He dined with a friend who had
got together a company of the poet's ardent admirers
to meet him. But he was in a difficult mood: he
declined soup and fish and meats of all kinds. "What
then will you eat?" asked his host, getting impatient.
"Oh, a potato," said Byron. And when a big potato
was put before him, he broke it up, drenched it in
vinegar and ate it, and this was his dinner. And
dinner over, he took himself off, to the deep dis-
appointment of all those who had come to gaze and
listen and worship.

"How long," said one of them to his host, "will
his lordship be able to keep this dietary?"

"How long—how long!" said his host. "As long
as people think it worth while to pay any attention
to what he eats."

The story goes on to say that, quitting his friend's
house, the poet walked to his club in Piccadilly and
told the waiter to bring him an underdone beef-
steak. He had perhaps discovered that a potato
drenched in vinegar was good as an appetiser, but
he probably did not know how much better it would
have been with the addition of oil.

The other most interesting memory of the potato
refers to its chief enemy, an insect called in the ver-
nacular *Bicho moro*—a blister-beetle or Cantharides,
its full scientific name being *Epicauta adspersa*. Not
every year but from time to time this pest would
make its appearance in numbers, and invariably just
when the potato-plant was at its best, when the

bloom was coming. On a warm, still, bright day, when the sun began to grow hot, all at once the whole air would be filled with myriads of the small grey beetles, about twice as big as a house-fly, and the buzzing sound of their innumerable wings, and the smell they emit. It was something like the smell of the fire-fly when they are in swarms—a heavy musty and phosphorus smell in the fire-fly. The blister-beetle had the mustiness but not the phosphorus in its odour; in place of it there was another indescribable and disagreeable element, which perhaps came from that acrid or venomous principle in the beetle's pale blood. Though we heartily detested it, the insect was not without a modest beauty, its entire oblong body being of a pleasing smoke-grey, the wing-cases minutely dotted with black.

The sight and sound and smell of them would call forth a lamentation from all those who possessed a potato-patch and had rejoiced for weeks past in their little green plants with their green embossed leaves, since now there would be no potatoes for the table except very small ones, until the autumn crop, which would come along after the grey blister-fly had vanished like smoke from the earth after leaving his evil seed in it.

The beetle feeds on the leaves of solanaceous plants and prefers the potato above all others, so that when he comes in a slow-flying swarm over the potato-field, you see the beetles dropping in thousands like a grey rain upon it, and know that before the sun sets the whole of the leaves will be devoured, the stalks being left till the following day, when he will eat them pretty well down to the ground before passing on to attack the tomatoes. Attempts were sometimes made to drive them off by lighting smoky fires of half-dried weeds round the potato-patch, but never once did we succeed in saving the plants.

As a small boy I was naturally incapable of entering into the bitter feelings of our elders with regard to the blister-beetle. Its appearance excited me and had the exhilarating effect produced by any and every display of life on a great scale. At the same time I hated it, not because it devoured the potato-plants, but for the reason that I had been feelingly persuaded of its power to produce blisters. I was out running about in the sunshine all day, and the air being full of beetles, they were always dropping upon me and had to be brushed or shaken off my straw hat, my jacket and trousers and boots continually; but from time to time one would get into my shoe or slip down my neck or creep up my sleeve to get broken on the skin, and in due time a pain would set in just at that spot; then on pulling off my clothes a noble blister would come to light, a boss of a pale amber colour and a jelly-like appearance. It was ornamental but painful, and I would go sore for a day in that part.

Being a boy naturalist, I tried to discover the secret of its breeding habits and transformations, but failed utterly. However, they are known, and are like those of our familiar English oil-beetle, which stagger the mind that contemplates the strange case of a big beetle whose eggs produce mites—mere animated specks—endowed with an extraordinary activity and a subtle devilish knowledge and cunning in building up their own lives out of others' lives. I did, however, succeed in discovering one singular fact when on this quest. There is a family of big rapacious flies common all over the world, the Asilidæ, and we have several species on the pampas, some arrayed in the colours and markings of bees and wasps. One is black and has bright red instead of transparent wings, and appears to mimic our common red-winged wasp. I found out that this fly preyed on the blister-beetle, and it amazed me to see that almost every one of these flies I could find had one grasped in its feet and was diligently sucking its juices through its long proboscis. Yet those juices had so potent a poison in them that a few drops of them on a man's skin would raise a big blister!

Although the potato was very much to me in those early years, all my feelings regarding it having originated in the chance discovery of the meek-looking little flower with a delicate perfume among the grasses, it grew to be more when I heard the history of the plant in cultivation, and how it had been used as food by the aborigines both in North and South America for long centuries before the discovery of the great green continent, and just as the yellow-haired Demeter, the Corn Mother, and her loved lost daughter Persephone, the Corn Maiden, were worshipped in ancient Greece; and as the Rice Mother is worshipped in the East, in many lands and islands; and as the Maize Mother and God were worshipped in all the Americas, by nations savage and civilised, so did the Peruvians, who built temples glittering with gold to their chief god, the sun, and to the sun's children, the lightning and rainbow, worship the Potato Mother, and pray to her to look kindly on their labours when the seed was committed to the ground and to give them good increase.

Finally I came to know the history of the introduction of the potato into these islands by Sir Walter Raleigh. This action served to make him appear to me the greatest of all the shining Elizabethans—greatest in all he thought, said, and did, good or evil; as courtier, poet, explorer and buccaneering adventurer and seeker after a golden city in savage wildernesses; as prisoner in the Tower and author of that most eloquent *History of the World* ; and, most beautiful of all, on the scaffold, by the block, the headsman with his glittering axe standing by him, when, like a king who was to come after him, he nothing said or did on that memorable scene to cast a shadow on his lustre or cause any lover then and in the ages to follow to grieve at even a momentary weakness on his part.

All this served to make the potato so important to me that when I stood among the plants, growing higher than my knees, in their lush-green embossed leaves and purple bloom, with a cloud of red and black and yellow and orange and white butterflies hovering about them, it seemed to me that America had given the two greatest food-bearing plants to the world—maize and potato; and which was the greatest I could not say, although the great maize-plant was certainly the most beautiful in its green dress and honey-coloured tresses, which the hot sun would soon turn to gold and by-and-by to a Venetian red of a tint which one sees but rarely in his life, in the hair of some woman of almost supernatural loveliness.

The potato, then, as I have said before, was very much to me. How natural, then, when I came to England that I should have been shocked at the sight of my first dish of potatoes on the table.

"Is *this* the way potatoes are cooked in this country?" I asked in astonishment.

"Why, yes; how else would you have them cooked?" I was asked in return; and they too were shocked when I said the sight of that sodden mass of flavourless starch and water made me sick —that it looked like the remains of a boiled baby in the dish, boiled to a rag. For up to then I had seen potatoes on the table as they appear when boiled in their skins, peeled, and placed in a large shallow dish with a little butter on them; and in that way they have the appearance of large cream-coloured fruit, and send out an agreeable smell and have a nice flavour.

Here was quite a different thing: this was the "homely potato" of the British journalist—homely indeed!—stripped of its romance, spoiled in the cooking, and made nasty to the eye. Yet this is how it is eaten in every house in England! In Ireland and

Scotland I found that the potato was usually cooked
in the proper way by people of the peasant class.
But what do the doctors, who make our digestions
their life study, say of this misuse of the potato?
I don't know. All I hear them say about the potato
is that if your digestion is bad you must not eat it.
What, then, will they say when I tell them that I
have a weak digestion, and whenever I have a bad
turn I cure myself by dining for a day or two on
nothing but potatoes? Cooked in their skins, I
scarcely need add, and eaten with pepper and salt
and butter. No soup or fish or meats or sweets—
nothing but potatoes for a day or two and I'm well
again. Perhaps they will say that I am not a normal
subject. But we needn't bother about the doctors.
Just now, while writing this chapter, I asked my
landlady's daughter in the village in Cornwall where
I am staying if she had ever tasted a potato boiled
in its jacket. Yes, she had, once only, and didn't
like it because it didn't taste like a potato—such
a funny flavour!

That "funny" flavour, so unlike the taste of the
tuber boiled and water-logged in the homely English
way, is precisely the flavour which makes it so nice
to eat and so valuable as food; also, if I may slip in
the personal pathology or idiosyncratic abnormality,
so perfect a cure for indigestion. It is, in fact, the
taste imparted by the salts which mostly lie close
beneath the skin, and are consequently thrown away
when the potato is peeled before boiling. You cannot avoid this waste by scraping your potato, since

scraping removes the waterproof skin, and, the skin gone, the boiling water saturates the potato and carries the salts away.

This is a serious matter in these days, when—as some of the newspapers say—we are trying to economise in the matter of food, and when the potato is beginning to be talked about. I suppose that there are about thirty or forty millions of us who consume about half a pound of potatoes every day; and it is not only the case that hundreds of tons of excellent food are thrown away every day in the peeling process, but that the most valuable elements in the potato are wasted. Perhaps the war will teach us to value the potato properly, as, I believe, it is and always has been valued in most countries outside these islands.

CHAPTER XXVII

A LONGISH name for a flower — one of its three names! After all it is not saying very much; we have another better, more familiar one with at least six names, and one of them not composed of six words like our John's, but of ten!

When it is spring I walk in sheltered places, by wood- and hedge-side, to look for and welcome the first comers. Oh those first flowers so glad to be alive and out in the sun and wind once more— their first yearly ineffable spring freshness, remembrancers of our lost childhood, dead and lost these many dim and sorrowful years, now recovered with the flowers, and immortal once more with spring's immortality!

Do we not all experience a feeling something like that in an early spring walk? Even a stockbroker or stockjobber knows a primrose when he sees one, and it is a yellow primrose to him too—and something more. A something to give him a thrill. It is as if he met a fairy-like child in his walk who tossed back her shining tresses at his approach to look up into his face with eyes full of laughter.

To me they are all like that. Look at this celandine, how it shines with joy and starts up to meet you half-way, throwing its arms out for the expected caress! And here too is my dear old little white friend, the wild garlic—a whole merry crowd of them by the stone hedge; happy meeting and happy greeting! Let me stoop to caress them and inhale their warm breath. It is true there are those who don't like it and take their nice noses away when the flower would be glad to kiss them. But when a flower has no fragrance to it, like the hyacinth and blue columbine of these parts, or even red valerian—Pretty Betsy herself blushing bright pink all over—it does not seem that they love as warmly as the flower with a scented breath—sweet violet and sweet gale and vernal squill and cowslip and many more, down to the water-mint by the stream and my loving little white friend here by the stone hedge.

And when the first early blooms are gone with March, April, and May, when it is full June, I wade in the lush meadow (when the farmer is not about) to greet and talk to the taller ones, and alas! to say good-bye to them at the same time, seeing that the mower will soon come to make hay of them. One of the old friends I diligently seek at this season is John, or Johnnie, tall as any there—tall as the flaunting ox-eye daisies. Not that it is a particularly attractive flower; I have never regarded it as pretty, but merely as one of those yellow dandelion-shaped flowers which are so common with us. And it is indeed in appearance a lesser dandelion on a thin tall plant, the blooms, half a dozen or so to a plant, on long fine stems. It interests me chiefly on account of its singular, unflowerlike behaviour, which the name describes; also on account of its other queer name and the meaning thereof. I don't mean goat's-beard, but its third old English name which now, like many another, has grown offensive to ears polite, and has long been banished from our flower books, and even the dictionaries. One must go back to the old writers to find it in print: not necessarily so far back as Chaucer, who is too disgusting for anything, but to the Elizabethans and Carolines. The banned name, however, is still in use in the rural districts.

What I have written so far was all I could have said about this yellow flower until last summer; and if in time gone by anyone had said to me that a day would come when Johnnie would appear to me as a wonder and delight, I should have laughed. Yet the strange experience actually came to me last June.

At a Cornish village there was a field near the cottage where I was staying, where my host had allowed his half a dozen cows to graze during the winter months: in April he turned them out, and a month later, passing by the field, it appeared to me that it would yield him a heavy crop of grass. One morning in June, looking at the field from a distance, it struck me that the hay would not be of a very good quality since the entire area had now turned to bright yellow with some tall flower that looked like ragwort among the grasses.

"What's happened to your field—what is that yellow weed in it?" I said to my man.

"Oh, that's only——" then he pulled himself up, thinking in time that I might be of the polite-eared tribe. "That's a yellow flower," he finished.

"Yes, I see it is," said I. "I'll have a look at your flower after lunch."

But the pleasure of luncheon, especially of the omelettes my landlady made so wonderfully well, caused me to forget all about it.

About three o'clock I was out walking, half a mile from the house, when I looked back from the high ground at the village beneath me, and my eye rested on the field about which we had talked that morning. "Now what was it about that field?" said I to myself, trying to recover something all but forgotten. Then I remembered that at noon it had appeared all a sheet of yellow colour and was now of a uniform deep, rather dull, green! It was very odd, but I had no time to investigate until the following morning when, on visiting the field about ten o'clock, I saw it in all its glory, the whole area resplendent with its multitudinous crowded blooms of the dandelion orange-yellow, the most luminous colour in nature; and but for the wind that waved the tall plants like a field of corn, mingling the vivid flower-tint with the green beneath, the colour would have been too dazzling in that brilliant sunshine. But it was the sunlight and the motion imparted by the wind which made it so wonderful. A sheet of yellow butter-cups or a field thickly grown with dandelions does not produce this effect owing to its want of motion. The stiffer the flower on its stem the less vivid in appearance is its sentient life—the less does it enjoy the air it breathes. These flowers, on tall pliant stems, danced in the wind with a gladness greater than that of Wordsworth's daffodils. It was only when the first shock of wonder and delight was over, that, looking closely at a flower, I made the discovery that it was the goat's-beard, the homely John-go-to-bed-at-noon, and the hardly respectable —I dare not say what!

After that I visited the field three or four times a day and found that the flower begins to open some time after sunrise and comes into its fullest bloom about ten o'clock; that at noon it begins to close, but for an hour or two the change is imperceptible, after which one notices that the field is losing its lustre, the dimness gradually growing until by three o'clock the field is all dark green again. John's in bed, tucked up, and in a deep sleep which will last quite seventeen hours; then he won't wake with a start, but slowly, slowly, yawning and rubbing his yellow eyes and taking at least two hours to get out of bed.

I do not know what has been said by the authorities on the physiology of plants on this habit of the flower, but it strikes the ordinary person as something abnormal or unnatural. We all know many flowers (the familiar daisy is one) which close in the evening, folding themselves up or covering their round discs with their petals as a child covers her face with her fingers, and this seems right and natural and consistent with Nature's plan. We are not yet acquainted with all the secrets of a flower, but we at least know that its life and growth are from the sun and suppose that when the light and heat are withdrawn the work of elaboration going on within it is suspended, that the flower is asleep and at rest until the vitalising influence returns. Why then the extraordinary waste of daylight by this one flower, when all others require all the light and heat they can get? Has Johnnie's "unconscious intelligence" found out an easier way—a method of work by means of which he is able to accomplish in his day of three or four hours as much as others can do in their twelve to sixteen hours' day? Johnnie then should be the right flower for the Socialist to wear on his day, which would have to be in June.

I had asked my man how he could have let his field get into such a condition, since the tough wiry stems of the goat's-beard could not be very good for his cows as winter feed, and all he could say was that it "had come like that of itself"; that in the two previous years there had been a slight sprinkling of the yellow flower—he didn't like to name it. But how it had come about was now plain to see, for before he started mowing balls of down could be seen all over the field, shedding myriads of seeds which would produce another undesirable but exceedingly beautiful crop the following summer. The lazy stay-in-bed-for-seventeen-hours goat's-beard was actually ahead of the other flowers in ripening its seed!

That shining yellow field, which continues to shine

in memory, just now serves to remind me of other plants and flowers that, commonly seen, have no special attraction, but which occasionally find their day of fullest perfection and triumph on some abandoned and waste ground—a field perhaps once, long years ago, under cultivation.

I have described some cases of this kind in *Nature in Downland*, where the turf was ruined for ever by the plough on the high South Downs a century ago, then left for Nature to work her will on the desolated spot. But we are most familiar with the sight of her beautifying processes in the remains of mediæval buildings scattered about the land, in old castles and abbeys and towers, draped with ivy, the rough stone walls flushed with green and grey and yellow colours of moss and lichen and rainbow-tinted algæ, decorated too with yellow wallflower, ivy-leafed toad-flax, and red valerian. Thus Nature glorifies our "builders of ruins."

And going back to remoter ages, I have in my rambles come upon two wonderfully beautiful flower effects, one in a Roman road, unused probably since Roman times; the other more ancient still on a British earthwork. I found the first one spring day when cycling over the high down country near Dorchester. I caught sight of what looked to me like a broad band of snow lying across the green hills. Coming to it I found the old Roman road, which is there very distinct and has a closer turf and a brighter green than the downs it lies across, so thickly overgrown with daisies that the crowded flowers were actually touching and had obliterated the green colour of the ground under them. It was a wonderful sight, for all these millions of small blossoms occupied the road only, not a daisy being seen on the green down on either side, and the loveliness was of so rare a quality, so rich yet so delicate, a beauty almost supernatural, that I could not bear to walk or ride on it. It was like a road leading to some unearthly brighter place—some paradise of flowers.

In the other case the site was an earthwork in Wiltshire, built probably thousands of years ago, and the flower selected to decorate it was the yellow bird's-foot trefoil.

There are in that part of Wiltshire many such remains, grim dykes, with or without walls at the side, and walls with a foss on one or in some instances on both sides. This one was a very deep ditch at the side of a wall ten to fifteen feet high, with a flat top eight to ten feet broad. It winds over a large down, then dips down to a broad level valley, and rising over the hill opposite disappears at last in the arable land on that side. Standing on the high down or on the top of the wall it has the shade and appearance of a vast green serpent with its mile-long coil lying in a series of curves across the earth. As in the case of the old Roman green roads, the turf of the earthwork is a different and brighter shade of green than that of the valley.

At this place I once met and had a long talk about the far past with a man of a singularly lively mind for a Wiltshire peasant. He told me that on numberless occasions since his boyhood he had stood looking at this great earthwork in wonder, asking himself who and what the people were that made it. "I have often," he said, "had the idea that they must have been mad; for allowing that they had a use for such a wall and ditch why did they make it go winding all over the place instead of carrying it in a straight line and saving more than half the labour it cost to build it?" I could only suggest in reply that it was no doubt a very ancient earthwork, dating back to the time when metal tools were unknown in England, and that the chalk had to be scooped up with sharp flints; that when they came to a very hard bit they had to make a bend to get round it. I also assured him that they could not have been mad as no such disease was known to the old ancient people.

Now in spring the flat top of this earthwork in all that space where it lies across the level valley, the broad level top of the bank is grown over with the bird's-foot trefoil, the yellow flowers as crowded as the daisies on the old Roman road, with not one flower to be seen growing on the green sloping sides. A green serpent still in appearance, but its whole back now a shining yellow.

When I dream of South Wiltshire in spring, when the wild flowers are in bloom, it is to look again on that wonderful green and yellow serpent.

CHAPTER XXVIII

THE CHEQUERED DAFFODIL AND THE
GLORY OF WILD FLOWERS

NEVER a season passes, never a month nor a week, nor even a day, when I'm wandering in quest of the sights and sounds that draw the field naturalist, but I stumble on something notable never previously seen, or never seen in the same charming aspect. And the fact that it is stumbled on when not looked for, that it comes as a complete surprise, greatly enhances the charm. It may be a bird or mammal, or some rare or lustrous insect, but it is in plant life where the happy discoveries are most frequent, even to one who is not a "painfull and industrious searcher of plantes" and knows little of their science. For not only are the species so numerous as to be practically innumerable to one who desires to see all things for himself, but many of the most attractive kinds are either rare or exceedingly local in their distribution. I will give a few instances.

What a delightful experience it was one cold sunny day in April when I sought shelter from the furious wind at a huge rocky headland at Zennor on the Cornish coast, and found the turf at the foot of the rocks jewelled with the first vernal squills! And what a thrill of joy in Scotland one June, when coming to a narrow green valley between high rocks and woods I had my first sight of the exquisite grass of Parnassus flowering in profusion!

One day, cycling from Salisbury to Winterbourne Gunner, I found a pretty red flower new to me growing by the roadside in great abundance; for a distance of three or four hundred yards the hedge-side was thickly sprinkled with its lovely little stars. It was a geranium, prettier than any red geranium known to me, the delicate colour resembling that of the red horse-chestnut. It was the *Geranium pyrenaicum*, native of central and eastern Europe, and by some botanists supposed to be indigenous in this country. Probably the colour varies, as some of the books describe it as purple or pale purple.

My delight was greater when I first came upon the large blue geranium growing among the South Wiltshire downs. The large loose plant with large flowers and deep-cut leaves reminded me of the geranium-leafed scented mallow, one of my favourites, and these two plants became associated in my mind, but the mallow is rosy pink and the geranium a pure divine (or human) blue.

One of the rarest, and to my mind one of the most beautiful, flowers in England is the bastard balm; I have never found it but once, and it was the way in which it came before me that has given it such a lustre in my mind. I was motoring with friends from Land's End to London, when in coming through the hilly country near Tavistock I caught sight of a flower unknown to me on a tall stalk among the thick herbage at the roadside, and shouted to the chauffeur to stop. He did so after rushing on a farther hundred yards or so, but very reluctantly, as he was angry with the hills and anxious to get to Exeter. I walked back and secured my strange lovely flower, and for the rest of the day it was a delight to us, and I'm pretty sure that its image exists still and shines in the memory of all who were with me in the car that day—the chauffeur excepted.

I am bringing too many flowers into this chapter, since only one is named in the title, but once I begin to think of them they keep me, and a dream of fair flowers is as much to me as that Dream of Fair Women is to the Tennysons and Swinburnes who write poetry. Or perhaps they are more like fair little girls than grown women, the beautiful little dear ones I loved and remember—Alice and Doris, and pensive Monica, "laughing Allegra and Edith with golden hair," and dozens more. But I must really break away from this crowd to concentrate on my chequered daffodil, only I must first be allowed to mention just one more—the blue columbine, the wild flower, always true blue and supposed to be indigenous. I don't believe it; I imagine for various reasons that it is a garden escape dating back to the Roman occupation, which gives it a better title by some eighteen centuries to be described as British than dozens of our wild flowers. The charming sainfoin, common as the gipsy rose in our fields, the wild musk that flourishes by a thousand streams from

Land's End to the Western Islands, the winter helio-
trope that spreads its green mantle over so much
of England, are by comparison aliens that emigrated
but yesterday to our shores.

It was in Wiltshire again that I found my first
columbines, in a vast thicket of furze, may, and
blackthorn covering about twenty acres of ground.
The plants were tall, the thin wiry stems being two
or three feet long, and produced few leaves, but
flowers as large as those of the garden plant. An
old keeper who had charge of the ground told me
he had known the flower from his boyhood, and
that formerly he could fill a barrow with "collar-
binds," as he called them, any day. It was a rare
pleasure to see that columbine in its own home—
the big blue quaint flower that looked at you from
its shelter of rough furze and thorn bushes; and
for the first time in my life I admired it, since in
the garden, where as a rule its peculiar beauty is
dimmed by other garden blooms, it has an inhar-
monious setting. But I must say of the colour that
albeit a true floral blue it is a blue of the earth, the
material world we inhabit, not the divine (or human)
blue of the blue geranium nor the more ethereal blue
of the vernal squill on the sea-cliffs, and of the wild
hyacinth seen in sheets of colour under the woodland trees. These are the floral blues that bring
heaven down to us.

It is not strange perhaps that this flower should
be known by bird names, but it is odd that the names
should be of birds so wide apart in our minds as

eagle and dove. *Aquilegia*, because the inverted tubes at the base of the flower are like the curved claws of an eagle; and columbine from its dove-like appearance, each blossom forming a cluster of fine dark-blue fairy fan-tails, with beaks that meet at the stem, wings open, and tails outspread.

This great find made me think that I had come into a columbine country, and I set out to look for it, but failed to find or even hear of it anywhere in that district except at one spot on the border of Wilts and Dorset. This was a tiny rustic village hidden among high downs, one of the smallest, loveliest, most out-of-the-world villages in England. In the small ancient church I found a mural tablet to the memory of the poet Browning's grandfather, whose humble life had been spent in that neighbourhood. So rare was it for a stranger to appear in this lost village that half of the population, all the forty school-children included, were eager to talk to me all the time I spent in it, and they all knew all about the columbine. It had been abundant half a mile from the village by the hedges and among the furze bushes, and every summer the children were accustomed to go out and gather the flowers, and they were seen in every cottage; and as a result of this misuse the flower had been extirpated.

They wished it would come again!

If comparatively few persons have seen the blue native columbine, just as few perhaps have found, growing wild, that more enchanting flower, the snake's-head or fritillary. Guinea-flower and bastard

narcissus and turkey-caps are some of its old English
names, the last still in common use; but the name
by which all educated persons now call it is also
very old.   Two centuries and a half ago a writer
on plants spoke of it as "a certaine strange flower
which is called by some Fritillaria." Another very
old name, which I like best, is chequered daffodil.
As a garden flower we know it, and we also know
the wild flower bought in shops or sent as a gift
from friends at a distance.   In most instances
the flowers I have seen in houses were from the
Christchurch Meadows at Oxford.

> I know what white, what purple fritillaries
> The grassy harvest of the river-fields
> Above by Ensham, down by Sandford, yields,

says Matthew Arnold in his beautiful monody; the
wonder is that it should yield so many.   But to see
the flower in its native river-fields is the main thing;
in a vase on a table in a dim room it is no better
than a blushing briar-rose or any other lovely
wild bloom removed from its proper atmosphere
and surroundings.

It was but a twelvemonth before first finding wild
columbine that I had the happiness of seeing this
better flower in its green home, a spot where it is,
perhaps, more abundant than anywhere in England;
but the spot I will not name, nor even the county;
the locality is not given in the books I have con-
sulted, yet it is, alas! too well known to many whose
only pleasure in wild flowers is to gather them greedily
to see them die indoors. For we live indoors and reck

not that Nature is deflowered, so that we return with hands or arms full of some new brightness to add to the decorations of our interiors.

Coming one May Day to a small rustic village, I passed the schoolhouse just when the children were trooping back in the afternoon, and noticed that many of them were carrying bunches of fritillaries. They told me where they had got them, in a meadow by the neighbouring river; then one little girl stepped forward and asked me very prettily to accept her bunch. I took it and gave her two or three pence, whereupon the other children, disregarding the imperious calls of their schoolmistress, who was standing outside, all flocked round and eagerly pressed their nosegays on me. But I had as many as I wanted; my desire was to see the flower growing, so I went my way and returned another day to look for the favoured spot. I found it a mile from the village, at a place where the lovely little river divides into three or four, with long strips of greenest meadowland between the currents, with ancient pollard willows growing on the banks. These were the biggest pollards I have ever seen, and were like huge rudely shaped pillars with brushwood and ivy for capitals, some still upright, others leaning over the water, and many of them quite hollow with great gaps where the rind had perished. I saw no chequered daffodils, but it was a beautiful scene, a green, peaceful place, with but one blot on it—a dull, dark brown patch where ground had been recently ploughed in the middle of the largest and fairest meadow in sight.

A sudden storm of rain drove me to seek shelter at
one of the old crumbling pollards, where, by cramming
myself into the hollow trunk, I managed to keep dry.
In half an hour it was over and the sky blue again;
then, coming out, that brown piece of ground in
the distance looked darker than ever amidst the wet
sun-lit verdure, and I marvelled at the folly of
ploughing up a green meadow in spring; for what
better or more profitable crop than grass could be
grown in such a spot?

Presently, as I walked on and got nearer, the unsightly brown changed to dark purple; then I discovered that it was no ploughed ground before me,
but a vast patch of flowers—of fritillaries growing
so close that they darkened the earth over an area
of about three acres! It was a marvellous sight, and
a pleasure indescribable to walk about among them;
to stand still in that garden with its flowers, thick
as spikes in a ripe wheat-field, on a level with my
knees; to see them in such surroundings under the
wide sky in that lucid atmosphere after the rain, the
pendulous cups still sparkling with the wet and
trembling in the lightest wind. It would have been
a joy to find a single blossom; here, to my surprise,
they were in thousands, and in tens and in hundreds
of thousands, an island of purple on the green earth,
or rather purple flecked with white, since to every
hundred or more dark-spotted flowers there was one
of an ivory whiteness and unspotted.

But it is not this profusion of blossoms—which
may be a rare occurrence—it is the individual flower

which has so singular an attractiveness. It is, I have
said, a better flower than the blue columbine; in
a way this tulip is better than any British flower.
A tulip without the stiffness and appearance of
solidity which makes the garden kinds look as if
they had been carved out of wood and painted, but
pendulous, like the harebell, on a tall slender stem,
among the tall fine-leafed grasses, and trembling
like the grasses at every breath; in colour unlike
any other tulip or any flower, a pink that is like a
delicate, luminous flesh-tint, minutely chequered
with dark maroon purple.

Our older writers on plants waxed eloquent in
describing their "fritillaria" or "Ginny-flower,"
and even the driest of modern botanists writes that it
is a flower which, once seen, cannot be forgotten.
That is because of its unlikeness to all others—its
strangeness. In the arrangement of its colours it
is unique, and furthermore, it is the darkest flower
we have. This effect is due to the smallness of the
tessellated squares, since at a distance of a few feet
the dark violet maroon kills or absorbs the bright
delicate pink colour, and makes the entire blossom
appear uniformly dark.

The flower which, combining strangeness with
beauty, comes nearest to the chequered daffodil is
the henbane, with an exceedingly dark purple centre
and petals a pale clouded amber yellow delicately
veined with purple brown. But in the henbane the
dark and pale hues are seen contrasted. In flowers
like these, but chiefly in the chequered daffodil, we

see that the quality of strangeness, which is not in itself an element of beauty, has yet the effect of intensifying the beauty it is associated with. Thus, if we consider other admired species—briar-rose, pink convolvulus, rock-rose, sea-poppy, yellow flag, bugloss, blue geranium, water forget-me-not, flowering rush, and grass of Parnassus, for example — and many more might be named—we see that in beauty, pure and simple, these equal and exceed the fritillary; yet this impresses us more than the others, and surprises us into thinking it more beautiful because its beauty strikes us more sharply. It is not sufficient to say that the sharper impression is due merely to the unusual appearance. I rather incline to believe that the source of the vivid interest excited is that faculty of the mind supposed to be obsolete, but which still faintly lives in all of us, though we may be unconscious of it—a faculty which see a hidden meaning or spirit in all strange appearances in the natural world. It is the "sense of mystery," and is with us in sight of a magnificent and strange sunset, and of any unusual atmospheric strangeness, down to the smallest objects that engage our attention—an insect, a flower, even our chequered daffodil of the river-fields.

CHAPTER XXIX

I AM not a lover of lawns; on the contrary, I regard them, next to gardens, as the least interesting adjuncts of the country-house. Grass, albeit the commonest, is yet one of the most beautiful things in Nature when allowed to grow as Nature intended, or when not too carefully trimmed and brushed. Rather would I see daisies in their thousands, ground ivy, hawkweed, and even the hated plantain with tall stems, and dandelions with splendid flowers and fairy down, than the too-well-tended lawn grass. This may be regarded as the mental attitude of the wild man from the woods, but something may be said for it. Sir Walter Raleigh explained, centuries ago, the reason of our desire for and pleasure in trim gardens, lawns, parks, and neatly cut hedges of box and privet and holly: those surroundings of the house were invented as a refuge from the harsh, brambly outside wilderness, the stinging nettles, scratching thorns, sharp hurtful stones and hidden pits—from all the roughnesses and general horriblenesses of an incult Nature.

But that's all a feeling of long ago, it may be answered; it has gone out now, and we have come

back to Nature—the dear old beautiful mother!
Have we indeed? Lawns have not gone out; on
the contrary, it appears to me that the idea of the
lawn, like the idea of clothes, has entered into our
souls and manifests itself more and more in all our
surroundings, our dwellings, our persons, our habits.
Sir Almroth Wright cried out a little while ago
against our habit of scrubbing our bodies every day
and rubbing them dry with rough towels to polish
and make them shine like our glass, china, and plated
table-ware. When Nathaniel Hawthorne came to
the Old Home from an outlandish United States of
America where this idea of the lawn had not yet
penetrated so deeply, he spent some time at a great
country-house where he stayed in running about the
lawns and park in search of a nettle, or weed, or
wilding of some kind to rest his eyes on. The novel
smoothness and artificiality of everything made him
mad. And if Sir Walter Raleigh himself were to
return to us in all his glory and splendour, and if
someone, opening the *History of the World*, should
read that passage about lawns to him, I think he
would cry out: "Oh, but you have now gone too far
in that direction! Your rooms, your tables, all the
thousand appointments of your establishment, your
own appearance, your hard-scraped skins, your conversation suffocate me. Let me out—let me go back
to the place I came from!"

What then of all the beautiful things we say of
Nature? It may be asked. Why, only this: it
amounts to as much as all the beautiful things we

say about painted pictures, jewels, tapestries, old lace, Chippendale furniture, and what not. We are not *in* Nature; we are out of her, having made our own conditions; and our conditions have re-acted upon and made us what we are—artificial creatures. Nature is now something pretty to go and look at occasionally, but not too often, nor for too long a time.

So much in defence of my attitude concerning lawns. There is no doubt that, seen at a right distance, a fine country-house or mansion, standing isolated from other buildings and from trees and gardens, looks best on a level green expanse. At this moment I recall Shaw House, Avington House, and two or three others, but every reader who knows England will have the image of half a dozen or more such buildings in his mind.

Now I think that this grass setting would be just as effective or more effective if left more in its natural state. Seen closely, the smooth lawn is a weariness to the eye like all smooth monotonous surfaces; like the smooth or oily unwrinkled sea, for example, which the eye refuses to dwell on; or like the blue sky without a cloud or a soaring bird on it. Such a sky may be good to be under but tiresome to the vision after three seconds. If you look at it for a whole minute, or for an hour without weariness, it is because you are thinking of something, which means that you are occupied with seeing mental images and not the sky. An acre or so of green linoleum or drugget, drawn evenly and smoothly

over the ground surrounding a large house, would
probably have as good an effect as a perfectly smooth
grass lawn. But into this question I am not going
any further. I write about lawns because there are
such things, and I have to see them and sometimes
live in sight of one. I have had one before my eyes
for hours this very day while staying at a friend's
house in the country. A week ago I went up to
London for a couple of days, and on my return my
hostess informed me that I had no sooner left than
the gardener presented himself before her to ask
her if now that her visitor had gone away for a day
or two she would allow him to sweep the lawn and
make it tidy.

It was a good-sized lawn, with a group of well-
grown birches on the west side, and one day in early
November the south-west wind blew and carried
thousands of small yellow heart-shaped leaves over
the green expanse, making it beautiful to look at.
By-and-by, the gardener came with his abhorred
brushwood-broom and swept that lovely novel
appearance away, to my great disgust. Then the
blessed wind blew again and roared all night, sway-
ing the trees and tossing out fresh clouds on clouds of
the brilliant little leaves all over the monotonous sheet
of green, and lo! in the morning it was beautiful
once more. And I stood and admired it, and it was
like walking on a velvet green carpet embroidered
with heart-shaped golden leaves. Naturally, when
I saw the gardener coming on with his broom, I
cried out aloud and brought the lady of the house

on the scene, and she graciously ordered him off. It was only when I went up to town that he was allowed to work his will.

I now propose to tell the story of another lawn of which I had the supervision for two or three months; a small lawn at a cottage surrounded by green fields lent to me by a friend one summer end; it was mowed and looked after generally by a man who came once a week from the village, and he also had the garden to see after. In July and August, when the sun was low enough to allow one to sit out of doors and of the shade of trees I lounged and read and drank my tea there, and noticed that it was abundantly sprinkled with plantains. Now I don't mind plantains on a lawn because, as I have already said and ingeminated, lawns are nothing to me unless flowers are allowed to blossom and leaves blown from coloured woods to lie on them, but I remembered my friends who had lent me their paradisaical retreat with its green lawn from which, idling in my canvas chair, I looked on a green valley and a swift chalk stream with coots and moorhens disporting themselves on it, and beautiful hanging woods beyond. I remembered them, and in my desire to do something to express my gratitude I said I would clear this one lawn of its plantains.

Going to the tool-house, I found a long, narrow, sharp-pointed trowel, which was just what I wanted, and also saw there an important-looking weed-killing instrument and a can of poison, which I certainly did not want. I started taking up the plantains, working the trowel down to the end of the root so as to leave nothing of the tenacious cunning creature in the ground. By-and-by the man from the village came and saw the beginning of my work—my little harvest gathered from four or five square yards of lawn. He smiled, and when I asked him why he smiled, he said the lawn had been in that condition for the past ten years and nothing could be done to get rid of the plantains. He couldn't say how many quarts of poison had been squirted into the roots, but they refused to die, and so on and so forth. On his next visit he found a huge heap of uprooted plantains in the middle of the lawn, left there for his special benefit, and not one growing plantain left on the lawn.

"Ah, yes," he said—it was just what I had expected him to say—"the fact is I've never had the time to do it properly. Always too busy with the rose garden, and plantains take a lot of time, you know. Certainly we did what we could with the weed-killer, but it seems it didn't amount to much."

What it amounted to was this: here and there all about the lawn were round brown spots, the size of a crown-piece or larger, where the grass had perished and refused to grow again. These unsightly spots marked the places where plantains had been destroyed by the weed-killer, the metal point of which is thrust into the centre of the plant and the poison squirted in. Now this poison does not kill the plantain only but the roots of the grasses as well—hence the naked brown spots. How long does the poison keep its potency in the moist mould?

A long time, I should think, seeing that these naked spots were some months old. I also wanted to know if the poison was deadly to other forms of life in the soil, especially to earthworms. To ascertain this I took up mould enough from one of the barren spots to fill a flower-pot, then filled a second flower-pot with mould from outside the lawn, then went to the rose-garden at the back to dig for worms, and selecting two full-grown vigorous specimens, put one in each pot. The following day I turned them out and found that the first one had lost its vigour, and not only was it languid in its motions, but the colour had changed to a dull pink and had wholly lost the rainbow bloom of the healthy earthworm. There was no change in the healthy colour and activity of the second worm. I put them back in their respective pots and examined them again next day: the first was dead, its body a dull red and flabby. The second was still just as strong and active and of as fresh and healthy a colour as when first taken from the earth.

I was satisfied that weed-killers are even more potent than I had thought them. As a bird-lover I had always hated them on account of their destructiveness to the small birds of the homestead, the blackbird and song-thrush, chaffinch, robin, dunnock, and other species that are accustomed to seek for small morsels on the gravelled walks where these poisons are so much used by gardeners to extirpate the small hardy weeds that root themselves in such places.

I didn't pursue the matter further, and the subject of lawns and earthworms was out of my mind for two or three weeks when something happened at the end of August to revive my interest in it. There came a wet day followed by a gale of wind which lasted a part of the night, and next morning I found that the wind in its violence had well-nigh stripped a row of young false acacia trees growing on the south side of their still living green leaves and sprinkled them abundantly all over the lawn. As I sat out of doors that afternoon I didn't quite like the disorderly appearance of the long green leaves torn off before their time lying all about me, and I took it into my head to sweep them away, but when I set myself to do it with the brushwood broom, not a leaf could I sweep from its place! I then discovered to my surprise that the leaves were all made fast to the ground; every leaf had been seized and dragged by an earthworm to its run, the terminal leaflet rolled up and pulled into the hole, but no further could the leaf go, since the next two opposite leaflets on the stem were like a cross-bar and prevented further progress. In every case the terminal leaflet was buried and the rest of the leaf lying out on the grass.

We know that earthworms live on the vegetable mould in which they move and have their being, and nourish themselves by passing the earth they remove in excavating their tunnels through their bodies. It is assumed by naturalists that they extract certain " salts " on which they live from

X 2

the soil they swallow. But as the worm is not a vegetable I prefer to believe that they exist on the microscopic organisms in the mould. Be this as it may, the worm does not live by mould alone; he is also a vegetable eater and feeds on decayed leaves of trees when they fall in his way, dragging them into his hole by night. But the leaf he prefers is the decayed one, and it struck me that these lawn worms were in an extraordinary state of leaf-hunger to seize upon and drag these fresh living leaves into their holes as soon as the wind had torn them off.

The conclusion I formed was that the lawn earthworm is a starved worm, and I began to examine and compare the lawn worms with those living in the soil away from the lawn. I found that when I dug for worms in the moist earth in likely spots away from the lawn, the mere act of striking the spade or fork deep into the soil brought the worms with a rush to the surface, and in many instances the rush was so rapid that at the moment when the spade was being driven deep down by the foot, a big vigorous worm would appear on the surface thrusting half the length of his long body straight up and looking like the round polished stem of some species of squill or lily springing miraculously from the earth. Worms, I found, are extraordinarily sensitive to earth vibration: thus when one walks upon or strikes the ground with a stick, they go deeper down; but when the vibrations come from beneath or from the earth around them, they rush to the surface to escape from a subterranean enemy pursuing them in their own element. On the lawn I never succeeded in making the worms rush up to the surface by striking a spade or fork into the soil; and when I dug up a number of worms from the lawn and compared them with others from the soil outside, I found a great difference in them. The lawn worms were much smaller and were not nearly so vigorous in their movements as the others. The wonder was that worms should be found living in such numbers in the lawn soil in these somewhat unnatural conditions, when just outside the lawn there was a soil easier to penetrate and abundance of decaying leaves for them to feed on.

These incidental observations on earthworms in their relation to lawns caused me to regret that I had not made a better use of my opportunities of studying these creatures on former occasions, as it now appeared to me that much yet remains to be discovered anent their habits and effect on the soil and vegetation. My knowledge of them was little more than that of the ordinary person, and how much *he* knows about the subject let the following incident show.

One evening I was with Mr. Frank E. Beddard at his club, and taking advantage of the occasion, asked him some question about earthworms, he being the greatest authority in the universe on the subject. It happened that another friend of his, a famous angler, was sitting near and overheard our conversation.

"Ah, yes—worms," he said. "Before I forget

all about it, I want to ask you if the worm we dig up in the sand for bait is the same as the common earthworm."

"No," said the other.

"Well, but they are both worms, are they not?"

"Yes."

"And if they are both worms, what's the difference?"

"They are both worms, and differ as much as a cat from a squirrel—both mammals."

And that was all he would say: the subject of their differences could not be profitably discussed on that occasion and with persons who knew so little.

Like everybody else I had read Darwin's classic, but what one reads does not inform the mind much unless one observes and thinks for oneself at the same time. The wonderful story of the action of earthworms on the earth's surface only came home to me during the excavations at Silchester, when year after year the pavements and floors and foundations of houses and temples and public and private baths were uncovered until the entire two hundred acres within the walls had been disclosed. It is not necessary to describe here, since we have it all in Darwin, just how the worms succeeded in burying in a century or two all that remained of a ruined Silchester —the outside wall excepted—to a depth of three to four feet beneath the surface. We know that for the last eight hundred years the ground has been cultivated above the buried city. When watching these excavations I discovered one fact about worms which

Darwin missed. Among the best finds at Silchester were the large and in some cases uninjured mosaic floors of the more important houses, some of which were removed intact to Reading Museum, and may be seen there.

When one of these fine large floors was uncovered it remained *in situ* until the late autumn, when it was taken up and removed. Observing these floors, after they had been washed and scrubbed until they looked as fresh as if made yesterday instead of nigh on twenty centuries ago, it surprised me to find that worms were quite abundant beneath them, that they came to the surface through small borings which were not noticed unless closely looked for; they came up by night, and in the morning the workmen had to sweep the castings away to make the floors clean. The question that suggested itself was: why did the worms continue to penetrate beneath the stone and cement floor after it had been buried so deep in the ground, and when they had, and had enjoyed for over a thousand years at the least, a soil formed of vegetable mould as deep as earthworms require to live and flourish in? A depth of three or four feet of mould is as much as they require, but they will, Darwin says, occasionally go deeper to five or six feet, and he gives nine feet as the greatest depth at which they have been found. Now at Silchester I saw some taken from a depth of twenty-five feet, and very many at eighteen to twenty feet. This was when the old Roman wells and other deep pits were cleaned out.

It struck me that these Silchester observations made a valuable contribution to a history of the earthworm's life habits. For it should be borne in mind that the soil covering the buried city is a rich mould, which has been under cultivation for the last nine or ten centuries, and is the kind of soil in which the earthworm finds his best conditions and attains his greatest size and vigour. Consider next that the soil in the deep pits and everywhere beneath the Roman pavements is a cold, heavy, hardly-pressed earth undisturbed for many centuries, unpierced by root of plant or ray of sun, and probably to a great extent devoid of the microbic life which makes the upper soil alive. When you turn over this long-buried soil with the spade it has a heavy damp smell, but not the familiar earth-smell of *Cladothrix odorifera*. Yet down in this dark dead soil the worms will insist on descending, although their only way to it is through the few small cylindrical holes they have succeeded in boring through the partially rotted cement between the tiles, or where a minute stone has dropped out of the tesseræ pavements. Their descent into these difficult places and down into the old pits involves long double journeys daily when they are forced to come up to deposit their castings on the surface.

What then is the force impelling them? Why do they leave a rich feeding-ground for a poor one? I take these facts in their relation to other well-known facts, as for example that of the quite extraordinary difference in size and vigour and colouring in the earthworms inhabiting different soils. They are like different species. Let us take the case of the London earthworm to be found in every few square yards of earth unbuilt on, even in the very heart of the City itself. Judging from all the specimens I have examined, this worm attains to about half the full normal size and is comparatively languid in his movements and rarely exhibits the brilliant play of colours seen in the large country worm in rich soil—the colour which is the sign of intensity of life. Doubtless he was once a big vigorous worm, but that was long ago in an old London, or Londinium, and he has had ample time to degenerate. In this state he is now biding his time, under our feet, and his time will come when our seven millions have faded or drifted away; then indeed he will recover his power, and slowly, patiently, unhasting and unresting, day and night, year by year, century after century, he will labour to sink away brick and stone beneath the surface and cover it all with a deep rich mould and a mantle of everlasting verdure.

Then we have the earthworms inhabiting heaths and all sandy soils throughout the land. They are no better than the London earthworms. One day last autumn I found the gardener at the house in a pine wood where I was staying at Ascot digging potatoes. I took a spade and went to him and started digging for worms at his side. There was a magnificent crop of potatoes, as it has been everywhere this autumn of 1918, but the earthworms we turned up were few in number and very poor specimens. "It is useless," said the gardener, "to look for a big worm here—I never see one. It is the sand that starves them."

I am not sure that this is a sufficient explanation: in the rich soils in these highly cultivated gardens in this heath and pine district where wealthy people have their homes, the worms, one would think, must find sufficient nourishment. It is more probable that their poor condition is due to something inimical to earthworms in the sand itself.

On the chalk, where the soil is thin, as in the sheep-walks, the earthworms are comparatively small in size, but vigorous and quick in their movements amidst the interlacing fibrous roots of the close turf. In the hollow places between the hills, where a deeper soil has been formed, the worms attain to their full size—all which goes to show that chalk itself is not inimical to worms. In heavy clays the appearance of the worms show that the conditions are not favourable.

Thus we see that earthworms are perpetually invading and peopling all soils, good and bad; also that if you have a piece of hard ground barren of food for worms and free of worms, where for long years they have not been permitted to exist, they will constantly flow in from all the surrounding rich soils where worms abound and flourish in order to get possession of it. The cause, I take it, is that the earthworm abhors the soil frequented by other worms, which is impregnated with the acid the worm secretes and discharges into the soil. The acid spoils the ground for him, and he prefers to go outside into the most barren and unsuitable places to remaining in it. And the perpetual desire to get away and seek pastures new is the reason of the wide distribution of the earthworm, of its universality, so that there is not a clod on the surface of the earth without a worm for inhabitant.

Three or four days after witnessing the remarkable phenomenon I described some pages back—the rush of hungry earthworms to secure a windfall of leaves torn before their time from the trees and consequently not well suited to their masticating powers—I paid a visit at a country-house a few miles away, and found there one of the finest lawns I had ever seen. The old Georgian house was built on an eminence overlooking the valley and stood in the centre of a square and perfectly flat piece of ground, which was all lawn; then the ground sloped on all sides to a terrace, and slope and terrace were all lawn too and one with the level ground above. The great extent and marvellous smoothness of this lawn filled me with admiration—when I saw it at a distance; but I no sooner set foot on it than I began to quarrel with it. To begin with, the ground was hard; there was no elastic, no real turf; it was like walking on flagstones. Nothing but grass grew on that lawn, not in a matted turf, but each grass or grass plant by itself, so that when looking closely down at one's feet one saw the hard ground between the blades and roots. On all that ground there was not a daisy to be seen, nor any of the small creeping plants and clovers usually found on lawns.

Before my visit was over I succeeded in getting hold of the gardener and asked him how he managed to keep his large lawn so clean and smooth. He took it that I was praising his work and began to tell me what a tremendous task it was to keep it in that perfect condition.

"But I think," said I, "that if you would call in the earthworms to help you and did less yourself you would have a better lawn."

At first he thought I was joking and was much amused. Earthworms, he assured me, were the worst enemies of lawns—they made such a mess! His greatest trouble was to keep them down. He was always going round with a bucket of brine, particularly about the lower borders, where they were always trying to come in, and poured the brine down their holes. Brine was the best worm-killer he knew; and the result of his care and use of it was that you wouldn't be able to find a worm on all that immense lawn.

I asked him if he could not understand that it was no pleasure to walk or sit or lie on a lawn where the ground was always dry and hard in spite of all the watering he gave it. To walk on his lawn tired and depressed me, whereas on the chalk-hill behind the house I could walk miles with pure delight, simply because it was a close-matted turf and was felt beneath the feet like a pile-carpet drawn over a thick rubber floor. It lifted me when I walked on it, and was better than the most luxurious couch to lie on, to say nothing of the pleasure one received from the sight of its small gem-like flowers and from its aromatic scent. As to the castings, they were unpleasant only when the lawn was wet in the morning, and only then when the grass was too thin. You do not see the castings on the thick turf on the downs, although if you take up a sod you find earthworms at the roots in abundance.

Well, he answered, a lawn could not have a turf like a chalk-hill fed by sheep, because—such a turf wasn't the right one for a lawn to have. Then, as this seemed a rather poor argument, he suddenly brightened up and said: "And what about the moles? Do you know that with a large lawn like this, with grass fields all round it, you are always in danger of getting a mole—that is to say if there are any earthworms to attract him. And a mole can disfigure a lawn as much as if you had made a furrow with a plough across it."

No doubt he was right there; but when I said that moles could be kept out by sinking a rabbit net to a depth of two or three feet beneath the surface and would save a lot of labour and expense, he only smiled and shook his head.

The gardener, like the gamekeeper, is never a person who will allow you to teach him anything, but after our conversation I was more convinced than ever that it would be better for the lawn if, instead of killing and starving the worms, we were to feed them and allow them to make and keep a turf.

With this idea in my mind I tried a fresh experiment. I pegged out a strip of the lawn at the cottage, about ten feet wide, and ran a cord on each side to keep it distinct from the rest of the ground, and over that strip I sprinkled leaves from the acacia and other trees abundantly. I examined the ground on the following day and saw no change. Leaves were still lying thickly on the ground, and it was impossible to tell whether any had been carried away or not. The next day it was the same. On the morning of the third day there was something new to note: it looked as if the worms inhabiting the quartered-off ground had suddenly developed a wonderful vigour and activity, or as if a rush of worms from all over the lawn to that favoured spot had taken place. The ground was thickly sprinkled over with castings, mostly under the herbage, although after a careful search I could not find a single casting anywhere else on the lawn. It was evident that the worms had been taking the leaves into their runs and feeding greedily on them, and I confidently expected that the result would be that in a little while the turf on the marked strip of ground would be thicker, greener, more elastic to the tread. Unfortunately I was obliged to leave the place when the experiment was just at its beginning, so that nothing was proved; and I hope that some reader of this paper, who possesses a lawn, or is about to form one, will carry the matter further and try to find out whether or not a better result may be had by encouraging the earthworms to work with and for us instead of regarding them as enemies and trying to suppress them.

INDEX